New Religions and the Nazis

This book highlights an important but neglected part of Nazi history—the contribution of new religions to the emergence of Nazi ideology in 1920s and 1930s Germany. Karla Poewe argues that Nazism was the unique consequence of post-World War I conditions in Germany, a reaction against the decadence of nineteenth-century liberalism, the shameful defeat of World War I, the imposition of an unwanted Weimar democracy, and the postwar punishment of the Treaty of Versailles. Aiming towards national regeneration, leading cultural figures such as Jakob Wilhelm Hauer, Mathilde Ludendorff, Ernst Bergmann, Hans Grimm, and Hans F. K. Günther wanted to shape the cultural milieu of politics, religion, theology, Indo-Aryan metaphysics, literature and Darwinian science into a new genuinely German faith-based political community. Instead what emerged was a totalitarian political regime known as National Socialism, with an anti-Semitic worldview. Looking at modern German paganism as well as the established Church, Poewe reveals that the new religions founded in the pre-Nazi and Nazi years, especially Jakob Hauer's German Faith Movement, would be a model for how German fascism distilled aspects of religious doctrine into political extremism.

New Religions and the Nazis addresses one of the most important questions of the twentieth century—how and why did Germans come to embrace National Socialism? Researched from original documents, letters and unpublished papers, including the SS personnel files held in Berlin's Bundesarchiv, it is an absorbing and fresh approach to the difficulties raised by this deeply significant period of history.

Karla Poewe is Professor Emeritus of Anthropology at the University of Calgary and a specialist in new religious movements. Her publications include *Reflections of a Woman Anthropologist: No Hiding Place* (1982 as Manda Cesara), *New Religions as Global Cultures* (1997) and *Charismatic Christianity as a Global Culture* (1994).

New Religions and the Nazis

Karla Poewe

Routledge
Taylor & Francis Group

NEW YORK AND LONDON

First published 2006
by Routledge
2 Park Square, Milton Park, Abingdon, Oxon OX14 4RN

Simultaneously published in the USA and Canada
by Routledge
240 Madison Avenue, New York, NY 100016

Routledge is an imprint of the Taylor & Francis Group
© 2006 Karla Poewe

Typeset in Sabon and Gill Sans by Bookcraft Ltd
Printed and bound in Great Britain by
Antony Rowe Ltd, Chippenham, Wiltshire

British Library Cataloguing in Publication Data
A catalogue record for this book is available
from the British Library

Library of Congress Cataloging in Publication Data
Poewe, Karla O.
   New religions and the Nazis / Karla Poewe.
      p. cm.
   Includes bibliographical references and index.
   1. Germany—Religion—20th century. 2. National socialism—
   Religious aspects. 3. Germany—Politics and government—
   20th century. I. Title.

   BL980.G3P64 2005
   200'.943'09043—dc22   2005006119

ISBN10: 0-415-29024-4 (hbk)
ISBN10: 0-415-29025-2 (pbk)
ISBN13: 978-0-415-29024-1 (hbk)
ISBN13: 978-0-415-29025-8 (pbk)

Contents

List of illustrations

Abbreviations

ADGB	Arbeitsgemeinschaft Deutsche Glaubensbewegung
AF	Adler und Falken
AfBF	Arbeitskreis für biozentrische Forschung
AfFRP	Arbeitsgemeinschaft für freie Religionsforschung und Philosophie
BAB	Bundesarchiv Berlin
BAK	Bundesarchiv Koblenz
BdF	Bund der Freireligiösen
BDU	Bund deutscher Unitarier
BF	Bündischen Front
BFG	Bund der freireligiösen Gemeinden
BfG	Bund für Gotterkenntnis
BFGD	Bund freier religiöser Gemeinden Deutschlands
BfFG	Bund für freireligiöse Gemeinden
BGDG	Bund der Gemeinden Deutschen Glaubens
CDU	Christlich Demokratische Union
CNAG	Christlichnationale Arbeitsgemeinschaft
CR	Conservative Revolution, Conservative Revolutionaries
DC	Deutsche Christen
DCA	Deutsch-Christliche Arbeitsgemeinschaft
DG	Deutscher Glaube
DGG	Deutschgläubige Gemeinschaft
DGB	Deutsche Glaubensbewegung
DKB	Deutsch-Katholizismus Bewegung
DLA	Deutsches Literaturarchiv, Marbach
DNVP	German National People's Party
DRB	Deutschreligiöser Bund
DUR	Deutsche Unitarier Religionsgemeinschaft
FA	Freie Akademie
FKG	Freundeskreis der Kommenden Gemeinde
GDE	Gemeinschaft Deutscher Erkenntnis
GGDC	Glaubensgemeinschaft Deutscher Christen

JNB	Jungnordischer Bund
KG	Kommende Gemeinde
KGRNS	Kampfgemeinschaft revolutionärer National Sozialisten
KVP	Konservative Volkspartei
NPD	Nationaldemokratische Partei
NRA	Nordisch-Religiöse Arbeitsgemeinschaft
NSDAP	Nationalsozialistische Deutsche Arbeiter Partei
NSLB	Nationalsozialistischer Lehrerbund
RDDJ	Reichsausschuss der Deutschen Jugend Bünde
SD	Sicherheitsdienst
SF	Schwarze Front
SPD	Sozialdemokratische Partei Deutschlands
SS	Schutzstaffel
VFG	Verband der freireligiösen Gemeinden

Preface

This book was written to answer the question that has been burning in my mind for several decades, namely, how Germans came to support the National Socialist worldview that ended in the Holocaust and the loss of countless lives. How could Germans of the time think themselves into such a dead end?

I began to glimpse the beginnings of an answer when, after my most recent research trips to Namibia and South Africa, I decided to study Berlin missionaries who had served there. In the Archive of the Berlin Mission Society I came upon Knak's unpublished history of the Berlin Mission from 1924 to 1949. Knak described heated debates held during the 1920s in the new auditorium of the then Berlin University between representatives of the Mission or Christianity and fanatical defenders of Germany's new religions. Apparently supporters of the *völkisch* movement, especially academics, were trying to turn Icelandic sagas into an alternative type of religion that was given respectability by linking it to German mysticism, Luther's perspective on faith, and the religious perspective of German classical writers such as Goethe (Knak n.d.: 28b). I had seen the making of new religions before, and became curious (Hexham and Poewe 1997).

According to Knak, pseudo-scientific constructions of new religions were so widespread that Rosenberg (1930) saw it as opportune to build his *Mythus* upon them. The use of their "religions" as political weapons by people who described themselves as neo-pagans and, as I discovered later, by seemingly agnostic Nationalists clearly served to prepare the religious politics of the Third Reich. Here seemed to be the answer to my question.

When I came upon the work of Jakob Wilhelm Hauer, who, along with Ernst zu Reventlow, founded the German Faith Movement, I dropped my research on the Berlin Mission. The problem had to be dealt with from the perspective of people who participated in the *völkisch*, neo-pagan, and German Faith movements that culminated in National Socialism. Consequently, I spent regular four-month periods over eight years doing research in various archives that housed the diverse documents dealing with Nazism, including the Bundesarchiv Koblenz, the Bundesarchiv Berlin, the Deutsches

Literaturarchiv in Marbach, the Deutsche Bibliothek in Leipzig, the Staats-
bibliothek Berlin, and various smaller archives. My husband Irving Hexham
and I interviewed several descendants of the worldview ideologues whose
letters I researched in archives. We also traveled to various locations and
cemeteries where evidence of their past still existed. We do not agree with
their politics, but are grateful for polite receptions and intelligent conversations, and particularly thank Wigbert Grabert and Gert Sudholt.

The book describes the development of the New Faith that its creators
thought to be the essence of National Socialism, from its beginnings in the
youth group (*Bünde*) phase to Nazi takeover and to its traces in the present-
day New Right.

I thank Ulrich van der Heyden, a first-class historian whose conferences
gave me the opportunity to present my early Hauer findings and whose
exquisite knowledge of German archives helped my research. Likewise, I
thank the exciting anthropologist Karl-Heinz Kohl, Director of the Frobenius Institute in Frankfurt/Main, and his colleagues and students, for
listening to and discussing my papers on the topic of this book. The religious
studies scholar Horst Junginger, who wrote a brilliant book about Hauer's
academic life, was kind enough to let me use some Hauer material and a
Hauer photo that are housed at the university in Tübingen. While I do not
agree with everything found in Junginger's book, it rests on superb research
and is inspiring.

German federal archives and their archivists respect research and the
pursuit of truth. With this they do humanity a great service. I am particularly
grateful to the energetic and enabling archivist Gregor Pickro, and I thank
him and Manuela Vack of the Bundesarchiv Koblenz (BAK) for permission
to use and cite from the Hauer holdings. Likewise I thank Jana Blumberg for
permission to use my research findings at the Bundesarchiv Berlin (BAB). I
am grateful to Dr Jochen Meyer and his assistants of the Deutsches Literaturarchiv (DLA) in Marbach for permission to research the Hans Grimm
holdings. Unlike the federal archives, the DLA upholds the right to protect
persons. Therefore, it can restrict citation from unpublished documents and
demands citation permission from even distant living relatives. Its regulations, which may be needed to obtain holdings, let distant living relatives
decide what about their ancestor's words and deeds should be withheld from
the critical eye of scholars. Such regulations limit public knowledge. Nevertheless, where relevant, I received permission to cite or make reference to
Hans Grimm's correspondents. Here I thank Dr Holle Grimm, who
graciously allowed me to cite from Hans Grimm's letter to Ilse Hess and,
earlier, for talking with my husband and me about her father and showing us
his home and study.

I am grateful to Monika Geilen of the BAK and Rosemarie Kutschis of the
DLA for permission to use photos from their respective archives. Likewise, I
thank the Verlag Hohe Warte for allowing the publication of two Ludendorff

photos. Given my different politics, they might have refused their help, but they did not.

Indeed, many other archivists and librarians in Marbach, Berlin, Leipzig, München, Kassel, and Koblenz have been helpful. Without their assistance and goodwill this research would not have been possible.

Special thanks go to my husband Irving Hexham. He accompanied me on this sometimes exciting but often painful journey of discovery.

I thank the editors of Routledge Press for their patience when, owing to severe and unexpected adversity, the schedule of this work was interrupted. In particular I am grateful for the sound advice from Routledge readers and, in the latter stages, for the help from Lesley Riddle and Gemma Dunn, and the copy editor Richard Pickvance.

Finally, I thank the Social Sciences and Humanities Research Council (SSHRC) of Canada and Research Services at the University of Calgary for their financial support.

Acknowledgment

Chapter 11, *Scientific neo-paganism and the extreme Right then and today*, was originally published as "Scientific Neo-Paganism and extreme Right then and today," *Journal of Contemporary Religion* 14.3 (1999): 387–400 (http://www.tandf.co.uk) and has been revised for this publication.

Chapter 1

Introduction

General remarks

It took thirteen years to make National Socialism a major political and religious force in Germany. How it became a political force is well understood and brilliantly analyzed by historians; how it became a religious force is not. Religion is the weapon par excellence of revolutionaries, and how else can we explain the abject moral failure and dead end that Nazism represents? And just as religion represents the failure of Nazism, religion also tells the story of how its leaders captured the imagination of millions of young Germans for National Socialism.

This book is about gifted intellectuals who simply would not accept, as Bonhoeffer had, "that the world had come of age," meaning that Germans, like all suffering humankind, had to recognize their true situation and manage their lives in weakness and with grace (Bethge 1970: 773). Instead, these self-appointed intellectual guardians of the defeated saw themselves as an elite determined not only to shape and usher in new myths and religions, but to use these to underpin National Socialism—indeed, to be its sacred, religious center.

Most academics assume that German pagan faiths, expressed in countless new religions, by diverse leaders and adherents both inside and outside of the official church, were too small in number to make an impact on National Socialism. This book dispels that myth. The religious elite of the twenties and thirties found a new form for their ideas that would then be disseminated to, and acted out by, young radicals—a technique still practiced today by the New Right.

Jakob Wilhelm Hauer (1881–1962), Mathilde Ludendorff, Ernst Bergmann (1881–1945), Johannes von Leers, Dietrich Klagges, best-selling novelist Hans Grimm (1875–1959), and popular anthropological writer Hans F. K. Günther (1891–1968), their millions of followers, listeners, and readers, not to mention many other intellectuals, writers and propagandists, had occasional problems with the crude, indeed brutal, tactics of the National Socialist Party (NSDAP). Several did not become Party members.

1.1 Jakob Wilhelm Hauer, founder of the
German Faith Movement

But more than disliking the NSDAP on occasion, they despised the decadence of nineteenth-century liberalism, the shameful defeat of World War I,
the imposition of an unwanted Weimar democracy, and the postwar punishment in the form of the Treaty of Versailles.

What they wanted was national regeneration. Clumsily at first, they
contributed to creating what the sociologist of western secularization, Colin
Campbell (1972: 122–3), called a "cultic milieu," namely, that "cultural
underground of society" that is kept alive by everything from mysticism to
unorthodox science, to new religions, to new literature and the propagandists who propagate it. Although they meant different things by it, Hauer,
Grimm, Günther, and other hard-nosed Social Darwinists wanted to shape
this milieu into a new, genuinely German (Nordic) faith-based political
community, a community of one *Volk* that would privilege, in their view, the
almost lost Germanic or Nordic culture and ancestry. What emerged was a
totalitarian political religion known as National Socialism and an ultra-
nationalist press that supported it.

Most historians of German history prefer the term *völkisch*[1] to that of
cultic milieu. They do so for at least three reasons. First, it was used in the
pre-Nazi environment by Germans themselves and constituted a regenera-
tive movement. Second, the term *völkisch* served to uphold the belief that
what happened in Germany, specifically the Holocaust, was unique to that

country. Thirdly, *völkisch* referred to the fact that, especially after 1930, race and religion were fused in popular thought and propaganda. Indeed, race, which then meant a specific cultural, historical, territorial, and in some sense biological and ancestral identity, became the buzzword of the thirties. While the term *völkisch* is retained in this book, we should not lose sight of the fact that the concepts of cultic milieu and political religion are useful and apply both to the German and other situations (Payne 2002).

Generally speaking, political religions or cultic milieus were and, where they occur today, continue to be eclectic (Burleigh 2000: 8; Hexham and Poewe 1986: xi).[2] Its leaders take or reject opportunistically bits and pieces from Yogic and Abrahamic traditions, justify their selective appropriations and rejections on the basis of diverse epitomizing experiences (defeat or other severe deprivations), and mix into it popular notions of science—or rather pseudo-science—such as the concept of "race," "eugenics" or "evolution" (Hexham and Poewe 1997: 99; Black 2004: 28). These eclectic religious ideas and epitomizing experiences are the underground that nourish new mythologies of would-be totalitarian regimes, in this case National Socialism.

By contrast with the above-mentioned individuals, some National Socialists intended to force (although they gave lip service to the word 'grow') a new Germany into existence immediately. To this end, Joseph Goebbels added with missionary zeal a propaganda strategy that proclaimed the "positive" qualities of *Kampf*, intolerance, and speakers capable of "convincing" audiences with their "sermons." He preferred hard-hitting terse texts on placards, terror and brutality in halls and on the streets, and an army of what he called "*völkisch* apostles and revivalists" who strategically, but unobtrusively, especially weeks before and after rallies, distributed flyers, brochures, and slogans. This painstaking detail work he called *Kleinarbeit* (Goebbels 1927: 18–28).

Hauer too saw his religious work and Grimm his political poetics as propaganda, but they adapted it to their more sophisticated audiences. Be this as it may, by the late 1920s all were clear that their faith in the Third Reich had to triumph over those who had different views. As Goebbels wrote, "if you are not for me, you are against me" (*Wer nicht für mich ist, der ist wider mich!*) (ibid.: 14).

Looking for examples of a new beginning (*Anfang*)

Hauer was already aware of the political force of new religious phenomena in the early 1920s, when he studied the then very popular anthroposophical movement of Rudolf Steiner (Hauer 1922b: 59). He saw anthroposophy as an outgrowth of the theosophy of Blavatsky and Besant. They mixed occult ideas (that is, Spiritualism, or according to Hauer, Egyptian, Jewish, and medieval magic) with old sagas, natural science hypotheses such as

1.2 Rudolf Steiner, founder of
Anthroposophy

human evolution, elements of Greek and Egyptian hermetic philosophy, and
Jewish Kabbala (ibid.: 7–9, 16–17, 21, 56, 61). While he saw anthroposophy as moving things in the right direction, he had three disagreements
with it: anthroposophy was an occult science (*Geheimwissenschaft*) (ibid.:
26–27);[3] it contained Jewish and, generally, Near Eastern elements (ibid.:
27); and it lacked the profound religious emotion (*religiöse Ergriffenheit*)[4]
that Hauer regarded as part of all great and old (pre-Christian) cosmogonies
(ibid.: 27, 50). Despite these disagreements, Hauer saw anthroposophy as
the beginning of a new era, an epoch of new and powerful intellectual and
spiritual creation (ibid.: 30).

By contrast with anthroposophy, Hauer based his own movement on the
concepts of being grasped by the sacred (*Ergriffenheit*) and of having a
powerful personality (*kraftvolle Persönlichkeit*) capable of experiencing and
understanding the needs of a time (ibid.: 5). Such a person was a religious
genius who experienced himself as grasped by the living intellectual heritage
of his country that empowered him to solve his people's needs.

Hauer's core concepts are rooted in a pre-Christian past from which they
are carried forward by a line of heretics. This notion is not too different from
that of Grimm, for whom the sacred past is carried forward in the form of
sagas. According to Hauer, his alternative religion was established by his
society's great romantic and idealistic literary figures and philosophers.

The same is true for Ernst Bergmann, the protagonist of German Faith, who during the First World War looked for empowerment in German Idealism. By contrast, Grimm deemed himself a political poet in a new sense, whose task it was to give shape to that which had been destroyed, ruined, dissolved, and upset by, specifically, the First World War and Versailles (Grimm 1938: 79).[5]

The motivation of men like Hauer, Bergmann, and Grimm was regeneration of their people following the defeat and denigration of the Great War. From present grimness and the hardening experiences that came with working in other parts of the world, they turned to the roots of an assumed authentic Germanic and therefore pre-Christian past. This return to roots justified seeing their actions as destined.[6] Both Grimm and Hauer, like Heidegger, believed that the *Volk* (meaning the new German existence) could only become authentically what it is by struggling to retrieve its roots in history, literary works, language, and landscape. But rather than being mere imitators, they intended to create a form and fiction that addressed the painfully experienced present. And these respective activities they saw as destined. Their revolutionary work began during and after the Great War and was completed in 1933.

When Rudolf Hess (1894–1987) said at the 1933 Party conference in Nürnberg, "All force emanates from the *Volk*," (*Alle Gewalt geht vom Volke aus*) (Schmitt 1933: 9), he underlined that the German Revolution (*deutsche Revolution*) was legal and authentic (ibid.: 8). It had transitioned from a religious movement to a political religion.

The coalescence of ideas from intellectuals in diverse disciplines during the 1920s and 1930s is remarkable. Coming from the legal profession, Carl Schmitt (1888–1985) talked about National Socialism as being the essence of a *völkisch* totality (*völkischen Totalität*), which was a people's consciousness of itself and of the whole of its own political existence (1938: 614; 1934; 1936). Hauer said the same thing differently. What we might see as terror of the mind is approved by Carl Schmitt (1933: 42). He argued that the *Führer* (Leader) concept, which Hauer saw foreshadowed in Rudolf Steiner, was a unique product of the National Socialist movement; only with the *Führer* concept that emerged naturally from the movement could a totalitarian *Führer*-state be maintained. It was based on an unconditional cospecificity or racial identity of *Führer* and followers.

According to Schmitt, cospecificity (*Artgleichheit*) rests on the continual unfailing contact between *Führer* and followers as well as their mutual loyalty. Only this absolute biological-cum-spiritual identity could prevent, so Schmitt argued (1933: 42), the *Führer*'s power from becoming tyrannical and despotic. It is this *Artgleichheit* that justifies the differentiation of National Socialism from every foreign power no matter how intelligent or advantageous (ibid.: 42). Law would no longer be bound to norms, but to race and, therefore, to type of judge and administrator—to a powerful personality. According to Schmitt the link between law and abstract words in legal paragraphs had been overcome. Instead law was bound "to ourselves and our own race" (ibid.: 46). Schmitt coming from law, Hauer from religion, Heidegger from philosophy, Grimm from Icelandic sagas, and others from different disciplines, were incapable of seeing that cospecificity assumed unquestioning loyalty and silenced criticism. It could only do what it did do, namely, lead to disaster.

National Socialism

National Socialism is in fact a relatively coherent worldview and practice determined to erupt, by radical and violent means, through an existing regime to a new one. The political scientist Carl Schmitt, who became a Nazi in 1933, saw Weimar democracy as bent on becoming a totalitarian state. According to him, only an authoritarian state, which Germany was before the defeat of World War I, would have been able to counteract the unstoppable democratic tendency toward totalitarianism (1938: 613). Furthermore, it may well be that, as Schmitt argues, the totalitarian state is not so much a state as it is a moment in the life of a state. That is, in the life of any state it is a potential moment that results when the state has to exert itself in a specific direction. Potentially, therefore, each form of state is total and in specific dangerous situations moves through totalitarianism (ibid.: 614). According to Nationalists and Nazis, the Weimar Republic, with its structurally flawed constitution and enforced liberal tolerance, was a cultural morass. Goebbels (1927: 14) spoke about Weimar's rotten spirit of Liberalism that made the Republic slide into the mud.[7] And there were no authoritarian institutions, except perhaps the Catholic Church, that could or would stop its slide.

For those who need an image, one could characterize National Socialism as a Hydra, a multi-headed serpent from Greek mythology. Its neck, so to speak, consisted of three vertebrae: *Volk*, *Volksgemeinschaft*,[8] and *Führer*. Its body was movement (*Bewegung*). Its various heads represented variations of the National Socialist worldview that were controlled and propagated by the movement's predominant ideologues in charge of diverse offices (*Ämter*). Thus Alfred Rosenberg (1893–1946), the chief ideologue of the NSDAP and the *Führer*'s Delegate for the Supervision of the Entire Intellectual and World View Education and Training of the NSDAP, gave preference to myths and medievalism (Hutchinson 1977). His view and anti-Christian attitude overlapped with Jakob Wilhelm Hauer. Both grounded German faith in the line of Christian heretics starting with Meister Eckhart.

Where Hauer differed from Rosenberg is in Hauer's greater emphasis on Hinduism and Buddhism, which, as part of the Indo-Germanic tradition, were particularly popular among Heinrich Himmler's SS and specifically his Research Institute called *Ahnenerbe* (Ancestral Heritage). Hauer belonged to

1.3 Alfred Rosenberg, Nazi ideologue

the SS and, like the head of *Ahnenerbe*, Walther Wüst (1900–1991),[9] worked Indo-Germanic ideas into National Socialism, especially its ethics—or rather lack thereof.

As head of the propaganda ministry, Joseph Goebbels (1897–1945) exercised enormous influence on the media and those engaged in the cultural sector. Like Rosenberg and Hauer, Goebbels also became increasingly anti-Christian, anti-Catholic, and with it anti-Semitic (Bärsch 1995; Reuth 2000). Nevertheless, by contrast with the above, he used Christian images and symbols to express distinctly aggressive National Socialist ideas. For example, he characterized the spirit of the resurrection as yearning for the *Führer* (*Führersehnsucht*) (Bärsch 1995: 81). As Bärsch points out, like many German *Bildungsbürger* who experienced genuine despair, Goebbels followed the stations of political ideologisation from Catholicism toward freer forms of a Christian view of the world and self (as in liberal theology) and then National Socialism (ibid.: 81). He mixed Christology with Vitalism and directed his adoration not toward God or Christ but toward the Führer (ibid.: 85). National Socialists knew that being against Christianity was the most authentic and deepest form of anti-Semitism, and how better to denigrate someone than to use their form against them. Turning the Christian office of preacher into a political one, Goebbels loved to say that there are two kinds of political speakers: parliamentarians and preachers. The parliamentarian defends the swamp. The preacher destroys in order to rebuild (ibid.: 87, quoting from Goebbels 1926).

Controversies

According to Bärsch (2002: 18), arguing that National Socialism is a political religion is controversial. Today scholars quarrel over this question.

There are several reasons, some rational and others a matter of faith, why this question comes up. The topic of National Socialism always, no matter how sound the empirical evidence on which certain works may sit, pushes against three articles of historical faith. First, historians are loath to accept that the Weimar Republic was a failure as a democracy. Second, it is also an article of faith, ferociously held against all evidence to the contrary, that anti-Semitism has its source in Christianity (Goldhagen 2002; Rychlak 2003). Third, to say that National Socialism is a political religion is to besmirch the word "religion." When these faith boundaries are crossed, many people become very nervous for fear of relativizing the Holocaust.

Nevertheless, this research shows that the new religionists or paganists, as Steigmann-Gall (2003: 76) prefers to call them, were decidedly anti-Christian because they saw Christianity as a Jewish phenomenon and as fundamentally un-German. As some of the correspondence in this book will show, it is not going too far to say that in the 1920s to 1940s to be anti-Semitic meant being anti-Christian and vice versa. Steigmann-Gall (ibid.: 84, 86) goes out of his way to minimize Rosenberg's popular influence and Ludendorff's determined paganism just to preserve the argument that Nazi anti-Semitism is rooted in Christianity. His argument amounts to saying that Ludendorff's early Protestant upbringing and sectarianism are the source of his various anti-internationalisms, including anti-Semitism. The notion that these people learned their anti-Semitism outside of the church, then hated the church because it would not affirm their anti-Semitism, and finally developed their outright rejection of Christianity over time, is ignored. Yet it is precisely this process of development that is carefully traced by Bärsch (1995) and Reuth (2000) vis-à-vis Goebbels. Likewise, these studies, and those about *Deutsche Christen* who, as Hauer knew, were not Christians but pagans, show just how powerful a force anti-Christianity and paganism was. Most important in this regard is Germann's (1995) study of the political religion of Dietrich Klagges.

Youths against Weimar

Hauer and Grimm, among others, motivated by such young radical Right intellectuals as Carl Schmitt, Wilhelm Stapel, Edgar Jung, Moeller van den Bruck, Joseph Goebbels, Alfred Rosenberg, and Werner Best (1903–1989), portrayed Weimar as having been forced on Germany by its international enemies. Although some eventually quarreled, right-wing ideologues, including Hitler, Himmler (1900–1945) and Heydrich (1904–1942), were also friends. Hauer was particularly close to the SS ideologue and legal mind Werner Best, and met and corresponded with Himmler, especially about his propaganda to establish German Faith instruction within the whole Reich.[10] Stapel, but also Goebbels, corresponded or met with Hans Grimm, who worked with and shared experiences on the front in World War I with Moeller van den Bruck. Grimm met personally with Hitler and Goebbels, although his relationship with them later soured, while Hauer wrote Rosenberg, met with Rudolf Hess, and attempted meetings with Hitler. All knew of one another's works and opinions.

Their radical perceptions began and hardened with two events: (1) the Treaty of Versailles in 1919, which placed sole responsibility for the Great War on Germany, even after Germans themselves revolted against the existing regime, causing the abdication of the Kaiser, and (2) the occupation by the French of the Ruhr in 1923 (see also Brady 1969). Versailles and the occupation of the Ruhr came to be seen as a war against the vanquished by other means (Müller 2003).

To make sure that the denigration stuck, Versailles—as both Jan Smuts and John Maynard Keynes observed—sanctioned the allies plundering Germany of its resources, territory, colonies, and self-respect. Not surprisingly, many German youths soon saw themselves as the victims of liberal modernism. As Müller (2003: 11) points out, young conservative Germans made it their business to "unmask liberal universalist claims", seeing behind it the play of power politics in a very present and concrete situation of despair. For Hauer, too, looking reality in the face became as sacred an activity as uncovering the godliness within. He and the Ludendorffs saw German Faith as having been trapped (*verschüttet*) under Jewish-Christianity.

Müller (2003: 11) calls young radicals such as Schmitt and his cohorts "anthropological conservatives." They were not focused on preserving centuries-old universalist traditions. Rather their focus was on present action (*Tat*) to reshape the immediate needs of their co-sufferers—of those, in other words, who belonged to their specific, one might say primordial, nation. Such anthropological categories as *Volk*, *Volksgemeinschaft*, *Volkstum*, and *Kampf* captured the reality that they thought they experienced on their home ground. Among these youths was Hauer's later friend in the SS, Werner Best (Herbert 1996: 40) and of course the propagandist Joseph Goebbels (Steuckers 1990: 61). No fledgling local national movement could have been handed better tools than those of deprivation, denigration, and occupation with which to take revenge on their global liberators.

Unpublished sources, especially letters, as well as published brochures and books written by Hauer and other determined founders of a *deutsch-Germanic* Faith show what they wanted to unmask, destroy and replace.

Marked for destruction was what Hauer called "Jewish-Christianity." Given that religion was assumed to be culture- and race-specific, what National Socialist sympathizers wanted in Weimar's place was a Faith-based community (*Volksgemeinschaft*) that was seen to be connected directly to its original (*Ur-*) religious inspiration, on the one hand, and to the *Führer*, a German version of an Indo-Germanic guru, who embodied people, nation, and faith, on the other. There were variations on the theme of what each "propagandist" meant by *Ur*-religious inspiration and *Führer*, but their intent to destroy Weimar and replace it with a *Volksgemeinschaft* was as constant as it was lethal.

Although the book concentrates on Hauer, it shows more broadly how young intellectuals and founders of new religions shaped the ideology and organizations of an emergent National Socialist state. First, young Germans, many of whom had lost their middle-class moorings, gathered in little groups (*Bünde*) to listen to self-appointed political-religious leaders teach the importance of honor, heroism, sacrifice, godliness, and struggle (*Kampf*). Soon members of these little groups were drawn into petty street wars and formed or joined private militias to defend themselves against other ideologues and their followers. And sooner than anyone anticipated, a ruthless Party built the war machinery that destroyed uncountable millions of lives.

Clash of cultures and faith-worlds

To this generation of British and North American students who have read Huntington's (1996) *The Clash of Civilizations*, it should not be surprising that Hauer, and the Nazi leadership generally, pictured a structurally analogous scenario. But it was not a clash between Western civilization and culturally assertive non-Western civilizations such as Islam and Chinese Communism that Hauer saw. To begin with, the word civilization had negative connotations for Germans of the 1920s and 1930s and was commonly equated with a general Europeanization and Americanization. These stood for leveling and atomizing processes that were seen to be effacing the specific national character of distinct peoples (Braun 1932). Gutmann (1928: 12) and Knak (1931), both missionaries with anthropological interests in Africa, equated civilization with secularization, commercialization, and mindless imitation, with denial of existing cultural practices, loss of values and self-worth, and Spenglerian decline. Civilization was culture hardened into administration. Even scientific creativity was subjected to the demands of industry and profit (Spengler 1920: 43–4).

By contrast, culture was conceived as an organism, subject like all organisms to the four seasons of life. Each culture was characterized by a specific spirit and a distinctive sense of space. In short, since civilization was a culture's old age, it was hardly worth clashing with. Rather, from the beginning, global politics were configured along cultural lines. The clash was one

1.4 Dietrich Klagges, Nazi ideologue and
founder of the Working Community of
German Christians

between cultures and therefore, depending on where one was in the National Socialist spectrum, between faiths, ethnicities, and/or races. By 1934, Hauer equated religion with race.

The picture of the world that Hauer sold his followers was one of a fundamental clash (*Kampf*) between two faith-worlds (*Glaubenswelten*), the Near-Eastern Semitic and the Indo-Germanic. Of these he experienced negatively and rejected the former, and experienced positively and affirmed the latter. Hauer's category of a Near-Eastern Semitic faith-world included Judaism, "Jewish-Christianity,"[11] and Islam. The Indo-Germanic faith-world included Hinduism, Buddhism, and a pre-Christian Germanic Faith. Having been a missionary to India before he became Professor of Religious Studies in Tübingen and the founder of the German Faith Movement, he personally experienced Hinduism and Buddhism directly and wrote about them professionally. His enchantment with the latter two faiths contributed to his intense, if in his pre-1930 works discreetly expressed, dislike of things and thoughts Jewish. He worked hard behind the scenes to remove Jewish and—what to him amounted to the same thing—Christian scholars from university positions.

By contrast, Hinduism and Buddhism were compatible with National Socialism. Together they blended into an ideological mix that dazzled not only the anthropologists and indologists of the *Ahnenerbe*,[12] people such as Walter Wüst, Ernst Schäfer, Bruno Beger, Ludwig Ferdinand Clauss (1892–1974), and of course Wilhelm Hauer, but pervaded the SS generally from Heinrich Himmler (1900–1945) on down (Kater 2001).

Germans who lacked contact with countries that Hauer placed into the respectable Indo-Germanic culture circle or who did not work with the anthropological imperative of using the non-West to destroy the West, used liberal theology, a religiosity that sanctioned free reflection, to divest Christianity of its Jewish elements. For example, Dietrich Klagges (1891–1971) was an important ideologue of National Socialism. Unfortunately, he is known primarily for having called a stateless Adolf Hitler to the position of Senior Executive Officer of the Brunswick Legation in Berlin, thereby making him a German citizen in 1932. Important here, however, is the fact that the free religious Klagges blended politics and religion to postulate that the Gospel of Mark was the *Ur*-gospel.[13] As the original gospel, Mark appeared to be innocent of Jewish distortion, is therefore *artgemäss*,[14] and worthy of being the foundation of a new German Faith (Klagges 1926). In a manner analogous to Hauer, Klagges then founded the Working Community of German Christians (DCA) who sought to show that the real Jesus was not Jewish but Indo-Germanic and whose true identity was distorted by later apostles who were under the spell of Jewish intellectual power (*jüdischen Geistesmacht*) (Germann 1995: 37–9).

The 'other' as tool to attack the 'own'

The route taken by Hauer and most of his students and followers, namely, from being students of theology to becoming determined enemies of Christianity had been mapped out for them by many of their intellectual mentors, including most prominently Nietzsche. While a student in England, Hauer claims to have been deeply affected by Plato. Upon his return to Germany, Nietzsche's works played an important role in Hauer's thought and that of his circle (Junginger 1999: 268–76).

Within Hauer's first major *Bund* founded in the 1920s,[15] called the *Köngener*, a select Nietzsche circle was formed, consisting initially of twelve people. In one of her letters to Hauer, Lene Rukwied mentions that Nietzsche is presented to them in a lively fashion and that he reminds her of Hauer.[16] Hauer's assistant, the doctoral student of the Nazi pedagogue Ernst Krieck, published on Nietzsche in Hauer's journal *Deutscher Glaube*.[17] To Nazi scholars Nietzsche was the prophet of National Socialism for the obvious reason that he undermined (*zersetzen*) Christianity and justified eugenics. A sick man, Nietzsche idolized life by equating salvation with religious, political, ethical, and social anarchy (Hofer 1934: 252). No Nazi would fail to recognize that Nietzsche's psychology of salvation was opposed to that of the Jew Paul. Even the Zionist Martin Buber, who was a friend of Hauer and

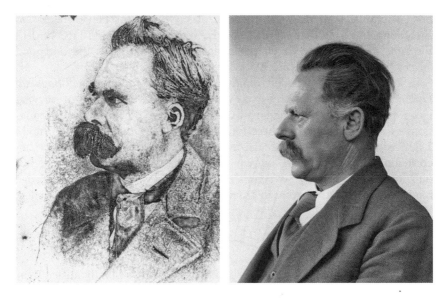

1.5 Friedrich Nietzsche

1.6 Jakob Wilhelm Hauer; liked comparison with Nietzsche

participated in his conferences, shared Hauer's interest in Nietzsche. To both of them, guilt, sin, and Jewish-Christianity were tools to destroy a natural human vitalism.[18]

The epistemological function that the Bhagavad Gita had for Hauer, Islam had for Nietzsche. Thus Nietzsche used Islam as a tool for attacking the " 'European disease' of Judaeo-Christian modernity," especially its "universalist claims" (Almond 2003: 43, 44). Hauer and other Nazis who had read Nietzsche understood correctly that the latter's virulent anti-Christianity meant that Nietzsche was passionately anti-Semitic or, if one might say, anti-Jewish. Usually the blame is put on Nietzsche's sister. At any rate, Hauer used the *Bhagavad Gita* and Nietzsche used Islam to express their respective dislike of things Jewish-Christian. More importantly, they used these to conjoin the holy with the bellicose, the *Sakralgemeinschaft* with the *Kampfgemeinschaft* (Almond 2003: 48; Hauer 1934a: 1).

Hauer (1932a; 1934a: 1) talks about wars of male defiance and male pride (*männertrotzige Kriege*) just as Nietzsche swooned about "the virility" of "Persian warrior-monks, unchained to any principle or ethic" (Almond 2003: 48). Both emphasize a life of tension between self-communion and self-surrender as in the self-communion with the creative depth of one's soul-cum-world from whence comes one's knowledge that one is doing right versus the self-surrender to a life of action and war (Hauer 1934a: 3). Like Nietzsche, from whom he probably took the idea, Hauer fuses mystic and warrior. In other words, mysticism or faith is the ultimate sanction for war, not "womanish Christianity" (Almond 2003: 48). Thus to Hauer there is no such thing as a deed that is only good. Each deed shelters guilt (1934a: 14). But guilt, like tragedy to which it belongs by its very nature, is "beyond good and evil" (*Bhagavad Gita* II, 50, quoted in Hauer 1934a: 21).

In sum, whatever Nietzsche found in Islam, Hauer found in the *Bhagavad Gita*. For them these faiths bypass moral prescription. Instead of obeying moral prescriptions, the Bhagavad Gita turns to the metaphysical foundations of all happening and these foundations are *Brahman* and god (ibid.: 25). Assigning such non-Western notions as "elite religious warriors" an epistemological function of knowing the enemy, Hauer and Nietzsche not only intended to destroy "womanish" Christianity so that a new knowledge might emerge but they were instrumental in creating that new knowledge. We know it as Nazism.[19]

Anti-Semitism

By blaming anti-Semitism on Christianity, scholars have badly misled their readers. In nineteenth- and early twentieth-century Germany it was not Christianity that was, nor Christians who were by virtue of their faith, anti-Semitic. Rather it was neo-pagans both within and without the church, who had an intense dislike of Christianity precisely because it is Semitic. By Semitic Hauer meant Jewish. Sometimes he used the term Jewish-Christianity; at other times Israelitic-Christianity or Israelitic-Jewry (1934e: 98, 102). As for neo-pagans, many remained officially in the church although they hated Christianity and were members of alternative religions such as Hauer's German Faith Movement.

The source of anti-Semitism lies elsewhere than with religion. It lies in a fundamental human divide between those people who love culture, by which I mean the poetics and politics that grew out of a very specific local condition and history, and those who love civilization, by which I mean the poetics and politics that are rooted in non-specific, universal laws meant to protect any civilian, local or foreign. Hauer's fight against Jewish-Christianity is based on this divide. Curiously enough, so is Hans Kohn's and Martin Buber's fight for Zionism. They saw the salvation of Jewry in the return to a more holistic, organic culture, and pictured a Jewish spiritual regeneration through a "return to the homeland—to the Orient" away from the corruption and cultural decadence of the Occident (Moore 2003: 31). Buber's and Kohn's interests in Hauer's German Faith ideas have their source in their respective *völkisch* notions of reclaiming the original cultural character of "their" respective peoples (Moore 2003: 30; Golomb 2004: 166).

The fundamental human divide, the fault line of human antagonism, is that between culture and civilization. Religion is the (cultural) weapon with which to fight the enemy. Huntington (1996: 125) is wrong when he sees this divide as new. The essence of National Socialism and fascism generally is that it draws its political boundaries to coincide with cultural ones. Huntington is correct in recognizing that this process is going on now, although the geographical centre is not Germany but the Middle East.

The culture-civilization game is more simple and general than the elaborate ideological deceptions spun by totalitarians. A simple analogy shows the human aspect of the divide. A house owner lives in a specific locality of which he is very fond and which he romanticizes. One day he receives an interesting worldly visitor whom he duly welcomes. Initially the visitor gives pleasure with his new ideas about how to improve this or that, and it is appreciated. But in due course the host notices that the guest has taken over the administration, as it were, of the host's house. The guest's knowledge has metamorphosed into power and the host does not like it. Soon he sees his guest as representing a foreign world which, if he accepted it, would mean the destruction of life as he knew it. Conflict is inevitable.

Anti-Semitism, then, is something that many people with strong local loyalties and attachments see personified in the concept of Jews. Increasingly, as also happened during the 1920s, they see it personified in America. In Indonesia, the Chinese are its Jews. Religion, ethnicity, and sexual orientation are weapons used to defend or gain something. Above all, they are what they were in Nazi Germany; powerful tools of propaganda and terrorism, especially terrorism of the mind.

Morality is another source of the intense dislike of Jewish-Christianity. To Hauer, Christianity hindered the natural growth of an "organic morality" that alone could produce the proper attitude to the "great realities of life," namely, the body, reproduction and love (1935: 101). According to Hauer the first book of Moses destroys an aristocratic conception of work and the Sermon on the Mount alienates the human being from earth.

Hauer finds particularly irritating that the morality of Christianity is captured in a holy scripture that enforces moral precepts first laid out by an Israelitic-Jewry. To him, these moral precepts are un-German. Furthermore, German morality has its own sources; first, its own people's will and nature and, second, the example of its own great men and women who are the embodiment of that nature. Importantly, German Faith finds anathema the notion of Ten Commandments chiseled in stone or of a word-based Confession signed by all. To Hauer's mind, morality and *deutsch*-Germanic Faith shape themselves continually like an allegory of lived life (ibid.: 103). There is no dogma, word or Scripture. German morality is not rigidly chained to words but changes as reality changes and as the original nature adapts to new conditions. It is a convenient moral relativism that Hauer and his cohorts developed. In the final analysis it is, as Herbert (1996: 98) points out, a fighter ethic that negates all moral ties except those with respect to the interests of one's own *Volk*.

Finally, the myth that Hauer perpetuated, namely, that scripted law is un-German, is belied by the deliberate efforts on the part of Werner Best, among others, to re-script law especially pertaining to human and people's rights or the rights of nations. Best rejected every form of codified rights of nations that was in some way based on universal values (Herbert 1996: 277). To Nazis universalism is abstract and therefore ineffective, even effete. What they valued was reality (*Wirklichkeit*), by which was meant the existence of actual power differences within society and among nations. And on these actual power differences they based their morality of "might is right."

Method

This book rests on years of work in German archives. Since 1995 I have spent four months of each year in Marbach, Berlin, Koblenz, or Leipzig reading, taking notes, or copying innumerable letters and other unpublished documents.

The method of this research and writing was informed by a question that burned in my mind for decades, namely, how did Germans come to embrace National Socialism? The answer to that question throws all the light one needs on the consequences of having held such a worldview—a disastrous war, millions of people dead, the Holocaust, and the post-war German generations burdened with guilt, an inadequately explained history, and unending quarrels about reparations. Only recently has a new generation of scholars embarked on the task of writing carefully researched and detailed biographies not only of the top Nazi leaders but, importantly, of the middle-rank Nazi ideologues. Among them are Ulrich Herbert (1996), Ralf Georg Reuth (2000), Holger Germann (1995), Claus-Ekkehard Bärsch (1995, 2002), Wolfgang Dierker (2003), Barbara Zehnpfennig (2000), and Fritz Heinrich (2002). The work of the Canadian historian Michael H. Kater (2001) is outstanding. They and others inspire this work. These scholars give us a clearer picture of what happened to a nation after a devastating defeat and a punishing peace. The aftermath of World War I should have provided clear lessons how not to treat defeated people. It should have taught us that ex-combatants and disaffected intellectuals make virulent politics and that their fanaticism inevitably takes hostage the hearts and minds of young men uprooted by war. But it did not.

This book is not a smoothly written history. As careful readers know, the latter tend to sit on published secondary sources, many of them being interpretations of interpretations, bringing little new food for thought. While analytical chapters play an important role, there are several chapters that primarily show how, especially, Jakob Wilhelm Hauer and those associated with him thought, changed, and deceived themselves and others.

I have no illusions about the limitations of the unpublished documents that their authors bequeathed to the archives that are studied here. Some papers, such as those of Ludwig Klages (1872–1956), for example, were clearly tampered with to remove evidence of his enthusiasm for the Nazi regime. Furthermore, a researcher who wants to quote from archived documents requires family approval. In the case of Hauer some significant documents are missing and, given what they likely contained, one doubts that it is accidental. Nevertheless, unpublished documents are "experience-near" (that is, they closely reflect real experiences) and this, in conjunction with published sources and recent scholarly work, gives the researcher and reading audiences a good sense of a man's development and motivations. It also puts us in touch with the unfolding catastrophe.

Organization

The various chapters of this book describe the gathering storm of resistance to Versailles under the banner of what was broadly called German Faith. It is the construction of this faith by diverse radical co-plotters that helped usher in National Socialism. Most chapters are centered on the intense time from 1919 to 1932 when National Socialism invaded the hearts and minds of Germans and from 1933 to 1936 when National Socialism became established and sloughed off those it had once needed. The last chapter links what became the political religion of National Socialism to similar ideas, differently worded, of the New Right today. While the book does not discuss anti-Semitism directly or deliberately, it is of course present throughout.

Following this Introduction, Chapter 2 gives an overview of Hauer's life and work based on published literature, Hauer's own accounts, and archival research. Chapter 3 describes the takeover of popular politics by the young during the *Bünde* phase and shows Hauer's own politicization. The fiery dialectic between *Bünde* leaders, Nationalists, and National Socialists is illuminated in Chapter 4. Hauer's German Faith is described in Chapters 5 and 6. Here the Hindu influences on Hauer's movement and on the SS are highlighted. Chapter 7 describes how the *Wehrwolf Bund* and SS helped to organize the German Faith Movement on the ground.

Hauer's war of attrition against Church and Christianity and the activities of the *Deutsche Christen* are discussed in Chapter 8. Chapter 9 looks at the SS intellectual Werner Best. It is to him that Hauer addresses his concerns about Catholicism, Zionism, and the free religious who, within his movement, were to be the bulwark against the power of the Roman Catholic Church. Chapter 10 discusses the "new faith" of novelists, especially that of Hans Grimm. It is here that the maleness of National Socialism is seen most clearly. Chapter 11 looks at Mathilde Ludendorff's scientific neo-paganism and, by describing the works of Sigrid Hunke, takes the diverse ideas of German Faith believers, whom we shall call Faithlers, forward to the New Right today. What Hauer called German Faith is now called Europe's own religion. A brief Conclusion links past to present.

Chapter 2

An overview

Introduction

Jakob Wilhelm Hauer was a missionary with the Basel Mission Society from 1900 to 1911. He became a student at Oxford University in 1911 and eventually an academic and founder of a new religion called the German Faith Movement (DGB).[1] Among German academics, Hauer is known primarily as having been a professor of religious studies[2] and Indology (*Indologie*) at the University of Tübingen and, for a short time, at the University of Marburg (Werner 1986). The American Scott-Craig and the Englishman Davies (see Hauer *et al.* 1937: 8), however, saw Hauer as a "prophet and leader" of a "Neo-Pagan religion."[3]

Hauer's real passion was Indo-Germanic religion, with emphasis at least as much on the Hindu as on the Germanic part. His stated aim was for his religion to become the essence of National Socialism and the New German man, especially as formed by the SS.[4] The parallel careers of being an academic and a founder of a new religion took off in 1919 after the "November Revolution and its aftermath"[5] and when he left the service of the church. At that time Hauer turned his Bible Circle into a worldview organization called *Bund der Köngener*.[6] Unsure whether it was philosophical or religious in nature, Hauer initially opted for the former and rooted his youth group in the German Youth Movement (Laqueur 1962: 106; Neurohr 1956: 158; Stachura 1981: 82). According to Hauer (1935: 10), the Youth Movement was struggling for a new Germany. It was the proper context, therefore, within which to plant the seed for the intellectual and religious breakthrough of the German revolution.[7] In 1933 he brought together various *Bünde*, Germanic and Nordic religions, and other groups such as the free thinkers or free religious (*Freireligiöse*) under one umbrella known as the ADGB[8] or simply German Faith (DG) after his flagship journal of that name.[9]

Hauer in the existing literature

Hauer and his SS colleague Walther Wüst were determined to make Religious Studies their instrument for the construction of a new Indo-Aryan-Germanic

religion based on a racial foundation. Today some scholars are just as determined to sell Hauer's work as "science" by downplaying his early affinity
for *völkisch* thought and National Socialism.

The biography of Hauer by Margarete Dierks (1986) is a good example of
this approach. Therefore, because Dierks is determined to rehabilitate
Hauer, her readers must know something about her. Born 1914, Dierks officially left the evangelical-Lutheran church in 1932 and joined Mathilde
Ludendorff's new religion called The German Perception of God (*Deutsche
Gotterkenntnis*). Like Hauer she inclined toward *völkisch* views, became a
devoted National Socialist, and joined a radical new religion. After the war,
Dierks was interned for 2½ years and denazified in 1948.[10] From 1951 to
1959, we find her again in Old and New Right circles in correspondence, for
example, with Hans Grimm,[11] in whose semi-religious literary gatherings
(*Dichtertagungen*) she participated.[12] She was also found in Unitarian circles,
one of the new religions that became popular in Germany after the war—
especially among surviving Nazis, because it gave them an intellectual outlet.
She wrote Hauer's biography in the spirit of appreciation for men such as
Hans Grimm and Hans Baumann (1914–1988), because they and their
works were ostracized after 1945.[13]

To understand the limitation of Dierks' otherwise detailed work on Hauer,
we have to know what she meant by the "science of history" as she described
it in her 1939 Ph.D. dissertation on Prussian archconservatives and the Jewish
problem (Dierks 1939). According to Dierks, German historiography had to
fulfill two tasks: one, "the exact, imperturbable and merciless investigation of
facts," and two, "the appraisal of historical processes and personalities in
terms of their meaning for the rise and greatness of the empire, for the health
and growth of the *Volk*, and for the purity in type of all German life" (1939:
7). In other words, Dierks practiced the scientific pursuit of history from a
Nazi worldview perspective and for its benefit. She believed that doing so
created a *völkisch*, in the deepest sense, political deed that would have an
effect on the future (ibid.: 7). What she did not do, however, is subject Hauer's
life to a "merciless investigation of facts." As is shown here, his pettiness,
spying, lack of truthfulness, his over-ambitiousness to make his political mark
through religion, his radical destructiveness toward Christianity and things
Jewish, all these qualities are omitted or glossed over in Dierks's work.

When she became interested in rehabilitating Hauer and other former
Nazi scholars and writers after the war, she systematically played down what
formerly she had emphasized, namely their National Socialist affiliations
(1986). With respect to Hauer, she downplayed important activities that
particularly shaped his National Socialist development, for example, his
lively involvement with the *Bünde* and the Youth Movement. His *Köngener*
group is mentioned, but in a work that overflows with Hauer's correspondence, his letters to some *Bünde* leaders and disagreements with Rudolf
Otto, are conspicuous by their absence (Dierks 1986: 66, 160).

While the works of Horst Junginger (1999), a scholar of religious studies in Tübingen, and Hubert Cancik (1982), one of Junginger's mentors, are academic in a way that Dierks's work is not, their notion of scholarship means that they quarrel about concepts, attribute National Socialism to the failures of Christianity, and downplay the fact that the new religions of Weimar helped usher in National Socialism.

Horst Junginger's excellent study (1999) of the shift from a philological to a *völkisch* approach in religious studies highlights Hauer's academic career and contributions and shows how deeply his academic work was shaped by his religio-political ambitions. It also describes his National Socialist involvement, but largely ignores his role in founding a new religion.[14] Consequently, Junginger does not make room in his analysis for individuals in religious studies who, far from being researchers, are in fact advocates or founders of new religions.

Cancik's (1982) paper, from which Junginger took off, attempts to show that, despite their cooperation with National Socialism, *völkisch* groups, including Hauer's, were not the beginning of the Third Reich, but a sign of the end of the liberal Weimar Republic (Cancik 1982: 180). This statement is made despite Hauer's explicit obsession not only with radically breaking down old forms but with creating new ones: a new *Bund*, a new Community, a new *Volk*, a new undemocratic Germanic state. Hauer's portrayal of himself as a conservative revolutionary, which, despite Mohler, was a code word for a National Socialist, is ignored.[15]

Cancik makes his end-of-Weimar argument because he sees in Hauer's anti-colonialism—his sympathy for Gandhi and India's insurgent movement, among other things—the last vestiges of Weimar liberalism (Cancik 1982: 179). In the process, Cancik overlooks two attitudes shared by the Old and New Right to this day. First, he ignores Nazi empathy for underdogs precisely because they saw themselves as underdogs during the Versailles treaty era (see von Leers n.d.). Second, he fails to understand that it was precisely Hauer's and other Nazis' radical liberalism that led them to National Socialism (Salomon 1999: 637).[16] More about this later: suffice it to say with Haffner that Hitler could as easily be ordered into the extreme left as the opposite. In fact, the traditional conservative opposition saw Hitler as standing left (Haffner 2001b: 70).[17]

To buttress his argument, Cancik points out that the Hauer people were closer to the left, Strasser, wing of National Socialism (1982: 180). Not looking at the continuously shifting political battles of those years, he fails to mention that so were Goebbels, Himmler, Reventlow (Reuth 2000: 140, 162–5, 166) and Dietrich Klagges (Germann 1995), all of them determined and uncompromising National Socialist ideologues and practitioners.[18] Confidently Cancik asserts that since that wing was squeezed out of the party in 1930, Hauer's followers had little in common with Hitler and were therefore unimportant to the future development of National Socialism and the Third Reich (Cancik 1982: 180).[19] This is like saying that because Goebbels and Himmler worked with the Strasser brothers, their Nazi propaganda and policing did not further National Socialism.

Countervailing factors are ignored,[20] namely, (1) that Hauer's contact with Gregor Strasser was minor in comparison with that between Hauer and Reventlow; (2) that Reventlow, Hauer's co-founder, promptly rejoined the Hitler circle after Otto Strasser's and later Gregor Strasser's resignations; (3) that the respectable historian Kershaw (1998: 397) has shown that Gregor Strasser's differences with Hitler were not ideological;[21] and, finally, that Hauer's "liberalism" (his knowledge of comparative religions) was a convenient springboard from which to launch his right-wing religious radicalism. In Hauer's view one was "reactionary" or "radical," and the escape from the former to the latter was through liberal theology and, if one went further back in time, through numerous nonconformists of the Roman Catholic Church (Heer 1982: 46). Thus, Liberalism broke the ground enabling the emergence of radicalism.[22]

Regarding liberal theology, Hauer knew what he was talking about. Like Rosenberg (1930), who found inspiration and forerunners of radical religious political movements among twelfth- and thirteenth-century heretics (Heer 1982: 46; 1998), so Hauer found Catholic discontents in the nineteenth century. He mentioned Johannes Ronge's story and the German-Catholic Movement (DKB) in a letter to Werner Best.[23] Around 1844, liberal citizens of both confessions promoted the DKB (Leesch 1938: 1). Ronge, a small-town provincial boy, who at the University of Breslau learned to hate Catholicism but nevertheless studied theology, was the originator of the Break-with-Rome movement. Like Hauer later with his DGB, Ronge originally attempted to unite the DKB with the free Protestants (*freien Protestanten*) who in 1858 became the League of Free Religious Communities in Germany (BFGD). The fusion failed, as did Ronge's movement. Nevertheless, Leesch saw in the DKB movement a sincere connection between *radical* political ideas with *radical* religious perspectives (Leesch 1938: 3). This also applies to Hauer.

Interesting is Leesch's argument that the DKB grew out of a precritical rationalism of the popular enlightenment philosophy, not from the critical rationalism of Kant (1724–1804) (Leesch 1938: 39). Popular or vulgar rationalism assumed, for example, that the human being is by nature good. By contrast, Kant argued that within the human being, owing to his own fault, but simultaneously as inner necessity, rests a radical evil (Leesch 1938: 40).

Hauer mirrors the DKB in two ways. He recognized the power of liberalism to lead to radical politics.[24] Unlike the DKB, he compounded his radical politics with vulgar Romanticism, in common with such CR authorities as Paul de Lagarde (1827–1891), Houston Stewart Chamberlain, L. F. Clauss, H. F. K. Günther (1935a), Alfred Rosenberg, Herman Wirth (1885–1981), Gustav Neckel (1878–1940) and many others of this ilk.

2.1 Ludwig Ferdinand Clauss,
anthropologist and race psychologist

According to Hauer, the German Christians (DC) practiced liberal theology.[25] For example, responding to a report in which the Nazi Uniate *Reichsbischof* argued "that Christianity is not an outgrowth of Jewishness but originated from the constant battle with it, and for the first time since the emergence of Christianity has a *Volk* dared to declare war [*Kampf*] on Jews." Hauer replied as follows. "The thoughts that the Uniate *Reichsbischof* developed here are a typical result of liberal theology."[26] And against Cardinal Faulhaber's New Year sermon which rejected any racial connection to Faith and identified the assertions of German Christians and of Rosenberg's *Mythus* (1930) as "a new Germanic or Nordic Religion," Hauer answered: "Consciousness of the power of Blood that is the expression of the godly primordial will [*Urwillen*] in us cannot be stopped by any human agitation."[27]

Junginger, giving figures about the religious affiliation of SS officers, supports the claim that the DGB and other new religions of the time did not advance National Socialism. The number of SS officers who claimed to be *gottgläubig* (a general term used for *deutsch*, Nordic, or Germanic believers) rather than Christian is in dispute. Suffice it to say here that Herbert F. Ziegler (1989; 2001) claims that on the average 76 percent of the SS were subject to new religious ideas (*gottgläubig*), while Junginger (2001:30) claims 75 percent were Christian. Using the personnel files of SS leaders[28] in the federal archive in Berlin, this research confirms Ziegler's figures. It is the case, however, that some of those who were *gottgläubig* did not officially leave the church, although they expressed their hatred of it in letters. Their not leaving was opportunistic. For example, they, or someone in the family, received an income from the church. What motivated them, however, were *deutsch*-Germanic ideas of Hauer and his associates.

Cancik's and Junginger's arguments that the DGB had little in common with Hitler and National Socialism, and did not further the latter, is belied by all of Hauer's efforts and thinking between 1933 and 1936. Thus he states, for example, on 27 March 1936, "I myself am convinced that German Faith of necessity demands the National Socialistic worldview, that therefore every German Faithler must be a National Socialist ... Likewise, I am convinced that the National Socialistic worldview, when it is understood and lived in depth, leads to German Faith."[29] But, being Hauer, he added, "To say this publicly or to foreground it in our advertisements would be misguided and disastrous so long as National Socialism supports a 'positive Christianity' ... consequently I have forbidden ... anyone to say that National Socialism and Christianity are irreconcilable."[30]

Nanko (1993: 273), who wrote his dissertation at the University of Tübingen in 1991 and then published it as a book, seems to recognize that the DGB and Hauer were determined to be in effect the essence of National Socialism. His book is a sociological and historical analysis of the organization of the DGB. He is sensitive to the internal rivalries and outside pressures, and gives some statistics about the socioeconomic background of its leaders and followers. Three economic groups were *not* found in the DGB. They were workers, the old bourgeoisie, and capitalists (Nanko 1993: 292). By contrast, civil servants and the self-employed, the latter including many university students, made up most of the membership (38 percent civil servants, 44 percent self-employed: of the latter, 10 percent were students). Employees represented about 20 percent of the membership and 16 percent of the leadership (Nanko 1993: 291). Civil servants were especially over-represented in the leadership.[31] On Hauer's Board (*Führerrat*), 69 percent were civil servants (teachers and professors), 16 percent were self-employed (lawyers, physicians, engineers, journalists, publishers and artists), and another 16 percent were white-collar workers. The self-employed made up 53 percent of the speakers (Nanko 1993: 290, 291), and of these 80 percent did work that was somehow book-centered (Nanko 1993: 293).

Nanko concludes that DGB members and especially leaders were predominantly in disciplines and professions that were predisposed to be ideological (Nanko 1993: 298).[32] Leaders were primarily political activists and writers as well as managers of interpersonal or inter-group relations with a special talent, and importantly with the time for and vested interest in propagating their ideas widely. Their influence far exceeded their numbers in the groups —something toward which Hauer, and for that matter all *völkisch* writers, worked consciously and systematically from the beginning (Nanko 1993: 103–5). Together their influence greatly exceeded that of German Christians and Confessionals combined.

The effort made to reach large audiences is shown in the correspondence between Erwin Ackerknecht (1880–1960) and Hans Grimm during the 1920s and 1930s. Ackerknecht took it as a sacred duty to promote the ideas of *völkisch* and Nationalist writers by organizing countless readings and talks throughout Germany. In the twenties, Ackerknecht was the director of the public library of Stettin. Like most *völkisch* thinkers who outlived their usefulness, Ackerknecht eventually fell into disfavor with some Nazis.[33]

My disagreements with Nanko—who, like Junginger, is a religious studies scholar—and with the historian Burleigh (2000) are over their goal of removing discussions about the DGB from the church struggle (Scholder 1988). Burleigh (2000: 257) argues that the church struggle belongs to a "discussion of resistance." I disagree. Since Nazis and Nationalists regarded Christianity as being "Jewish," the church struggle was a core element of the Nazi offensive to remove all traces of "Jewish" life from German society at the time. And this offensive was led not only by Rosenberg, who had enormous influence over what was read by students and the German public, but by Hauer, Wüst, Beger, Best, and numerous other SS intellectuals as well as Nationalist writers for whom German poetry was religion.

The rivalries and religious differences between Goebbels, Rosenberg, Himmler and Hauer are often used to justify the idea that there was no consistent, religious-based National Socialistic ideology. This is wrong (Nassen 1987). True, the variant core elements of Goebbels' religiosity consisted of Christological symbols and Vitalism, Rosenberg's of Nordic religion and mysticism, Himmler's and Hauer's of aspects of the Yogic and Germanic traditions, and Grimm's of Icelandic sagas. But in their awareness of living in a time of devastating crisis, all shared a radical determination to destroy existing structures and traditions that they claimed were imposed by an alien enemy, the Jews. They also shared a desire to harness the mysterious depths of the German *Volk*'s primeval power to build the Third Reich.[34] Therefore it was necessary to destroy the Jewish *Weltanschauung* found in the so-called Jewish faiths of Christianity, Marxism, Materialism, and economic Liberalism (Bärsch 1995: 80–3; Goodrick-Clarke 1998: 122).

Johannes von Leers (1902–1965) was an SS officer, briefly agrarian history professor at Jena, chief editor of the National Socialist journal *The Will and Way* (*Wille und Weg*), and a key figure on Hauer's Board (*Führer-rat*) of the German Faith Movement (Rimmele 1999). Leers' sole purpose was to ensure that high school and university students read pro-Nazi literature.[35] People such as Walter Darré (1895–1953), Hans F. K. Günther, Ludwig Ferdinand Clauss, and numerous literary figures including Hans F. Blunck (1888–1961), Gustav Frenssen (1863–1945) and Hans Grimm, among many others, all were directly or indirectly connected to Hauer, Leers, and the SS.

2.2 Gustav Frenssen, writer

2.3 Johann von Leers, anti-Semitic agrarian history professor at Jena, on the board of the German Faith Movement

All were committed to anti-Semitic ideas and a determination to free Germany from the imperialism of Jewish-Christianity (Bramwell 1985: 33, 49). Together they harnessed enormous listening and reading audiences, addressing anything from a hundred to over twenty thousand people at any one time.[36] To minimize their combined and proactive influence on the public to embrace National Socialism is absurd. As von Leers points out with Frenssen, their path to National Socialism went through the door of liberal theology.[37]

One of the letters to von Leers shows both the large influence of Hauer-like ideas on young minds and the wild liberalism vis-à-vis theology. *Help Out* (*Hilf mit*), a journal for youth published by the National Socialist Teacher Association (NSLB), reached approximately two million high-school students. It carried a clear racially based National Socialist message of blood and soil written so as to counter all Christian tendencies. Furthermore, it provided an information service for teachers that dealt with historical, racial-political, and cultural-political questions in the National Socialist sense. It was an effective tool against Christians in that it presented the church fathers as criminals and made the Nordic race central.[38]

Given the above, Nanko's argument that, since Hitler's takeover, Hauer and those that joined his ambitions "accommodated themselves as was necessary" or reacted automatically to "pressure from outside" (Nanko 1993:

109, 111, 112), ignores Hauer's determined proactive efforts to further National Socialism. Nanko also sidesteps questions of individual choice and moral responsibility (see Ustorf 2000: 262). Hauer developed in the *völkisch* and National Socialistic direction long before January 1933. And his increasingly intense dislike of the church was already apparent in 1919.

Following Buchheim (1953), who based his first postwar work on the DGB primarily on an interview with Hauer and his material, Nanko placed the blame for the "National Socialistic phase" of the DGB and for Hauer's forced resignation from it in 1935 on secret service (SD) radicals. The SD was the Security branch of the SS. Himmler was the head of the SS, Heydrich of the SD. Radicals in the SD were intent on coordinating (*gleichschalten*) DGB and SS ideology (Nanko 1993: 281). Unfortunately, Nanko ignores important events that contradict his "phase" theory. First, on 1 July 1935 Himmler founded the *Ahnenerbe*, whose goal was to further the "science of intellectual prehistory" (*Geistesurgeschichte*) (Kater 2001: 27). In order to succeed, *Ahnenerbe* needed to attract respected university scholars who would provide evidence for Himmler's theory that the world's great cultures originated in the North. Unfortunately, Hauer's publication in 1934 of *Deutsche Gottschau*, a book that was obviously ideological and unscholarly, put Hauer's usefulness to Himmler and Wüst into question. Wüst became leader of *Ahnenerbe* in 1936 specifically to save it from dilettantism (Kater 2001: 202; Wüst and Schrötter 1942). Hauer's book made him an ideological and organizational competitor rather than a loyal academic, and his charisma irritated leaders of the NSDAP. Early in 1936, therefore, Hauer was coerced into resigning his leadership of the DGB, but he continued to perpetuate his German Faith both at the university and within informal reading circles.

The missiologist Werner Ustorf (2000: 55–6), who also discusses Hauer, recognizes that the DGB was "critical of the churches and publicly claimed to be the religious soul of the Nazi party." Since Ustorf sees Hauer as having been a Christian missionary who did not "formally separate from the (Basel) Mission," he is inclined to agree with Cancik and Junginger on the matter of Hauer's sudden change from secular "liberalism" to National Socialism (ibid.: 67, 58). Worse still, according to Ustorf not only did Hauer not leave the mission, "but he remained a member of the church!" (ibid.: 59).

At least two of Hauer's letters either contradict Ustorf's findings or expose Hauer as a liar. First, on 20 November 1933 Hauer wrote Hans Brenke, a medical doctor who joined the DGB while yet being a church member that he, that is Hauer, had formally left the church (*Kirchenaustritt*), an act that he now regarded as a duty. He did so in the "early fall before Hess's decree."[39] Second, there is Hauer's short exchange with Hartenstein, the Director of the Basel Mission. On 29 November 1933 Hartenstein, having learned of Hauer's Nazi activities, wrote Hauer that, "because your name is still mentioned in connection with the Basel Mission" in public discussions

2.4 Walther Wüst, *Ahnenerbe* SS, talks about Hitler's *Mein Kampf* before SS leaders in München, 1937

and newspapers, "for example, the *Frankfurter Zeitung*," he (Hartenstein) is forced to declare publicly "that the connection between your name and the evangelical *Missionswerk* is dissolved."[40] Hauer answered, "Any public explanation that I no longer belong to the Basel Mission is hardly necessary."[41] After all, he continued, "no one in Germany would still link me to the mission." What he would prefer Hartenstein to do is simply remove his name from the list of the annual reports and thereby formally and entirely dissolve the connection.[42]

Junginger (1999: 120 n. 33) argues that a liberal-minded Hauer was in a transitional phase from Christianity to German Faith and to National Socialism in the fall of 1933. He sees its confirmation in Hauer's letter to his assistant and student, Herbert Grabert.

My findings disagree with this late date for Hauer's transition from Christianity to his new religion. Indeed, far from being critical of National Socialism, he embraced it. What Hauer wrote to one person was not necessarily the same as what he wrote to another. Furthermore, even Junginger's evidence shows that Hauer was in transition around 1919 when, after his second theological examination, he left the service of the church in October of that year (Junginger 1999: 54). Telling too was Hauer's answer to the Basel Mission's question, whether Hauer, who had returned to Germany with a BA from Oxford, England, in 1914, could imagine himself serving in a British mission society. Hauer declined categorically and wrote: "I feel German [*deutsch*], more German [*deutscher*] than I ever felt before in my whole life ...." And while Hauer protested that his feeling German was not political but "love of my *Volk*," political is precisely what it was (ibid.: 54). Even when Hauer relativized his answer later, arguing that he might serve in a British mission provided he could pursue his research interests (ibid.: 54), this was not so much an indication of Hauer's still being Christian as it was of his tendency to dissimulate. Hauer hedged his bets and, not infrequently, said one thing in one letter and, depending on circumstances, revealed something else in another. In 1935, when it was clear that the Nazis were there to stay, Hauer admitted in print that, "in reality I have never been a Christian" (Hauer 1935: 10).

Because the churches in Germany are supported via personal taxation, one can only leave the Church officially. This legal step, similar to a divorce, had serious financial consequences. For this reason, perhaps, Hauer and many other non-Christians dabbled with Germanic faith long before they officially left the church. This phenomenon of being official Christians while in fact despising Christianity and practicing non-Christian faiths has done the reputation of the German church untold harm (Wielandt 1908: 7).

Hauer's life according to Junginger, Cancik, Rennstich, and Hauer himself

Hauer grew up in the small town of Ditzingen near Stuttgart. His father, who according to Hauer was a devout Christian, had a small plastering business in which Jakob Wilhelm and his brothers had to help. The boy Hauer attended a village school. His interest in learning was furthered by a local Protestant minister. According to Junginger, he also attended the *collegia pietatis* of local pietists who traced their tradition to Johann Michael Hahn (1758–1819) (Junginger 1999: 53; Benrath 2000: 232).[43]

Since there was no money to send Hauer to university, the local church helped him to receive his further education at the Basel Mission from 1900 to 1907. He was regarded as intelligent, and while some of his teachers saw "no trace of a spiritual life" in him, they all hoped that his faith would deepen and mature (Rennstich 1992: 4). In his autobiographical sketches, Hauer described himself and his close friends at the mission as having been in a "struggle against all things narrow, including theology" (Hauer 1935: 564). "We were soon regarded as heretics [*Ketzer*] by our brothers," reported Hauer (Hauer 1935: 564).

Four other things are worth mentioning about his Basel Mission experience before 1905. First, instead of praying in the prayer nook, Hauer used it as a hiding place to read "forbidden" literature. The first book of this sort was Harnack's *Wesen des Christentums* (Rennstich 1992: 7).[44] While Nazis saw Harnack's work as the triumph of a freer and livelier conception of theology, its enemies called it "liberal theology."[45] The mission regarded the book as heretical. It denied the Godhead of Christ and was hostile toward theology that according to Harnack, "smother(ed) the true element in religion" (Harnack 1901: 43). To Harnack the "power of the personality" and religious "experience" were the motor behind religious breakthrough (ibid.: 48, 148). This is precisely the ground, namely liberal theology, in which Hauer's philosophy of religion is rooted (Rennstich 1992: 7).

Second, Hauer described how he and a close friend were powerfully attracted to the "struggle of social democracy" in Basel—which attraction was soon lost, however, owing to a hollow but inflammatory speech given by a "fanatic looking" Jewish lawyer (Hauer 1935: 564, 565). One cannot help but see here two latent tendencies, an interest in politics and, minimally, a mild form of anti-Semitism that would incline Hauer toward national, rather than international, Socialism. International Socialism, Marxism, and Communism were associated with Jews.

Third, Hauer mentioned that he was powerfully attracted by the figure of Socrates, especially by the fact that Socrates "obeyed his inner voice" (ibid.: 567). This love of Plato's work is confirmed by the correspondence from former English friends who addressed him as "My dear Plato" or "Beloved Plato."[46] But while these friends exhorted Hauer to stay in the Christian fold, he asked himself, although retrospectively, how it was that the figure of Jesus never grasped him in the same way that the figure of Socrates did (ibid.: 567). More importantly, however, Hauer's historicism, the notion of his nation's destiny as willed by fate, and his belief that the *Ur-* or original of the perfect state is found in the distant past, has its roots in Plato.[47]

Finally, Hauer wrote that his "encounter with Nietzsche" sealed his fate (ibid.: 570). By "encounter" he meant having read some of Nietzsche's poetry. The philosopher died in 1900, the year when Hauer entered the mission (ibid.: 569). Nietzsche showed Hauer the importance of breaking through, and affirmed his struggle of many years against religious convention (ibid.: 570). It is an irony that this young man, who from all accounts could never abide Christianity, would later make the argument that his German Faith is a genuine extension of, and beyond, Christianity.

Despite the grave doubts of his teachers, Hauer was sent as a missionary to the South Indian District of Malabar, where he acted as school principal from 1907 to 1911 and where he soon found influential benefactors (Junginger 1999: 54; Rennstich 1992: 4, 5). Given British policy in India that missionary teachers were to be university-educated, Hauer was sent to Oxford in 1911 at the Mission's expense. Just before outbreak of the First World War in 1914, Hauer took his BA at Oxford and was promptly interned. With the promise that he would not take up arms, he was released and sent to Germany in 1915. In Tübingen he received his PhD in 1918 and his *Habilitation*[48] in 1920, both under the professor of the history of religions, Richard Garbe (1857–1927), whose chair Hauer filled later. Garbe too had travelled extensively in India (1885–1887) and saw Indian culture in Christian practices, for example the organization of monasteries (Junginger 1999: 36).

Developing a German Faith

Hauer's inaugural lecture, 28 April 1921, was on the topic of "The Idea of Development in the History of Religion" (Junginger 1999: 55). He traced the development of the discipline through Lessing, Herder, Schleiermacher and the philosophers of German Idealism, which, significantly, he considered a religion. This lecture was an important signpost, as was his 1923 book, *Die Religionen* (Religions). It was the first hint of Hauer's effort to trace *that* lineage of thought going back to medieval mystics such as Eckhart (*c.* 1260–1328) that would later come to be known as German Faith.

When, therefore, in 1940 Hauer argued that "Jewish-Christianity" had to make room for the truly German faith which consisted of a line of "Indo-Germanic *Führergestalten*" and their specific (*arteigene*)[49] Indo-Germanic views that originated in the ancient Aryan world and flowed unerringly into National Socialism (Junginger 1999: 148), he was not saying anything that he had not already expressed in the twenties (Hauer 1923: 12). What he did do, because it was now public knowledge that Hitler had given up the idea of a "positive Christianity," was to say brashly what formerly he had said cautiously. The increasing brashness of his work is already explicit in his publication *The German Way of Knowing God* (*Deutsche Gottschau*) (1934e). Furthermore, given the increased importance of the concept of race since the early thirties, his notion of a German Faith based on "Germanic" *Führergestalten* allowed him to make the link simultaneously to the race principle, to the ancestor principle (*Ahnenprinzip*), and to a specific (namely Germanic) *Ur*-culture.

Like the Marburg theologian Rudolf Otto (1869–1947), with whom Hauer was friendly, Hauer saw the living essence of religion to be religious experiences and a sense of the Holy (*das Numen*) (Grabert 1932: 60; 1936; Hauer 1923: vii, 2). To grasp it, the method of intuition was used (Hauer 1923: 344; Junginger 1999: 57). Intuition was not original with Hauer, as Albert Speer told his American interrogator Captain Oleg Hoeffding, "The word 'intuition' was altogether in great vogue with us" (Overy 2001: 218–19). Even scholars such as the anthropologist Leo Frobenius (1873–1938) converted from the "mechanical" culture circle approach to the idea of cultures as living organisms, with individual souls, the essence of which had to be intuited (1921: 3–4). Instead of philological analyses of

2.5 Leo Frobenius, anthropologist who researched the organic life of culture accessed by living intuition

texts, Hauer put into the foreground the ecstatic side of religious experience (Hauer 1923: 344, 166) and worked with these in terms of the *völkisch* discourse.[50]

Besides the Germanic aspect of his religion and the importance of religious experiences, Hauer added Buddhist and Hindu ideas (1922a; 1932b; 1934e). His interpretation of the *Bhagavad Gita*, for example, influenced Himmler and the SS. Indeed, Himmler defended his lethal decisions and his detachment from their consequences with just those Buddhist and Hindu ideas (especially the words spoken by Lord Krishna to the warrior Arjuna) that Hauer popularized (See Padfield 2001a: 91–3, 403; Hauer 1923: 419–20; 1932; 1934a).

Hauer's 1934 publication on the *Bhagavad Gita* lays out systematically the justification for doing the deed that a man is called to do by fate even if that deed is steeped in guilt (Hauer 1934a: 60–1). Hauer calls such a deed innate or hereditary duty (*angeborene Pflicht*) and there can be little doubt that Himmler saw his destruction of the Jews in that light (Padfield 2001a: 402–3). According to Hauer, Krishna taught Arjuna that the "hereditary duty" has to be done even when it is interlocked with a repulsive fate (*Schicksal*) and with guilt (Hauer 1934a: 61). In Indo-Aryan times, said Hauer (ibid.: 62), this "innate duty" was equated with the duty that belonged to the caste to which a human being belonged (ibid.: 26). For Himmler that caste was the SS. As Padfield (2001a: 402) writes:

> While there were many paths to perfection, in essence they involved a man doing his caste duty in a disinterested passionless way, dedicating it only to God. And here, perhaps, is the key to the picture of Himmler, by nature a squeamish man, forcing himself silently to watch an extermination at Auschwitz. Performance of duty detached from passion was indeed what he continually sought from his staff at the death camps.

Hauer discussed his Hinduistic leanings with others before 1934. For example, already on 5 April 1930 Hauer wrote the Director of the Basel Mission, Hartenstein, that it was "the Apologia of Socrates that influenced my inner life in the Basel Mission. It was also nature. And when I worked in India, I realized what a strong attraction the *Bhagavad-Gita*[51] had for me ...."[52]

Hauer's deceit

As noted above, I differ with Junginger over the issue of Hauer's affiliation with National Socialism. According to Junginger (1999), Hauer joined Rosenberg's *Kampfbund für deutsche Kultur* in May 1933, and the *Hitler-jugend* in December 1933 (Junginger 1999: 128). In 1934 he was persuaded by Himmler and Heydrich to join the SS and SD, and in 1937 he joined the NSDAP. This is accurate as far as it goes. But there is more. Even if Hauer was not committed to *völkisch* ideas from the 1920s and to National Socialism before 1933, his correspondence up to 1937 sat on a lie. He always wrote his followers that he was not a member of the Party, implying, and sometimes stating outright, that he was not a National Socialist. Publicly, he sold himself as a liberal who was open to all religious and political persuasions. Behind the scenes he worked against "Jewish-Christianity" and for National Socialism with deadly seriousness.[53] With the exception of fellow SS officers, none of the people with whom Hauer corresponded were told that he was a member of the SS and SD and that he could, and would, spy on them. The most famous example was Martin Buber, who, probably not knowing that Hauer had spied on him, wrote him a generous letter of reference that helped Hauer get off easily during his denazification hearing (Junginger 1999: 137).

The consequences of this inseparable union between poetics and politics with which Hauer worked were horrendous. Hauer's research ceased to sit on empirical evidence. He used his SS friends to discriminate against any scholar who had less than a clear National Socialist worldview. To Jews he spoke with a forked tongue. On the one hand, he claimed that he and they shared a common bond in the sphere of religion. On the other, he wished that they be excluded from German public life.[54] At his moment of greatest

2.6 Hauer's SS-approved marriage to
Annie Brügemann, 1939

triumph in 1933, when he headed the ADGB, he accepted without hesitation the Aryan paragraph (*Arierparagraphen*) for the ADGB, thus excluding Jews automatically. One of Hauer's students, Paul Zapp, when he faced his trial for his active role in the murder of 13,499 persons in the Ukraine (Junginger 1999: 137, 139, 185, 214), claimed that he had committed the crimes in accordance with Hauer's philosophy (Hakl 2001; Kwiet 2004: 253, 255, 259). Almost the same could be said of Himmler.

Hauer's letters before 1933 were not predominantly ones between Hauer and other scholars, although he was then a very energetic academic, eager to make his mark.[55] Rather, they were between Hauer and leaders of various *Bünde*, as well as his followers and helpers in the *Köngener Bund* and the readers and contributors of his journal called *The Coming Community*.[56] Early on he identified himself as a type of 1920s German guru, that is a *Führer*. Although extremely guarded about his politics, Hauer nevertheless revealed something of his political position in a 1932 letter to Annemarie Gebser, whom he wrote that, although he does not use the word *National-sozialismus*, he has undergone a change toward being *völkisch*. Hauer also advised her to align herself with the party and affirm it.[57]

Hauer and others used terms like *Führer* and *Heil* long before Hitler came to power. Hauer's followers, particularly young women, even dreamt about him, much as disciples of Reverend Moon dreamt about the latter in the

1970s and 1980s (Hexham and Poewe 1986). From the perspective of Hauer's followers, it was fate (*Schicksal*) that had led them to their *Führer*, that is, their intellectual and spiritual guide.[58] In short, Hauer was a leader of men and women, including, for a short while, Marianne Weber, Max Weber's wife, who looked to him for religious, philosophical, and political (in the sense of worldview) guidance.

Hauer saw the 1920s as a time of struggle (*Kampf*) among diverse worldviews and religions.[59] The aim was to bring Christianity and the church into decline. It was a time of a new conception of God, not as one grasped by thought, but as the reality of inner experience.

Conclusion

Jakob Wilhelm Hauer and other founders of *deutsch*-Germanic religions at that time deliberately created a faith based on *völkisch* experiences, elements of the Yogic tradition, pre-Christian Germanic beliefs, and German philosophical idealism. The Indo-Germanic or Indo-Aryan myth not only guaranteed internal coherence, but convinced Hauer that his German Faith was the essence of National Socialism and National Socialism was the essence of his religion. His conception had no place for Jews.

Chapter 3

Hauer and the *Bünde*

Becoming a National Socialist

Popular politics and the *Bünde* environment

In the 1920s and until the end of 1932 Germans from all walks of life, but especially younger people, took politics into their own hands. They did this because intellectual and popular opinion held that the Weimar democracy was imposed by the enemy and was ineffective. The more vicious elements added that, because many Weimar leaders were Jewish, they were therefore not German and would not work for German interests. This takeover of popular politics in opposition to the new democracy ended in a terrible disaster.

That politics could be harnessed effectively by well-educated young people had to do with the existence of an ever-growing number of small organizations including the Youth Movement, reading circles, circles focused on the struggle (*Kampf Bünde*), and paramilitary groups (*Freikorps*), and an ever-growing number of philosophical, poetic, political, and/or religious *Bünde*. Respected intellectuals such as Heidegger (Bambach 2003), Haushofer (Herwig 1999), and Hauer built student circles around themselves. Less mainstream intellectuals such as anthropologists Ludwig Ferdinand Clauss, Hans F. K. Günther, and theologians who were still officially linked to the church such as Hermann Mandel (1882–1946) became itinerant speakers at *Bünde* meetings and conferences. Mandel also led a group calling itself Circle of Friends of the ADGB (Bartsch 1938: 47). The reading circles and literary conferences organized by Hans Grimm, Erwin Guido Kolbenheyer, Hans Friedrich Blunck, Hans Carossa, and others, and coordinated by the energetic library director of Stettin, Erwin Ackerknecht (1880–1960), likewise encouraged a nationalism based on notions of autochthony, that is, "the *völkisch* belief in the rootedness of the homeland and in ancestral kinship" (Bambach 2003: 10).

Hauer began to express his passion for Indo-Germanic religion gradually after his return from India and England. His view that German Faith should become the essence of National Socialism and the New German man, especially as formed by the SS, was not openly expressed until the end of 1933.[1] This chapter traces the development of Hauer's opportunistic rejection of

Christianity and his growing immersion in *völkisch* thought and National Socialism.

The parallel careers of being an academic and a founder of a new religion took off in 1919 after the "November Revolution and its aftermath"[2] and when he left the service of the church. At that time Hauer turned his Bible Circle into a worldview organization called *Bund der Köngener*.[3] Unsure whether it was philosophical or religious in nature, Hauer initially opted for the former and rooted his group in the German Youth Movement (Laqueur 1962: 106; Neurohr 1956: 158; Stachura 1981: 82). According to Hauer (1935: 10), the Youth Movement struggled for a new Germany. It was the proper context, therefore, within which to plant the seed for the intellectual and religious breakthrough of the German revolution.[4] His *völkisch* development reached its zenith in 1933 when he brought together various *Bünde*, Germanic and Nordic religions, and other groups such as the free thinkers or free religious (*Freireligiöse*) under one umbrella known as the ADGB,[5] or simply German Faith after his flagship journal of that name.

Starting at the turn of the century, counter-cultural and *Bünde* circles, including Hauer's, had in common with all emerging National Socialists the notion that society was moved in new directions, not by political parties, but by leaders of genius (*Führer*). Such leaders, it was thought, knew how to propagate their inspired ideas (propaganda).[6] They tested their ideas in the *völkisch* (folkish), *bündisch* (youth group), and Nordic-religious social environments, a "milieu" that consisted of an interwoven network of personalities (*Führergrössen*) who were political activists, writers, trained speakers, and/or managers of interpersonal and inter-group relations (Herbert 1996: 51; Fritzsche 1999: 188, 193). Hauer was very much part of what the sociologist Colin Campbell (1972: 122–3), looking at recent expressions of western religiosity, called the "cultic milieu," namely, that "cultural underground of society" that is kept alive by everything from mysticism to unorthodox science and the publications of those who preach it.

According to Stachura the "Bündische Youth was numerically the largest constituent of the Conservative Revolution" (1981: 50).[7] Likewise, the theoretical notion of "a 'third force' between socialism and old-fashioned nationalism" was inspired by the *Bündisch* group concept and by Moeller van den Bruck's idea of the *Bündisch* Youth as a microcosm of the future Reich (Stachura 1981: 50; Lauryssens 1999: 99, 100). Indeed Fritzsche (1999: 157) and Lauryssens (1999: 123) argue that the play with notions of *Gemeinde, Kameradschaft, Volksgemeinschaft, das Dritte Reich* and a "third force" had to do with the disintegration of the social and political fabric between 1928 and 1932, and with the popular mobilization of burghers into a "radical nationalist plurality." By taking notions of solidarity and a class-free society, on one hand, and "the chauvinism of the nation at war," on the other, National Socialists "twisted together strands from the political Left and the political Right" that increasingly captured the imagination of Germans from all walks of life (Fritzsche 1999: 213; Neurohr 1956). It should surprise no one that Hauer was among the twisters.

Hauer's *Bund* differed from others in minor ways. Youth and *Bünde* movements were homoerotic, and homosexual experiences were accepted and often even encouraged (Liebs 1976; Machtan 2001; Geuter 1994).[8] In the earlier years, Hauer's *Bund* seemed to share in the general sexual freedom that continued right through the Hitler era. Hauer's charismatic eros seems to have been heterosexually oriented, however, so that there were a high percentage of women in his Bund. Infatuation with their leader was not unknown, and some party members made fun of Hauer's predilections and his "influence over women."[9]

The homoeroticism of the *Bünde* and National Socialism is important. Nanko (1998: 75) uses Hauer's writing about secret societies (1923: 421) to differentiate him from the general nationalistic and socialistic politics and place him within a small and distinct stream of *völkisch* ideologues that pursued ideas of matriarchy. What Nanko does not mention, however, is that Herman Wirth, one of these ideologues, was installed by Himmler as the first director of the *Ahnenerbe*, the SS research institute (Kater 2001: 7), and that the professor of philosophy at Leipzig, Ernst Bergmann (1881–1945), not mentioned by Nanko, was a hard-line National Socialist and virulent anti-Semite despite his fascination with matriarchy.[10] They all had in common a fanatical desire to destroy the Judeo-Christian tradition in order to make room for a new-Germanic religion.

Mohler's focus on the Conservative Revolution obscures rather than clarifies its relationship to the *völkisch* phenomenon and National Socialism. Reflecting on his first publication about the CR, Mohler reveals his distinct perspective. First, he points out that he wrote the book to help the intellectual right in Germany who lost their voice after 1945 (1989b: 7). Second, he wanted to distinguish between the intellectually elite movement of the CR and the mass movement of the Nazis when, in fact, neither would have been possible without the other.

Important is Mohler's point that after 1918 the *völkisch* and youth movements inspired the CR, also called the German Movement (*Deutsche Bewegung*) (1989a: 32). Uncertain about the *Bündisch* phenomenon, he argued that it was a transitional phase for young conservative revolutionaries (1989b: 8; but see Haffner 2002: 65, 196, 207). Detailed biographical studies show, however, that the *völkisch* phenomenon and the *Bünde* phase were the place of transition to National Socialism. This is the case for Josef Goebbels (Reuth 2000: 81), Heinrich Himmler and Gregor Strasser (Padfield 2001a: 38, 76), Rudolf Hess (Padfield 2001b: 14, 47), Rudolf von Sebottendorf (Goodrick-Clarke 1992: 135), Martin Bormann (Stevenson 1973), as much as for Hauer and his followers (Martin 1991: 16).[11] Likewise, leading Gestapo officers such as Dr Emanuel Schäfer also came to National Socialism through the *Bünde* (Johnson 2000: 53–4).

No one makes this point more clearly than Hitler. In *Mein Kampf* (1940: 417–19), Hitler argues authoritatively that being *völkisch* is useless unless its followers understand *völkisch* ideas as being the basic elements of a political party. To Hitler as to Hauer, a worldview had to be transformed into a well-organised, unitary political faith and fighting community. After Hitler was freed from the Landsberg prison on 20 December 1924, he asked one question of his largely *völkisch* followers: "Who shall be the political *Führer?*" Those who answered "Hitler" became leaders of a new "fighting organization," which he wrote about in Landsberg prison (Hitler 1940: 378, 418, 419). The rest recruited followers that would sweep the party into power in 1933 (Kershaw 1998: 296).

According to Neurohr (1956: 22), National Socialism is a myth about the Third Reich that is a synthesis of several part-myths. People such as Oswald Spengler, Moeller van den Bruck, and intellectuals associated with the journal *Tat* (Deed) and its interlaced reading circles, became popular in the late twenties and early thirties. They inspired a whole generation of young Germans, including many of Hauer's followers. This process of capturing the imagination of students and the general public was continued by SS intellectuals such as Hauer, Walther Wüst, Hans F. K. Günther, Werner Best, Gottlob Berger (1896–1975), other intellectuals such as Ludwig Ferdinand Clauss, Ludwig Klages, founders of new religions such as Ernst Bergmann, and Hermann Mandel (1882–1946) (see also Herbert 2001; Kater 2001; Stachura 1981). Ian Kershaw puts it simply when he says the blend of *völkisch* and mainstream nationalism became "a frontal ideological rejection of democracy and the Weimar state" (1998: 132).

Hauer and *Bünde* attitude (*Haltung*)

Both Laqueur's book and Hauer's letters make it clear that the social landscape between 1925 and 1933 was shaped significantly by the German Youth Movement. The latter was not a unitary movement. Rather, it consisted of innumerable *Bünde* (organizations for different age groups), reading circles, and communities. The emphasis on personality (*Persönlichkeit*), genius (*Genialität*), and elitism made for incessant leadership competition so that the *Bünde* were subject to continuous splits and reunions. The ideal of leaders to form a united movement never materialized (Laqueur 1962: 144). Each little group had its own guide (*Führer*), "its own magazine or newsletter," its yearly camp meetings, "its distinctive banners and attire" (ibid.: 155).

If the *Wandervogel* was the first phase of the German Youth Movement lasting from 1896 to 1919,[12] the *Bund* and, especially, the Volunteer Corps (*Freischar*) was the main form of organization in the second phase between 1919 and 1933 (Laqueur 1962: xiv). Hauer and his *Köngener Bund* briefly joined the Volunteer Corps in 1926.[13] The second phase is the focus of this chapter.

The *Bünde* were uniquely German. What made them so during the years between 1919 and 1933 was the problem that neither onlooker nor participant could decide what they were. Were they religious, philosophical, or political groups? The answer is: all three. At any rate, it was here that Hauer sorted out his early political and religious priorities, and these require closer attention.

The correspondence between Hauer and such *Bund* leaders as Buske, Ahlborn, Borinski, Paetel, Schoeps, and others, showed that the one thing all *Bünde* were concerned to define was its specific *Haltung* or attitude toward state, party, comrades, and enemies. An interesting example is Hans-Joachim Schoeps, who, although he was Jewish-German, espoused an extreme German nationalism and was one of the central people in setting the political tone in the Youth Movement. On 26 August 1927 Schoeps[14] wrote Hauer, that the spirit of the movement whose attitude was marked by the term *freideutsch* (a specifically German freedom) required a particular type of human being that it was the mission of this Bund to bring about. At stake was a revolution of the conscience in all areas (of life) against the ethos of the middle class with its sense of satiation, rigidity, and moral narrowness. The picture of humanity that we want to convey "to our youth," wrote Schoeps, was that of brotherly love with, however, "the notion of a cultivated manliness. This attitude alone would bring into being a *Volksgemeinschaft*," a community of the whole folk, with social justice and mutual preparedness to help.[15]

In line with his belief that the essence of religious-political life is shared experience, Hauer defined *Bündische Haltung* as that attitude or ethos that emerged from those life experiences that all *Bünde* have in common. It also referred to the responsible service rendered toward major stages of life such as boyhood (*Jungenschaft*), young adult (*Jungmannschaft*), and manhood (*Mannschaft*).[16] It is easy to regard this emphasis on attitude and, generally, irrationalism as "metaphysical claptrap," but unfortunately this is what it was (see Laqueur 1962: xix).

In the years between World War I and World War II more philosophizing was done outside the university than inside it. Furthermore, because the "philosophy of the street" was one of opposition, things such as mysticism, irrationalism, vitalism, and biocentrism were used to oppose logocentrism, rationalism, and materialism (Neurohr 1956: 236). At the core of this effort was the graphologist and popular philosopher Ludwig Klages, who published his famous book *The Intellect as Adversary of the Soul* in 1929 and 1932. Already in 1899 when he first met Franziska von Reventlow, the sister of the man who would cofound the German Faith Movement with Hauer in 1933, Klages saw embodied in her the "element of Nordic Paganism" (Schröder 1966: 271). This meeting at a time when he was reading Bachofen's *Mutterrecht* was a major turning point in his life (ibid: 269). It also highlights the irrationalism that characterized the thinking of the time of the *Bünde*.

The Klages sentiment and the vague Schoeps statement show: (1) what the primary attitude was, namely, preparedness for a revolution of conscience;

(2) what the goal was, namely, the achievement of a homogenous racial (national) community (*Volksgemeinschaft*); and (3) what the *Bünde* were against, namely, the bourgeoisie. Although its leaders were all over the political map, especially when we think in traditional terms of left, center, and right, the *Bünde* were *völkisch*[17] (Paetel 1999; Borinski and Milch 1967: 33). Laqueur (1962) took *völkisch* to mean racist, although not necessarily in the biological sense. What was emphasized was the belief that specific *Bünde* or, on a larger scale, specific peoples should have specific cultural, historical, and environmental identities.

It was but a small step, which most National Socialists took, to add biology and social Darwinism and to imagine race hierarchies and race wars. On the whole, however, the nationalistic right thought more in terms of blood in the sense of giving priority to great Germanic ancestors, sometimes referred to as an aristocracy. This notion of ancestors in the sense of a core aristocracy as the essence of a nation goes back to Paul de Lagarde. Ancestors (*Ahnen*), but now in the sense of a line of great German heretical thinkers, was the essence of what Hauer meant by a distinct German religion, a German faith that, according to him, had always been there but had been repressed by the imperialism of Christianity.[18]

In the above letter, Schoeps stated that Walter Hammer, editor of the journal *Junge Menschen* (Young People), wanted to dedicate the whole November 1927 issue to the theme of "the religiosity of today's youth."[19] Younger theologians ranging from the Barth-Gogarten[20] schools of thought to religious socialists had agreed to contribute articles. Schoeps wondered whether Hauer, being part of the Volunteer Corps, would write a piece about the religious nature of the *Köngener*.[21] It is these prods to think about religion in the non-Christian context that encouraged Hauer to create a German faith that he intended to be the deep and solid roots of National Socialism. First it is necessary, however, to review Laqueur's (1962) description of the Volunteer Corps.

The Volunteer Corps (*Freischar*)

The Volunteer Corps, founded in 1926, was an umbrella group of diverse youth groups and young individuals (ibid.: 144). About 75 percent of its ten to twelve thousand members were under the age of eighteen. Eighty-five percent of the members were boys who came from Protestant middle-class families. Only a few were Catholic and fewer still Jewish. Fifteen percent of the members were girls from similar socioeconomic backgrounds.

The leader of the Volunteer Corps was Ernst Buske (1894–1930) who was born in Pomerania and was one of the editors of the periodical called *Altwandervogel*.[22] According to Laqueur (ibid.: 145), Buske was one of the few down-to-earth leaders of the youth movement. He studied law and became the legal representative of a large farmers' association. Because he had only one arm,[23] he did not participate in World War I. After the war, at the young age of twenty-four, he became the movement's main leader. What made him outstanding was the force of his personality. Of a practical bent, his leadership spelled the end of the "romantic excesses" to which the *Bünde* were prone (Laqueur 1962: 145). Unfortunately, Buske died in 1930. His early death shocked Hauer. "Since Buske's death," wrote Hauer to Frau Gertrud Rheinfels on 1 May 1930, "the German Volunteer Corps is in a state of crisis." Hauer took that to mean "I have to participate more actively in leadership [*Führung*]."[24]

Other young group leaders within the Volunteer Corps were Dehmel, a leader before and after Buske, Ahlborn, a sometime independent socialist, and the socialist Borinski, to mention only those with whom Hauer corresponded. Nor was it unusual for leaders to have been theologians or, generally, university professors (Laqueur 1962: 145). Several of them would in due course not only start new *Bünde*, but transform these into new religions, among them Ernst Bergmann and Hermann Mandel, Ludwig Fahrenkrog (1867–1952), Bernhard Kummer (1897–1962), Gustav Neckel, Herman Wirth, and of course Hauer himself. These men, among others, would become part of Hauer's German Faith Movement.

Hauer's participation in the *Bünde* scene started when he and a small group who called themselves "The Bible Circle with a New Direction" broke away from a Christian community around 1919. Soon they called themselves *Bund der Köngener*, after the Köngen castle on the Neckar River.[25] Addressed as Chancellor (*Kanzler*), even by his students, Hauer moved the headquarters of the *Köngener* from Stuttgart to Tübingen, where he taught at the university. In 1926, while Hauer was Professor at Marburg (1925–1926), the *Köngener* joined the Volunteer Corps.[26]

The organ of the *Köngener* was initially *Unser Weg* (Our Way), which soon was replaced by Hauer's periodical called *Kommende Gemeinde* (The Coming Community). In the former, Hauer made explicit his awareness of what they were and were to become, namely, a people whose basic ethos was religious. They saw themselves as having a common task within the larger *Bund* and the whole *Volk*. The religiosity of the *Köngener* was to be free of Christian doctrines. Instead it was focused on a vague notion of sacred eternal power. *Köngener* members rarely talked about God. Experience of surrender and faith was emphasized. Such faith was *not* based on respected theology, but on something called primal life (*das Urlebendige*), the creator spirit, who would create the community of the future.[27]

Already in 1929 Hauer pictured his journal *KG* as becoming the mouthpiece of a religious movement that was bound to neither church nor dogma.[28] He had similar ambitions for the Comburg[29] Workweek that was organized annually by the *Köngener*. It was to become "more and more the center of the new *Bündungen*."[30] Hauer was gaining recognition, in other words, for fighting for the view that the German revolution should be a non-Christian religious one carried by a united *bündisch* front.[31]

The *Köngener* also were part of the *Reich*'s Committee of the German Youth Leagues (RDDJ), a somewhat bourgeois umbrella organization consisting of 75 youth groups.[32] The RDDJ organized exhibitions for the purpose of showing the German *Volk* the moral, social, economic, cultural, and health condition of their youths. At the time, there were grave concerns about the malaise and misbehavior of youths. Their smoking and drinking, as well as general unruliness, was frequently mentioned in letters.[33]

It has to be remembered, wrote Laqueur (1962: 146, 151), that after 1929 Germany faced an "unprecedented economic crisis" with "millions of young Germans unemployed" (ibid.: 146–7). The middle class was pauperized and eighty percent of Germans had no private property (ibid.: 151). The confusing political identities of people then have to be understood in this context. They saw themselves as socialists, but not as proletarian socialists; as Bolshevists, but not as international Bolshevists. Capitalism, democracy, and internationalism were Jewish, foreign, and bad. What these people had in common were notions such as national control of the economy and, thus, a national kind of socialism. Virtually every letter written in those days expressed anger against Versailles (Paetel 1999: 139).

Long before 1929, the Movement for Christian Internationalism reported in April 1923 that the political condition of Europe had worsened. The occupation of the Ruhr area especially had not only "reignited the fire of hate," but also showed that "our civilization itself is in danger of becoming catastrophic."[34]

Did the *Bünde* have solutions? Perhaps the most attractive one was the creation of dozens of labor camps, especially after 1929, where young people "lived and worked together" for several weeks, earned their subsistence, and were offered "a rich educational program, a great many lectures, amateur theatricals, music, and above all discussions" (Laqueur 1962: 146). Participants came from across the political spectrum, from Communists to National Socialists, although most were of the moderate left to right of center (ibid.:146). To the activities of the labor camps the *Köngener* also contributed.[35]

While Laqueur mentions Hauer as having joined the Volunteer Corps and later becoming the ideologist of the German Faith Movement (1962: 148), he does not mention just how much the *Bünde* leaders and Hauer cooperated. Their correspondence reveals the form of the *Bünde*, their incapability of becoming larger organizations, and Hauer's search for alternative structures such as the annual Workweeks and comradeships around his journal *Kommende Gemeinde*. Hauer's alternative structures would let him not only measure, but also affect, the political temperature. In short, Hauer's activities within the youth group scene show a man determined to make his mark on a fluid political situation.

On 27 January 1930 Hauer wrote a long letter to Buske, who was then both the *Führer* of the Volunteer Corps and the *Führer* of the political guild.[36]

As pointed out earlier, the *Bund* was divided into age grades of boys, youths, and men. Apparently, Buske saw Hauer as the *Führer* of the Young Adult age grade that Hauer organized further into theological, political, foreign affairs, and teachers' guilds. He expected the political guild and the work abroad to be decisive for the next decade. More importantly, Hauer expected that the youth group phenomenon would be thoroughly politicized, a process with which he agreed. To avoid one-sidedness, however, Hauer suggested that the guilds must remain in touch with one another, and the best way to do that would be to organize annual Workweeks around a specific current topic. For the coming year he suggested something like, "the construction of society out of an ultimate sense of responsibility." Hauer pointed out that the *Köngener* at their annual Workweek had discussed a similar topic, and participants were riveted. He was particularly keen to have an effect beyond the local region of Württemberg and, to do this and to find speakers, he wanted Buske to rope in Dehmel, who was known to have organized "expeditions of the *Jungmannschaft*" to foreign countries (Laqueur 1962: 142). Hauer ended his letter with the then already fashionable "*Heil!*"[37]

Toward National Socialism and new religion

As mentioned earlier, the leaders and followers of most *Bünde* were middle-class youths who were attracted to ideas and discussion groups (Paetel 1999; Grimm 1954: 13).[38] And this, of course, was exactly what the *Bünde* offered. Youths gathered around elitist leaders, often intellectuals ranging from professors to writers, who edited their own journals that became the mouthpieces of specific groups. Consequently, ideas traveled like lightning and quickly became buzzwords. For example, the titles of Moeller van der Bruck's (1876–1925) popular book The Third Reich (*Das Dritte Reich*, 1923)[39] and Grimm's equally popular book People without Space (*Volk Ohne Raum*, 1926), became slogans. Since Otto Strasser, a former member of Moeller van der Bruck's *Juni-Klub*, made the *Third Reich* a watchword of the National Socialists, they and the youth groups had much in common. Youths and Nazis shared a deep hate of Versailles, and the literature they favored was against Liberalism, Marxism, and the parliamentary democracy of Weimar.

Grimm (1954: 12–13) mentions that Bünde youths read their own news journal called Future Generations (*Die Kommenden*)[40] in which was found, among other things, the sentence: "The fourteen-year-old finds no apprenticeship; the fully trained skilled worker carries around his certificate of apprenticeship with an unseen stamp 'unemployed'; the university graduate hears only warnings about overfilled professions; the young academic faces the same hopelessness as the rest."

Hauer's early National Socialist affinities were underlined further by the importance he, like Hans Grimm, assigned to a foreign policy that advocated

colonizing countries that had space (*Raum*)—something Germany supposedly lacked. The expression *Volk ohne Raum* soon came to stand for the idea
of returning former German colonies to Germany. Hans Grimm, who will be
discussed below, became a millionaire from the sale of his book. While
Grimm focused on South Africa and Namibia, and while Hauer focused on
South America and Argentina, where two of his children lived, both men
adopted the National Socialist line that they themselves helped to develop,
namely, to see internationalism primarily in the sense of maintaining connections to Germans living in other countries.

The correspondence between Hauer and the socialist Borinski repeated
some of the same themes. In June 1930 Hauer reminded Borinski that the
Adult Group of the Volunteer Corps was structured into guilds of which the
political one was the most important. Since Borinski was active in that guild,
Hauer asked him to find speakers for their political week in the fall. He
ended his letter by affirming that, since he saw himself as the *Führer* of the
Adult Group, "I must try and coordinate the different efforts so that they
work towards one goal."[41]

By July 1930, however, Hauer was totally disillusioned with the inability
of the Volunteer Corps and youth groups to cooperate. He wrote Borinski
that the failure to achieve a community (*Gemeinschaft*) had ruined the youth
movement: "The wheel of history has passed over us." From now on, he
continued, he would step back from doing any political work for the Volunteer Corps. Instead he would try to impact the whole (*das Ganze*) with what
he would harness from working within the tranquility of his *Köngener*.[42]

Hauer also had a lively correspondence with Knud Ahlborn, who in 1922
was one of the founders of the Free German League (*Freideutsche Bund*).
Ahlborn, who became a physician, shifted his political orientation several
times before 1933. Originally he was a right-winger; then in 1918, he
announced that he had joined the extreme-left independent socialists. He
saw the task of the *Freideutsche* as that of leading its members from bourgeois liberalism, through democracy, to socialism (Laqueur 1962: 111).
However, by the time of his correspondence with Hauer, Ahlborn had swung
back to his original position. He now led the moderate Right of the youth
movement (ibid.: 82).

During May 1930, Ahlborn and Hauer discussed topics for the next issue
of Hauer's journal, *Kommende Gemeinde*. Ahlborn suggested religion and
mentioned that he had the cooperation of the Swiss *Altfreischärler*, Dr Hugo
Debrunner, who was also the leader of the pan-idealist movement.[43] Hauer
was enthusiastic. "I would find the topic, 'the foundations of a new religion',
extraordinarily fascinating and a discussion with the pan-idealists highly
worthwhile. They have good ideas but, in today's situation, they are on the
wrong track, namely, that of system building."[44]

Then in July Hauer told Ahlborn that he had left the Volunteer Corps. He
found it impossible to stay on course with them because the *Jungnationalen*

in the Corps wanted no part of a large trans-*Bünde* team.[45] The topic was brought up once again in November of 1930, when Hauer explained to Ahlborn what his plan had been. In conjunction with numerous *Bünde* and unions he had wanted to create a trans-*Bünde* German Workgroup whose leaders would come together on a regular basis to find a common path. He realized, however, that they were living in an epoch of fragmentation and this was simply unrealizable. On the other hand, Hauer argued that the plan of integrating the diverse elements of the youth movement must not be abandoned. To that end, he built up the *Köngener* as a group within which "the thought of the whole and integration" remained alive.[46] Ahlborn responded that he too was attached to a plan like Hauer's, but also recognized that it was not realizable. He suggested, however, that they should talk about it face to face.[47]

At the beginning of 1931, Hauer was back in correspondence with Borinski. It was here for the first time that Hauer's focus on matters of religion and National Socialism came together explicitly. In January he wrote Borinski about the current issue of the *KG*, the main theme of which was "religious change among the proletariat." He asked Borinski whether he could not find more leaders among the working classes who would center their discussions on Hauer's journal.[48] More importantly, toward the end of February 1931, Hauer wrote Borinski to tell him the next theme of the Comburg Workweek was National Socialism itself. He wanted a discussion focused solely on "the basic worldview assumptions of National Socialism." Anticipating that people would go off on political and economic tangents, he asked Borinski whether his circle had "people of importance" who, along with him, would attend the Workweek.[49]

Also that month Hauer mentioned his continuing political development to the poet Anna Schieber who, some years back, seemed to have converted to Hauer's *Köngener Bund*.[50] Already in 1928 she told him that he is the first embryo (*Urkeim*) of the Community of Future Generations.[51] Hauer wrote her in 1931 that he had spoken about economic and political questions publicly for the first time: "It is like a new beginning."[52] Significantly five days earlier he also informed her that he had resigned from the Third Commission of the World Peace Conference to concentrate on the *KG*.[53] The significance of resigning from an international body to concentrate on a local one is discussed below. The resignation ended Hauer's interest in a universal brotherhood and concentrated his attention on national politics grounded in a very particularistic German faith.

In January 1930 and April 1931, Hauer had an interesting discussion with Gottfried Drescher of the *Kronacher,* a *Bund* like the *Köngener,* but with older professional and business people. Drescher complained that the union between the *Kronacher* and *Wandervögel* did not materialize. Hauer blamed the politicization of the youth movement. At the same time, Hauer also pointed out that communities that did not have a specific task such as wrestling with spiritual, religious, or political reconstruction would not survive. And this free-floating *Gemeinschaft*, wrote Hauer, "as is your and my ideal will have to sit, in final analysis, on a religious foundation in the widest and deepest sense of it." [54]

Hauer's goal and direction became even more explicit in an April 1931 letter to Drescher. The latter had complained that a discussion about National Socialism could not possibly fill a whole week. Here Hauer disagreed. Furthermore, he wrote, the program was arranged in such a manner that we could perhaps *help* National Socialism to become more true to itself, for that was the intention. He gave examples of issues where National Socialists had to become more decisive. For example, the movement needed to recognize more decisively the emergence of the *völkisch will* to unite with religion. The basic concepts and assumptions of National Socialism needed to be clarified: this would include their conception of *Volk* and the connection between *Volk* and religion; their conception of race and anti-Semitism; the question of *Führer* versus dictator; and finally the matter of whether or not the *will* to be Germanic and the *will* to be Christian could be united in a different way from the one pursued presently in National Socialist circles. [55]

In a letter to Hans Dannemann, a National Socialist who had run the *Köngener* youth grade since 1928, Hauer mentioned that he would visit Christian Mergenthaler (1884–1980), [56] who in 1931 was the leading representative of the Württemberg NSDAP, in order to persuade National Socialists to speak at the annual Comburg Workweek. [57] "If I don't succeed," he wrote, the topic would be changed to "The Spiritual Foundations of a National Movement." The aim would not be, however, "to analyze critically what National Socialism is; rather, it would be to depict positively our own ideas." [58]

By the beginning of 1931, Hauer had learned something about leadership. Thus he lamented to Rudi Daur, a Christian pastor within the *Köngener*, that the *Kronacher* did not have an aggressive man who could force change (*Durchschlagkraft*). By comparison, he realized that he had to maintain his leadership with a certainty that left no room for discussion. His experience with the Volunteer Corps taught him to be more skeptical and suspicious, and that there cannot be uncertainty.

When a female participant of the Workweek criticized it and him, he shot back that the Workweek was a central force capable of changing real, concrete situations. As for himself, he was not an academic by nature, but a highly practical man. He conceded, however, that since the Workweek had not yet succeeded in penetrating the large world, he now saw what was missing. He then suggested how the critic could help positively, namely, to win over people of meaningful intellectual or political dimensions with whom he knew her to be in contact. [59] Hauer was also thoroughly aware that attendees of the Workweek had to be people of importance. Thus he mentioned in his letter to Dr Rudolf Craemer of the *Jungnationale* that Dr Marianne Weber, the wife of the deceased sociologist Max Weber, had joined their cause. [60]

Choosing whom and when to tell

Hauer did not like telling his followers outright which party he supported at a particular moment in time. He feared that it might turn people away. Therefore, where he stood on the political spectrum we usually discover years later. Thus in a letter to Erwin Vogt written on 22 December 1936, Hauer reminded him that "already before the Revolution [of 1933] I was a member of the *Kampfbund* for German Culture and, consequently, also automatically a member of the National Socialist *Kulturgemeinde*."[61] Alfred Rosenberg, the worldview ideologue of National Socialism, had founded the *Kampfbund* for German Culture in 1927. Initially the National Socialist Society for German Culture, it was renamed *Kampfbund* in 1928. Apparently, it attracted extreme rightists who felt alienated from Weimar culture (Benz *et al.* 1997: 539). Unable to sustain itself, the *Kampfbund* joined in 1934 with other cultural organizations to become the National Socialist *Kulturgemeinde* (ibid.: 618–19). Hauer joined the *Kampfbund* some time between 1928 and 1932. These dates coincide with other Hauer activities. In October 1932, for example, Hauer participated in the German Faith (*deutschgläubige*) Conference in a place called the *Rauhen Alp* (Bartsch 1938: 44). At this meeting, all of the Nazi German-faithlers who would later join the German Faith Movement were present. Among them were Fahren-krog of the Germanic Faith Movement, Krannhals and the enthusiastic Nazi Krieck of the *Bund* of National Writers, Prinz zur Lippe of the Young Nordic *Bund*, and Röth, Scheffer, Schloz, and Stammler of the Black Front[62] (Bartsch 1938: 44).

In a letter of 19 July 1935 to Backofen, the man who would briefly take over the DGB when Hauer resigned, Hauer implied that 1928 was the year when he decided positively for National Socialism. " ... My positive attitude toward National Socialism is shown by the fact that I appointed, in the year of 1928, the old fighter and SA man, Hans Dannemann, as *Führer* of the Young *Köngener* of the *Köngener Bund*." In 1933 Dannemann "transferred the *Jungköngener*, without any friction, into the Hitler Youth." Later he wrote that, long before the Revolution (1933), "I stood up for National Socialism in our Komburger and Kassel Workweeks."[63] Here, as in many other letters, Hauer stated why he did not then become a member of the NSDAP; it was because the party was still committed to a "positive Christianity," something which he opposed.[64]

An important letter that further reveals Hauer's political position around 1932, and shows as well that he persuaded *Köngener*s to commit themselves to National Socialism, is one written to Annemarie Gebser, 31 March 1932:

> ... You talk about your development that is oriented very strongly toward National Socialism. Have you not sensed, in that which I said – and even though I did not use the word *Nationalsozialismus* a single

3.1 Martin Buber, *völkisch* philosopher
of religion and participant in Hauer's
Workweeks

time – that a change has occurred in me toward being *völkisch*? Ask
yourself how it is possible that a National Socialist SA man can be the
Führer of the *Jungköngener*,[65] is such today, and intends to remain it?
Perhaps you would have a different attitude toward the Bund, if you
yourself would not merely be with those who are strongly oriented
toward National Socialism, but stood yourself in National Socialism.
For those who are merely oriented toward National Socialism are generally questionable figures. Personally, I prefer people to align themselves
with, and affirm, the party, especially if they want to enter, and deal
with, political life at all.[66]

It is clear that he was committed not only to the *völkisch* movement but
also to the Nazi party some years before it took over the government in
1933. Later when he defended himself against what seemed to be attacks on
his person and reputation by the SS, of which he was a member from 1934,
he mentioned that he had fought "a clear and decisive battle against foreign
infiltration [*Überfremdung*] of our worldview and religious life for one and
one-half decades."[67] Thus Hauer saw himself as committed to the *völkisch*
movement since 1923. That this time frame is correct is shown in a letter of
recommendation for Hauer by Professor Bebermeyer, the state commissioner

at the University of Tübingen. He wrote that Hauer was a pioneer (*Vor-kämpfer*) of the *völkisch* movement.[68] Furthermore, two-thirds of the Board of Leaders (*Führerrat*) of the ADGB that Hauer led from 1933 to 1936 were National Socialists.

In sum, Hauer chose carefully to whom he revealed and how he revealed his strong *völkisch* and National Socialist affinities before 1933. To Gebser he wrote that he was *völkisch*. To Nikolaus Ehlen, a *völkisch* Catholic priest, he mentioned that he was captivated (*gepackt*) by *völkisch* thought.[69] What he wrote to the democratic Gertrud Bäumer and the Zionist Martin Buber was somewhat different. To the former he said "the present stream [*völk-ische Bewegung*] has captivated our youths, since I, however, am primarily interested in religion, I am captivated by the Germanic-Indo-Germanic movement."[70] He does not mention his direct fascination with the *völkisch* movement. To Buber, whom he persuaded to speak at the upcoming Comburg Workweek, he countered the impression that it was a *völkisch* function (*Veranstaltung*): "This is not right. It is just that the *völkisch* question was a concern."[71]

Chapter 4

The push toward Nazism
Youths and leaders

Introduction

Had Germans heeded the words that the 33-year-old Karl Barth spoke in 1919 at a small conference in an insignificant German town, the Nazi nightmare might not have occurred. Alas, most did not. Instead, they listened to those whom the youths favored. A fiery dialectic developed whereby *Bünde* leaders, Nationalists, and National Socialists listened to youths who listened to them.

What was so shocking about Barth's words? The title of his talk was *Der Christ in der Gesellschaft*. In German, *Der Christ* has two meanings: the Christ and the Christian. Thus the title could simply mean the Christian in society. But Barth pointed out immediately that a Christian must know that Christians are not meant: neither the mass of the baptized, nor the self-important Religious-Socialists, nor the most noble and pious Christians imaginable. *Der Christ* referred to the Christ. By moving the focus away from Christians to Christ, Barth turned theology away from the human being to God, the triune God who in his whole unbounded and unmitigated brusqueness and foreignness stood facing the world (Scholder 2000: 65).

To German theologians, who regarded themselves as having overhauled Christianity, this was worse than heresy. Barth, however, merely made a factual observation. Modern German theology was founded not on the Bible but on the human being: on ego-supporting human spiritual experiences and anthropological categories of *Volk* and *Volkstum*. Christ had been secularized many times over for the sake of political theology, racial science, academic fraud, new religions, and warring nations (Scholder 2000: 65). Now He was to be betrayed again for the sake of National Socialism. Barth refused (Barth 1938).

When asked about the German church situation, Hans Grimm referred the questioner to Barth and to his good friend Professor Emanuel Hirsch in Göttingen. In contrast to Barth, and although he was a Nationalist, Hirsch revered Hitler from the beginning. Like other *völkisch* theologians, Hirsch's method was determined by a fundamental anthropological assumption:

namely, the argument that, in order to understand the actions of a *Volk* and state, one has to immerse oneself in that people and measure their actions against their own ideas and culture (Scholder 2000: 153). Bible Christianity was passé and Grimm agreed with him: the church is a miserable emergency order while religion is a necessity. It was with the masses, and especially the youths, that Grimm was concerned. The strong will of youths to make something of the new state must not be disturbed. And Barth was likely to do that.[1]

In 1954 Emanuel Hirsch rethought the events of the 1920s, when Karl Barth was his colleague at the University of Göttingen. Hirsch classified Barth as belonging to the "secret political resisters" and "political opposition" who prevented Hitler's and Hess's plans to create a German Protestant *Reichskirche* that was receptive to National Socialism and would educate the youths in that direction. He held Barth, who since 1923 had raised a whole new generation of pastors and doctoral candidates, as co-responsible for the failure of Germany's new departure. Turning this thought around, Hirsch wrote Hans Grimm 19 September 1954 that, had Hitler's and Hess's plan succeeded, the whole front of resisters and conspirators would have been impossible and Hitler's political goals would have succeeded.[2]

At the second presidential election on 10 April 1932, Hirsch and six other Göttingen professors stated publicly that they would vote for Hitler.[3] None of them were party members. They "risked" voting for Hitler to free Germany from the foreign yoke, to save it from Bolshevism, and to allay the impatience of the young. They hoped that a large number of votes for Hitler would show the international community German determination to resist the slavery of Versailles.

November of that year, Hirsch worried that the Papen regime might steal Hitler from Germany's youths. In the context of Jünger's latest publication in a time of terrible crisis,[4] Hirsch wrote Hans Grimm on 2 November 1932: "that for which we waited a long time has arrived, a people aware of their Germanness and freedom, our youth are awake—and the self-laceration begins and calls forth the double danger, that the young will view their political ambitions as illusion and deride themselves, or that they will follow the path of voluntary self-proletarianization." Hirsch feared that Jünger's book might inspire the youth to become national bolshevists instead of national socialists.[5]

In a letter dated 12 September 1954 to Grimm, Hirsch wished that Grimm had written about how the youth experienced Hitler. It was one of Hitler's achievements, he wrote, that he gave these youths a goal and an ideal that made them more than they otherwise would have been. Many still remember that they were better people during their time in the Hitler Youth than now.[6]

There can be no doubt that German suffering between 1918 and 1933 was acute (Dönhoff 1994: 80). But so too was the vanity of their intellectual and religious leaders.

The Hauer–Mande correspondence

Like many other Germans of his status, from Grimm to Hugenberg to Hirsch, Hauer was pushed and pulled in various political directions. The greatest pull on Hauer toward the *völkisch* and National Socialist movements was his hope that these movements shared his dislike of the church and Christianity. Before 1933, however, the position of the Nazis toward the church seemed ambiguous and, from Hauer's perspective, too accommodating. But Hauer was also, it seemed, pushed toward National Socialism. This push came from some of his young followers who had converted to the NSDAP. The example of Hermann Maurer, in the letters known as Mande, is particularly illuminating.

A recent convert to National Socialism, Mande took offence at the prominence given to Communist and Marxist perspectives at the January 1931 Comburg Workweek. As usual, Hauer had speakers from all political camps, not only because he was acting in line with his philosophy about the benefits of discussions among adversaries (*Widersacher*); he was interested in Communists because workers were joining them in large numbers, and Hauer wanted help to persuade them to join the *Köngener Bund* and to read his journal.

On 8 January 1931 Mande wrote Hauer a dramatic letter. "After the stirring event that is called Workweek, I fell into disquiet that disturbs my conscience with the accusation: Guilt. Guilt because we did not oppose things which one cannot identify with the expression 'Sin as adversary of the Holy Spirit' but with the word: 'Sin as adversary of our blood'."[7] He was thinking of the feeling, he continued, "that has not left me all these days: the feeling that perhaps a plurality of our circle have lost their (political) instinct" and slipped to the left. To call Hauer back to what he thought the *Köngener* should be, Mande ended his letter with a reminder that comes as much from Rosenberg as from Hauer, namely, "that the *Köngener Bund* is not merely a community, but the germ [*Keim*] of a new worldview."[8] Underlining his point, he included a number of quotations from Rosenberg's book *Der Mythus des 20. Jahrhunderts*.

Before Hauer's answer, Mande sent him another letter. He reported that he had a talk (*Unterredung*) with a city pastor named Krauss and the *Köngener* Werner Sick about Martin Buber. During this meeting the city pastor, who was also a religious studies scholar (*Religionswissenschaftler*), dictated and signed something about Buber for Werner Sick. Unfortunately, this enclosure that Mande sent Hauer was not among Hauer's papers. It must have been uncomplimentary, since Mande wrote that it "confirmed" his suspicions about "Buber's formulations."[9]

Mande, in effect, suggested how Hauer could correct the fact that he had not given National Socialism a fair voice at that Comburg meeting. He asked that the next edition of the *KG*, which would publish the conference papers, include an essay from a National Socialist. To this end Hauer should get in touch with the NSDAP and ask for an essay about the conference topic from a National Socialist perspective. In brackets Mande added, "(Perhaps Mr Rosenberg would be prepared to write the essay, or perhaps someone else)." He even offered a Table of Contents in which the National Socialist essay about '*Volk*, Race, State, and Human Being' would be at the beginning of the volume, Hauer's at the end, thus highlighting what they had in common. "If Rosenberg participated," said Mande, "he would ipso facto be part of the next conference."[10] He suggested further that the National Socialist topic for Rosenberg, or whoever, might be "The emergence of the Organic State from within the *Volk* and the Human Being within this State."

Hauer thanked Mande for wanting to help with next year's Workweek. Regarding the last one, Hauer suggested that Mande was a bit "too fearful."[11]

> I think it good that people should know the suggestive power of Communism and analyze it for themselves. I believe that enough counterforce broke through at the meeting that people can handle it. If one or the other falls for Communism, no harm is done … Sacrifices must happen; they can't be prevented. It is not for nothing that I warned of the dangerous path we have entered. – Where Jews are concerned, I am of the same opinion. The innermost core of Martin Buber is genuinely essential and is of the same nature as the core of my own being that is being overcome by god [*Gottergriffenheit*]. What surrounds it empirically is Jewish and is in many ways repulsive or minimally foreign. I believe this was expressed clearly in my final talk. But we cannot do otherwise than to take this Jewish element and grapple with it. It too is a reality within our people. Whether we can remove it as the National Socialists want to do is in my view questionable. I have yet to achieve clarity here. Nevertheless, I see it as good that the Jewish reality presented itself so clearly. Today, National Socialism has nothing to fear. Three times I indicated how I see it.

"As for guilt," continued Hauer, "it is certainly present; anyone who dares to enter upon these things will be guilty. But, I believe, it is not larger than it should be in the circumstance."[12] Then a few days after Hauer had resigned his activities with the World Peace Conference, he sent Mande a 5½-page, single-spaced letter full of sound and fury. It started calmly enough. He pointed out that he was about to turn fifty and, given his inner peace, he saw the turbulent events of the day with greater calm and less fear than Mande. Despite his calm, he lived intensively in the present and "the fate of my people touches my heart." He trusts in the future because there is one, provided certain conditions are met. "Unfortunately, with the inner attitude held by the Nazis today … one cannot build a Reich. At best one could build class rule or group rule that may do for Russia or Italy, but not for the German *Volk*."[13] And this, argued Hauer, would bring civil war. Consequently he did not let himself be pulled into any of the present-day political streams. "Rather, I try to grasp the essence of these movements in order to make clear to those who want to listen to me that this essence has to be built into the total political target [*Zielwillen*],[14] if disaster is to be avoided."[15]

Then he went off at a tangent about liberalism, making three significant points. First, he argued that he was indifferent as to whether the worldview of those who valued freedom and conscience was liberal or conservative. This seemingly innocuous remark calls for an aside. It recalls the story of one of Hauer's colleagues in the *Ahnenerbe SS*, the Germanic scholar Dr Hans Ernst Schneider. Born 1909 in Königsberg, Schneider became a member of the SS from 1937 to 1945, where he worked closely with Himmler. After the war in 1945 he assumed a new identity under the name Hans Schwerte. Following his PhD and habilitation in the history of German literature,[16] he eventually became the President of the Aachen University of Technology (RWTH) in 1970. His real identity was discovered in 1995. What is important is that Schwerte was liked by his students and colleagues for his left liberal views. Many debates emerged about his "conversion" from National Socialism to liberalism. Hauer's view makes it clear, however, that no conversion was necessary. Nor did Schwerte admit guilt. In line with the tropes used by Hauer, conservative revolutionaries, and the New Right today, "guilt" is Jewish-Christian, "error" and "tragedy" is Germanic. And error is the root of greatness.

That said, in his letter Hauer praised liberalism for a related reason. He was referring to something that he had discussed with Otto and would discuss later with Werner Best. In the event that the church maintained its power no matter what the next government, Hauer saw the need to cooperate with the liberal Free Protestants and the free religious (*Freireligiösen*). He was in fact anticipating what he would do with the German Faith Movement.

Second, the letter made clear that Hauer's liberalism had little in common with that of Britain or France, namely, individual rights, limited state, laissez-faire economics, political liberty, and democracy. Rather Hauer referred to the new school of nineteenth-century German liberalism that was nationalistic and collectivistic. As Cranston states (1967: 460), "The French declaration of 1789 proclaimed the rights of man; the German liberals inspired in 1848 a declaration of the rights of the German People. The new German liberals thought in terms of collective, rather than individual, rights." As the Italian historian Guido de Ruggiero pointed out:

> It was the great merit of Hegel to have extracted from the Kantian identification of freedom with mind, the idea of an organic development of freedom, coinciding with the organization of society in its progressively

higher and more spiritual forms. ... The State, the organ of coercion *par excellence*, has become the highest expression of liberty.

Third, Hauer, like the journalist Hans Zehrer, whom he hoped to invite to the next Workweek and about whom more will be said, conflated liberalism with socialism. Thus Zehrer, another conservative revolutionary, favored cooperation with a Bolshevistic Russia, Gandhi's rebelling India, and with the Soviet-supported revolutionary movement in China. As noted in his correspondence with Otto, Hauer was in agreement with India's fight for freedom from English imperialism and capitalistic exploitation (Paetel 1999: 209, 213).

This pinpoints Hauer's notion of liberalism. He praised it for having broken down old traditions, especially those of the church, and for having created dynamic individuals, especially ones who would serve a religiously penetrated organic whole that was captured in the slogan, *Reich*. There is no break between Hauer's defense of liberalism and his National Socialism. The former flowed quite naturally into the latter. His liberalism found empathy in the left wing of National Socialism. As Paetel remarked about Otto Strasser, "The effort to free National Socialism from becoming a 'right' bourgeois-fascist parliamentary party and to reconstitute it as a 'left,' new, and concrete movement was still politically possible" during the crisis years 1930 to 1932 (Paetel 1999: 218). Hauer wanted to continue the revolutionary movement and warned Mande against being like those who were still engaged in party politics.[17]

Regarding the topic of Jews that Mande had brought up, Hauer explained that one could no more condemn all of Jewry based on the few sentences taken out of context and condemned by his Nazi leader Dannemann, than one could condemn all of Catholicism based on the *reservatio mentalis* of the Jesuits. In other words, Hauer knew that anti-Semitism based on textual interpretations of the Talmud was absurd. But connecting Jewry to Christianity and ridding Germany of both was not. If one embarked on this road, "then one would have to cut out, with as little consideration, the Catholic Church from the German realm, as one wants to eliminate Jewry from the German *Volk*. And that is why I pushed that we discuss the worldview foundations of National Socialism at the next Workweek."[18] And then Hauer wrote a telling ambiguous sentence: "Isn't it a fact that even you must respect that to this day National Socialists, Socialists, and Democrats,[19] in other words, 'cursed Liberals' are in the *Köngener Bund*, exactly where they should be." To Hauer, who viewed the *Reich* in terms of worldview rather than party politics, National Socialists were liberals. The Schneider/Schwerte case, thought to be strange, is the norm.

Referring to Mande and others being grasped by the *völkisch* wave, Hauer wrote, "I believe that none of you will surpass me in being grasped by the reality of '*deutsches Volk*'." He did not use the word *völkisch*; but that was what he meant. "When the chips are down, I want to see who would be the tougher and the most ruthless. ... I am more of a German in blood and spirit than many of those who are now writing about Germanhood. I am not referring to you, but to the many fellow-travelers of present-day National Socialism." Salvation, if it is to come at all, "can only come from within the whole [dem Ganzen]."[20] It also meant, however, that National Socialism as a völkisch movement was eternal. For that very reason we find it as an undercurrent in the New Right today.

Then Hauer continued with a long aside: "By the way, regarding the expression 'conservative revolutionary', I can tell you, if that expression is now popular, I am its source. I coined it during a conversation with the present Minister Treviranus when a small circle of old bigwigs [Bonzen] talked about conservatism ... some were surprised that I was there ... And when I threw into the conversation that there is such a thing as conservative revolutionaries, no one in the room doubted that I was one."[21]

Gottfried Treviranus (1891–1971) was a minister in Brüning's government between 1930 and 1932. Initially he was a member of Hugenberg's DNVP, then of the CNAG, and finally of the KVP. The last was made up of people who, together with the former DNVP leader and chairman, Graf Westarp, split from the DNVP and joined with Treviranus' faction to form the new Conservative People's Party (KVP) (Eyck 1956, vol. 2: 344). These indecisive people were conservative nationalists who disliked Hugenberg's desperado politics (ibid.: 323) and opposed the Hitler Party's brutal tactics during the 1930 elections (ibid.: 344). The friend of Hans Grimm, Emanuel Hirsch, remembers the lines of conflict somewhat differently. In 1929 on the occasion of a referendum against the Young Plan,[22] the small Treviranus group opposed Hugenberg and the referendum. Thereupon German Nationalist professors were called to Berlin, where Hugenberg and Treviranus presented their differing views. Treviranus soon left, but Hugenberg, who was at that time a genuine opponent of Hitler, remained. He argued that if the despair of Right nationalists was not solved and if the Right did not find a way to hold the young, they would flock to Hitler. This he wanted to prevent. The followers of Treviranus did not share Hugenberg's sense of urgency.[23] Obviously, Brüning's effort to extend his reach to the Right did not bear fruit.

Hauer corresponded with Treviranus. "He has also read the KG, as he wrote me recently. I have been asked to become a member of the Conservative People's Party. [24] I did not do it, because this party too began to make compromises. Lacking the courage to assume a new attitude, it joined up with Christianity and thus spoiled everything for me. One must have courage for something new. And this courage the Köngener have, at least I have it."[25] The complaint about the party appeasing the Church, Hauer also made against the NSDAP.

Both Volkskonservative and National Socialists, including ones from München, who belonged to the NSDAP read Hauer's KG. "And they suggested that I send *KG* issues to Rosenberg with the remark that there would be understanding for our plans [*Sache*]." Nevertheless, Hauer stated that the *Bund* would not unilaterally follow National Socialism or the *völkisch* movement. The *Bund* was both and more. The issue was "cleanness [*Reinheit*] despite stark contrasts." As for the power that came from this cleanness, it had to be brought to a "break-through [*Durchbruch*] in the German *Volk*, if something is to happen."[26]

Interesting here is that Hauer denied that the party-political differences were matters of degree. Instead, he insisted that they were "deep-reaching differences." Why did Hauer do that? No doubt it was because of the ridicule heaped on contemporary "Trotskyites," who rejected the goals of the Communist Party since the latter distorted them, but who would not join the SPD because they saw it as a watered-down bourgeois party. Analogous accusations were made about the "Trotskyites" within the NSDAP who fought distortions in that party, but refused to return to the bourgeois DNVP (Mohler 1999: 59).

Hauer did not like the church because most of its clerics were non-Christians. Likewise, he did not like the NSDAP because most of its followers were not National Socialists. Each religion, party, culture, or people had to be recognizably distinct. That was the basic *völkisch* and racial principle on which his thinking sat.

"You write," continued Hauer, "that my words tell everyone what they want to hear. I don't see that as a reproach, but as a great praise for me. ... That is how it was with all those who outlasted their time. I don't want to compare myself with any greats ... But in essence my effectiveness is the same." "Stirred people," continued Hauer, "find in the words of great men the meaning that is already within the reader. And still one reader does not act like the other. That is how it has to be."[27] These words contained a half-truth; but they also revealed Hauer's utter moral relativism.

Then Hauer followed with another suggestion. "Even if I were to become a member of the National Socialist Party, even if I were active in shaping politically this party, which actually I do not regard as impossible provided the National Socialist Party were to go the way that I want to help it go, even then the *Bund* has to continue." Hauer could, in other words, picture himself joining Hitler's party. However, two things diminish this shocking concession: the party must take his advice and the *Bund* must continue.

Many German politicians had the illusion that the party would take advice. Even Alfred Hugenberg, leader of the DNVP and close friend of Hans Grimm, thought that refusing to endorse Hitler officially as a candidate in the second Presidential election in 1932 was a necessary "corrective measure for National Socialists."[28] But why should the *Bund* continue? Hauer said it was a concentration of these conflicts from the deepest foundation of being human and a *Volk*. "I would regard it as a bad report, if anyone, through my doing, joined the National Socialist Party, unless he was driven from within himself to do it."[29] Hauer wanted to persuade his reader that the power within drove a person to act. It absolved him from any responsibility for his action. It was Nietzsche's *amor fati* (see p. 160).

Finally, Hauer asked Mande to help prepare the next Workweek "in order to tackle forcefully and without consideration, but in the most positive sense National Socialism." He called on all National Socialists in the *Bund* to prepare the next Workweek "in a totally positive sense and in strong trust."[30]

Mande's answer to Hauer was Moeller van den Bruck's book, *Das Dritte Reich*, which said in more depth and with more power what Mande meant.[31] He pointed out that the last chapter, entitled the Third Reich, carried the motto that resembled Hauer's: 'We must live within contrasts.' But Moeller van den Bruck also used the expression "conservative revolutionary" and, according to Mande, he lived it. Mande mentioned the journal *Der Ring* as a still active core of a circle of Moeller's followers. His letter is filled with other references to Moeller's works.

Mande had to correct Hauer again. He discovered from Werner Sick that Hauer was thinking of asking people from the *Tat-Kreis*, the circle of readers of the journal *The Deed* (*Die Tat*), to speak at the next Workweek. This Mande would "regret" because "Hans Zehrer, formerly editor of the *Vossischen Zeitung*, has now become editor of *Die Tat*."[32] Zehrer was also "a member of the splinter group with Dr Otto Strasser." Finding people in this group would have meant another injustice to National Socialism.[33]

Otto Strasser had left the NSDAP in July 1930 and announced in his newspaper in Berlin: "The socialists are leaving the NSDAP." Only thirty followers left, although in a few weeks this number increased to several hundred. But, significantly, none of the prominent Party members left with him; not his brother Gregor, or Graf Reventlow, or the notorious *Gauleiter* Koch of East Prussia (Paetel 1999: 211).

Initially Otto Strasser founded the Fighting Community of Revolutionary National Socialists (KGRNS)[34] (Benz *et al.* 1997: 885). Its theses about the German revolution were based on a loose interpretation of the anthroposophist of whom Hauer was critical, Rudolf Steiner, and broadly constituted the group's program (Paetel 1999: 211–12). Already in August 1930, however, this group joined with others including Zehrer's to form the Black Front (SF) (Peters 1998: 799). Strasser left Hitler's party because he was unable to push through his more socialistic ideas. In the meantime, Hans Zehrer had founded a loose group of national-conservative authors around the journal *Die Tat*, of which the writer Ernst Jünger was a part (Peters 1998: 816). Together they influenced conservative revolutionaries with their opposition to the Weimar Republic and their illusion, as it turned out, that they could find a third way between Hitler's National Socialism and Ernst Thälmann's Communism.

Although Hauer followed Mande's advice and invited Rosenberg to his conference, he received no reply. His Nazi acquaintance Mergenthaler also

refused participation because the democrat Gertrud Bäumer and the Jew
Martin Buber were invited. Exasperated, Hauer wrote Mande, "It is not
clear to me how we can gain some understanding at the Workweek of the
Jewish question, when a Jew who is, furthermore, a real expert, cannot
speak." And why, continued Hauer, "should a National Socialist refuse to
discuss the Jewish problem when it is the most burning question of his
Party?"[35]

Where Hauer stood in the political spectrum we learn a bit better in the
next paragraph:

> That you became a Party member I can only welcome, especially since
> you seem to be wholeheartedly in the movement. I am doing the same
> where the *völkisch* departure is concerned. ... Since I have observed the
> development of the National Socialist Party in the last little while,
> however, I believe now as then, and especially now, in a Working
> Community that must be built out of the best of the different directions,
> as was shown in our Comburg Workweek. For tactical reasons, I was
> quite happy about the formation of the National Opposition and hope
> that they will gain power, if for no other reason than that we would get
> different foreign and agrarian policies. But the compromises that were
> necessary to bring about a National Opposition, ones to which National
> Socialists also consented have, after all, made me somewhat dubious.[36]

Hauer was "wholeheartedly" in the *völkisch* camp and empathetic with
the National Opposition. He welcomed Mande's membership in the Nazi
party barely two weeks after the formation of the Harzburg Front that
created a National Opposition which had as its goal Chancellor Brüning's
downfall (Eyck 1967: 335). When Hauer wrote about the National Opposition, he was referring to the fact that on 11 October 1931, "one day after
Hitler's audience with Hindenburg, all the constituent elements of this
opposition"—Hugenberg's DNVP, Hitler's National Socialists, the *Front-
kämpferbund*, Seldte's *Stahlhelm*, parts of Dingeldey's DVP[37] as well as a
number of nationalistic associations—met in Bad Harzburg (Eyck 1967:
332). Their aim was cooperation to take over the government in Germany
and preserve the "country from the chaos of bolshevism" (quoted in Eyck
1967: 333).[38] As it turned out, the intense power struggle between Hugenberg and Hitler destroyed their chance of putting up a common candidate for
chancellor, and the Rightists' effort to send a motion of no confidence in the
Brüning cabinet failed later that week (Eyck 1967: 335–6). Ironically, the
three top Harzburg Front leaders—Hitler, Hugenberg and Seldte—would
form the cabinet on January 1933 that marked Hitler's access to power.

Nanko (1993: 92) insists that in 1931 Hauer was equally distant from
Socialism and National Socialism. This is incorrect. Hauer only complains
about being unwilling to put up with the petty ideological quarrels of

political parties. His support, even if only for "tactical reasons," of the National Opposition puts him squarely in the far Right camp with the National Socialists. His only complaint about them was that they engaged in a compromise.

Eyck (1967: 336) correctly pointed out the German population's loss of their "sense of right or wrong." He referred to the November 1931 revelations of the "Boxheim Papers," written by Werner Best, that showed "with frightening clarity just how the National Socialists intended to exercise their power" with brutality. But National Socialist brutality was known all along. Hauer received reports about it even from Birger Forell on the occasion when Nazis "broke windows of the poor Jews" in Berlin.[39]

Hauer had been rather timid in his previous letter, but now was much more critical. He had good reason to be. Hitler had just lost the presidential election of 13 March 1932 to Hindenburg. It was the Centre and the Social Democrats, Hindenburg's former enemies, who voted him in.[40]

The gains that the Nazis made were great. They got 30 percent of all votes cast. But at the second election, on 10 April 1932, Hindenburg got his absolute majority, even though Hitler's party now received 36.8 percent of the ballots (Eyck 1967: 360–1). Just as significant for Hauer's criticism was Hindenburg's decree of 13 April 1932 banning the National Socialists' private army consisting of the SA and SS (ibid.: 362). This decree followed the widely publicized reports about Nazi terror on the streets, and the discovery of a suspicious SA and SS plan to prepare for a German civil war (ibid.: 363–4). And while Hindenburg conceded the decree, it was an open criticism of Nazi tactics.

In the Prussian *Landtag* elections of 24 April 1932 the National Socialists moved up from nine deputies to 162, with the Center Party having the third largest number of seats (71) after the Socialists (94). No doubt some thought that an understanding between National Socialists and Catholics (of the Center) might have brought down the coalition government. Be that as it may, two things were in the minds of the public that took an interest in politics. First, there was Eduard Dingeldey's comment, made 25 April 1932, about the previous day's Prussian *Landtag* elections: "The political results of the election on the whole are that the citizens who found themselves between National Socialism and Center have in effect crossed over to National Socialism." Dingeldey was a Member of Parliament and leader of the liberal German People's Party (DVP). Second, what Goebbels wrote in his Diary on 26 April 1932 was no doubt in the consciousness of most National Socialists and their observers, namely that the Party was faced with a major decision, "to seize power with the Center or to oppose the Center and this power. From the perspective of parliamentary politics, nothing can be done without the Center, neither in Prussia nor in the Reich."

At any rate, it would appear that Hauer was well aware of all these developments and attitudes, for he wrote Mande: "If Hitler had made the effort to grapple with the Center, then the situation in the national and various state parliaments [*Landtage*] would be different, where people now confront one another and no one knows what one should do, I mean Center and National Socialism."[41]

Then Hauer answered Mande's objection to having the Communist Schneller speak at their conference. "You will not succeed in beating down Communism, nor beating down any direction. We are not Italians and Hitler is not a Mussolini." Likewise he defended the Pacifism of the *völkisch* Catholic priest Nikolaus Ehlen. "... You seem to have gone far in the attitude, one that I oppose by the way, that considers authentic Pacifism, which Ehlen's is, as treason." In Hauer's eyes Ehlen's Pacifism came from within, making him a real Christian. Such a person he would defend until blood flowed "... even though *I am neither a Pacifist nor a Christian*. – But all this is too superficial, too much a matter of tactical politics instead of politics in the grand style of creative politics [*schöpferisch-politisch*]."[42] Hauer believed in god-given or rather bio-culturally determined differences that were ineradicable, ones one could not simply label treasonous and dismiss. When were differences bio-cultural? When they were based on religious, cultural, and/or biological differences, and these differences had to be grappled with. And so he suggested to Mande inviting all National Socialists or National Socialist sympathizers in the *Bund* for a weekend meeting in Stuttgart or Tübingen.

Conclusion

Nineteen thirty-one was a desperate time when Nationalists, conservative revolutionaries and National Socialists vied for the souls of the young. Wilhelm Stapel, editor of *Deutsches Volkstum*, whose ideas were popular in young conservative circles, among *völkisch*-nationalists, and with some Christian-Lutherans, wrote to Hans Grimm imploring him to publish a popular version of his *Volk ohne Raum*: "The victory of our national convictions rests with the power of middle-class and farm youths. But already Communism is devouring those in the countryside and the *Young Stahlhelm*. Only two things can keep the youth on our path: Moeller van den Bruck's *Third Reich* and your book *Volk ohne Raum*."[43]

Like Hauer when he was pressed by Mande, the elitist Grimm thought the idea revolting. But in the end a popular version of *Volk ohne Raum* appeared. And while Grimm did not want a war, when it came, shorter versions of the book were sent to frontline soldiers.

Chapter 5

Hauer's view of religion

Introduction

In 1921, writing for a popular audience, Hauer seemed to see the regeneration of Germany in the rather unimaginative terms of an analogy with the Israelites of the eighth to sixth centuries BC. This kind of analogy has been commonly used by founders of new religions including, for example, African Independent Churches (Poewe 1993). According to Hauer, those centuries were a time of hostile invasions, mighty battles and political shake-ups, and it was prophets such as Amos and Isaiah, with their highly concentrated personalities and minds open to eternity, who gave new shape to the future of the Israelite *Volk*. It is something that Germany is in need of today.

While it would appear that reference to Old Testament prophets might reveal Hauer's Christian leanings, nothing could be further from the truth. Rather, what Hauer is doing here is offering an accepted sanction for his view that a *Volk* must be led by heroic individuals who emerged from their own specific cultural and bloodline tradition. He portrays these prophets as having been, like Hauer himself, against church, temple, and established ritual. While anti-Semitism may not have been intended here, separation of the Jew, as belonging to a *Volk* different from the German, is (1921a).

In a follow-up article, Hauer used the same material to sanction the primacy of religious experience as the authenticating trait of the *Volk*-saving hero. To this end he argued that "the deepest and most consequential insights are not products of thought but of 'revelations'" by which he means "powerful inner experiences" that convince the hero of "being grasped by a power or possessed by God in the highest and most holy sense of it." (1921b).

These two newspaper articles sum up some of the common thinking of the time, namely, that Germany was in a state of crisis from which only an inspired personality could save it, one who personally experienced the crisis and humiliation for which the answer comes from within. We see here a popular attitude of the post-World War I years, namely, the privileging of experience, irrationality and intuition above abstraction, rationality and thought (Speer 1969).

While the issue will come up later, the reader should note that Hauer's anti-Semitism does not have its source in Christianity. He does not sever the connection between Jew and his race-specific religion. Rather he begins to make clear already that Jewish religion, which includes Christianity, belongs to Jews not to Germans. The only way that Hauer can retain a modicum of respect for Jews, whose presence in the universities and arts he resents, is by keeping the link between Jew and primordial faith intact but rejecting their religion, namely Jewish Christianity, for Germans. In religious cultural terms the Jew is the wholly other.[1]

Hauer's position is more discreet than the radical view of Goebbels, for whom the connection between Jew and religion is severed and irrelevant. To Goebbels, the Jew is equated with capitalism, Marxism, and the Weimar parliament and democracy. He is part of the international community that is destroying Germany and from which only National Socialism, with its combination of socialism and anti-Semitism, can save it. Quite simply Goebbels is out to defeat the enemy, "... let's call him Jew, capital, whatever" (Goebbels 1927: 1, 7, 12). Religion is irrelevant; relevant are politics, youths, and terror.

In the academic setting of his inaugural lecture, 28 April 1921, Hauer started with the assumption that Idealism[2] is a religion. The topic of the inaugural lecture was, "The Idea of Development in the History of Religion." Here Hauer traced the history of the discipline through Lessing, Herder, Schleiermacher and the philosophers of German Idealism. The lecture was, therefore, the first hint of Hauer's effort to trace *that* lineage of thought (going back to medieval mystics such as Eckhart)[3] that would later come to be known as *Deutscher Glaube* (German Faith).[4] It is an approach that was repeated again and again among his students and those of other professors in the German Faith fold. Knak's observation, mentioned in the Preface, was correct. Hauer's student Herbert Grabert, among others, followed it (1932; 1936) as did Hermann Mandel's student Sigrid Hunke (1913–1999) (1969; 1987; 1997). Until her death, she was one of the important political philosophers of the New Right in Europe.

Hauer was already aware of the political force of current new religious phenomena in the early 1920s, when he studied the then very popular anthroposophical movement of Rudolf Steiner (Hauer 1922b: 59). He saw anthroposophy as an outgrowth of the theosophy of Blavatsky and Besant. They mixed occult ideas (that is, Spiritualism, or according to Hauer, Egyptian, Jewish, and medieval magic) with old sagas, natural science hypotheses such as that of human evolution, elements of Greek and Egyptian hermetic philosophy, and Jewish Kabbala (ibid.: 7–9, 16–17, 21, 56, 61). While he saw anthroposophy as moving things in the right direction, he had three disagreements with it: anthroposophy was an occult science (*Geheimwissenschaft*) (ibid.: 26–7);[5] it contained foreign and culturally incompatible, that is, Jewish and, generally, Near Eastern elements (ibid.: 27); and it lacked the profound religious emotion (*religiöse Ergriffenheit*)[6] that Hauer regarded as part of all great and old (pre-Christian) cosmogonies (ibid.: 27, 50). Despite these disagreements, Hauer saw anthroposophy as the beginning of a new era, an epoch of new and powerful intellectual and spiritual creation (ibid.: 30).

By contrast with anthroposophy, Hauer made three interdependent concepts, being *grasped by the sacred* (*Ergriffenheit*) and a *powerful personality* (*kraftvolle Persönlichkeit*) capable of experiencing and understanding the *needs of a time*, the core concepts of his own movement (ibid.: 5). By "powerful personality" he meant a religious genius who experienced himself as grasped by the living intellectual heritage of his country, which gave him power to solve his people's needs. This reliance on an ethnically specific lineage of thought, here a Germanic and more broadly an Indo-Germanic one, was the third concept of his religious construction (Hauer 1922a).

Isolating a lineage of thought as a religion and specifically as a German faith is a *völkisch* political act. This is particularly obvious when we compare Hauer's work with that of Walter Nigg, a disillusioned Swiss Reformed Church minister who wrote from the perspective of a free religious (free Protestant) sympathizer intent on defending individualism, which was in disrepute. In 1937 he published a book entitled *History of Religious Liberalism* (*Geschichte des religiösen Liberalismus*) in which he discussed the same free thinkers—ones opposed to the church, Rome, or Christianity generally—as did Hauer. What is important here is that Nigg, aware of Nazism, wanted to save liberalism and individualism from political destruction. He did not see what Hauer saw and approved, namely that liberalism, especially as used by anti-Christian radicals, was the agent of its own destruction.

Nigg admitted that the German Christian and German Faith Movements are part of modern theology, represent church Liberalism, and are liberal in their conception of God and anthropology. But he denied what Hauer affirmed, namely, that this religious liberalism prepared the way for Nazism (1937: 400). They had one thing in common, however, namely, a disguised will to destroy Christianity. This was part of their politics, so that what Nigg preferred to call the finale of liberalism Hauer understood as the triumph of National Socialism. The transition from one to the other was seamless.

Influence of India and loss of Christian authority

Some years later, on 5 April 1930, Hauer wrote to Director Hartenstein of the Basel Mission explaining how he applied his 1920s thinking to his own faith, his study of religion, and his public life. Although the letter started with a discussion of the differences between Vedantism[7] and Bhakti[8]-religion, Hauer soon brought it around to Christianity and his own faith, showing how his research of religion is not separate from his practice of it. To help Hartenstein understand the distinction between Vedantism and Bhakti-religion, Hauer drew an analogy with German Idealism and Christianity.[9]

Hauer argued that Vedantism is to Bhakti-religion as Idealism is to Christianity. These things, he said, "… were not clearly understood by researchers, because one does not always know from which perspective they studied religion." "During the course of my existence," he continued, "I realized ever more clearly that the *Bildung* [forming] of my life and thought did not *happen* through Christ. I thought as much even when I worked for the mission. Then it dawned on me slowly and broke through only within the last ten years: my faith is rooted in God's deed of revelation, which I recognized as a happening that embraced the whole of history."[10] "More than theology lectures, it was the Apologia of Socrates that influenced my inner life in the Basel Mission. It was also nature. And when I worked in India, I realized what a strong attraction the Bhagavad-Gita[11] had for me even though, at that time, I taught from the perspective of an apologist for Christianity."[12]

"From all this you can see," he wrote, "that I followed logically *that* path that was traced out for me *through my inner nature* from my youth on. There is such a thing as being seized directly by the omnipresent and never-ending revelation of God. And out of this sense of being seized, my faith was formed. And this faith [*Glaube*] determines my thinking."[13]

Some years before 1930 Hauer claims to have made another astonishing observation:

> The more consistently and ruthlessly I followed the direction emanating from the starting point of God's revelation, which removed me from Christian dogma and theology, the nearer I came to the person of Jesus, now however in a very different sense. It is not the case that I faced an absolute authority; rather, I discovered that what I called revelation, namely the living presence of God, was also the source and foundation in all matters of his [Jesus's] faith. I stand with him, so to speak, in the same sphere. And from within this domain, I judge my own religious experience and the religious experiences of others, that is, of the whole history of religions. It is therefore not the case that I approach things without presuppositions, in the sense of being in free suspension vis-à-vis all religions. Rather I have a very firm position from where I observe everything. But this position is not an isolated domain within which the life of God is concentrated; rather it is a region within the total domain of God's varied revelation. Consequently, I cannot examine the other religions without presumptions, but I can do it without prejudice since they are also the history of God.[14]

This is the method Hauer used simultaneously to approach (1) his own faith, (2) that of the religions he researched, and (3) that of the people who became his followers. It was a radical relativism, as is found in the *Bhagavad*

Gita, that allowed him to communicate across other religions and religious politics, without denying very real differences, but at the same time allowed him to establish a common ground that was shared universally by all. It is from within this common ground that he approached such Jewish colleagues as Martin Buber, Hans Kohn, and W. L. Horowits and also his very good friend and colleague who, however, remained a Christian—if a somewhat unorthodox one—Rudolf Otto.[15]

Regarding Hauer's method, it is necessary to refer briefly to Junginger's (1999) conclusions about them, then look at Dierks' understanding of Hauer's religion, and finally at how Hauer dealt with the religious question in letters and his journal *Deutscher Glaube*.

Junginger's and Dierks' views of Hauer's approach to religion

According to Junginger (1999), Hauer's approach to the study and practice of religion was phenomenological. Anthropologists can appreciate his having been deeply affected by Indian religiosity while he was in India. Few would follow him, however, in his recommendation that one should move beyond a merely philological and historical or psychological, symbolic and mythological approach to religions and instead study religion in a way that was appropriate to its nature. According to Junginger (1999: 299), Hauer's theoretical program at this time sat on the "search for truth that he assumed to lie behind the facts of religion and its history." The starting point and goal of Hauer's scholarly interest was the so-called "truth question in the history of religions." And this truth had to do with "genuine religious experiences." Unlike scholars such as Rudolf Otto, or the once Catholic Friedrich Heiler and even Pater Wilhelm Schmidt, however, Hauer's religious experiences were not measured against the canons of Christian dogma or those of the social sciences. As a result, his religious development moved away from even the free form of a radical liberal Christianity, to an Indo-Germanic and, later, to a German Faith (ibid.: 301).

As we saw earlier, Hauer's development toward founding a new religion started in 1919. When he and some of his followers split from a *Bible Study Group*, they called themselves the *New Ones* (*Die Neuen*). By this time, Hauer had already learned about the new religion of Annie Besant. It was based on establishing a relationship between Christianity and Hinduism by postulating the return of Christ in the person of a Brahmin youth. It was an interesting syncretism, but Hauer rightly believed it would never, for that very reason, receive any respect from the theological establishment, and this respect was important to Hauer (see Biehl 1990). Annie Besant's approach could therefore not be his.

Instead, Hauer juxtaposed the philosophy of religious experience as it is expounded in the "Indo-Aryan" *Bhagavad Gita* with (West-Indo)-Germanic mysticism, sagas, and literature and kept them in a state of creative tension. In Hauer's words, "What the Indo-Aryan man recognized then counts for the present-day human being in an even higher degree" (Hauer 1934a: 39). He meant the rhythm in the polar tension between orientation toward the world and immersion within the soul, which, he argued, was the basis of true life. But so too was the creative tension between the East- and West-Indo-Germanic tendencies (ibid.).

Christianity had no place in Hauer's religion except as opponent. It was as much a foreign faith and psychology imposed on Germany, as Islam was on India (1932a: 27, 30). With it neither syncretism nor creative tension was possible; it was too foreign. We saw this attitude earlier in his letters to Buber.

Dierks (1986: 70), who gave relatively little attention to Hauer's involvement with the *Bhagavad Gita*, argued that from his study of "anthroposophy in 1921 and 1922" Hauer (1922b) "learned something important about the constitution of a spiritual movement." According to Hauer, such movements tended to emerge in history when three powers met: "perceived need, a heritage of past thought that lay fallow but awaited the right hour for re-emergence, and a strong personality capable of shaping these ideas to suit the times" (ibid.). The heritage of past thought was particularly important to Hauer because it could be used to counter Christian criticism that new religions inevitably slipped into free thought because they had no tradition.

Around 1921–1922 Hauer worked out the importance of giving priority to religious experience. According to Dierks (1986: 75), he argued that things grasped intuitively or glimpsed psychically are incapable of intellectual proof. This line of thought allowed Hauer to legitimate and make room for the existence of free experience precisely because it cannot be unlocked with rational thought. To Hauer's thinking, religious experience was entirely different from thought. He rejected the developmental thinking of anthropologists who postulated many steps between initial experience and final recognition of the community of the eternal. Hauer systematically separated thought based on reason and experience of the psyche. The human being is religious to the extent that he experiences; he is a thinker to the extent that he researches and knows.

Using a geological image, Hauer argued that research done by historians of religion is worth something only when the historian digs down to the *Quellgrund*, the source of the spring of religious experience. The aim was to dig down below hardened layers of religious forms. Only "down there" can one grasp again the living element in otherwise old or foreign forms of religion. "'This process of uncovering requires careful and detailed philological, psychological and historical work [*Kleinarbeit*] that has to be illuminated, however, by a strong religious intuition if it is to reach its goal'" (Dierks 1986: 81, quoting Hauer 1922a: v).

We see here too why Hauer was sympathetic to Jung's depth psychology. Hauer always tried to grasp the religious experience that he assumed to be at the base of any and all forms of religion (Dierks 1986: 83). Somehow this basis had to do with psychological moments that needed to be illuminated (ibid.).

Unlike Edward Burnett Tylor (1832–1917), who thought that religion was science gone wrong, Hauer thought that primitive religion was evidence of the creative spirit. And while he was not in agreement with Wilhelm Schmidt's original monotheism (*Urmonotheismus*), he was in agreement with Schmidt's notion that religion "can be truly grasped only ... by one in whose inward consciousness an experience of religion plays a part" (Evans-Pritchard 1965: 121, quoting Schmidt 1931: 6). Hauer put it as follows: *Religion mit Religion anschauen* (to look at religion with religion). The case could not have been made better by postmodernists who argue for partial, that is, positioned knowledge. We are "positioned, partial, knowing selves" in the sense of "historically, socially, radically politically, economically, gendered, sexed" selves (Kulick and Willson 1995: 18), and here in the sense of radically religiously ones.

Hauer's approach was, in other words, to discover the religious source (*Urphänomen*) from below the many forms of religious appearances. This *Urphänomen* is the same in all religions. To be in the presence of the primal will is being in the grasp (*das Ergriffensein*) of an inexplicable present and determining (*zwingenden*) power (Dierks 1986: 86). Instead of an original monotheism (revealed *Urmonotheismus*), Hauer postulated at the beginning of all religions the experience of a "primitive *monism*," a faith in a powerful all (*Allkraftglauben*) (ibid.: 87). Revelation as acts of grace from above did not play a role in this line of thought (ibid.: 87).

On the lowest step of the religious ladder, Hauer attempted to grasp the *life* of religious experiences, which he then examined from psychological, ethnological, theological and philological perspectives. He wanted to let life speak for itself. "Life alone has the power to awake life; and the conviction that science has to serve life is very deep with me" (Hauer 1923: ix). As if announcing his future work as religious founder, Hauer ends the foreword to his book *Die Religionen* (The Religions, 1923: X) as follows: "The aim today is to gather up in total those who are spiritually alive to counter the threatening decline with a new constructive deed. ... Those who want to create, need religion. But religion is not a concept, rather it is the power of life [*Lebensmacht*]." Hauer's new constructive deed was to found the German Faith Movement in 1933.

German Faith (*Deutscher Glaube*)

Inquiries about what exactly German Faith was and how it differed from Christianity continued throughout 1934. Hauer answered these queries in some letters and then did so especially in his new journal *Deutscher Glaube*. To this material we turn now.

On 10 February 1934 the wife of a pastor, Hanna Hiller, wrote Hauer that she had carefully listened to his talks on the previous day and was astonished that instead of focusing on the distinction between a German Faith and an authentic Christianity he exclusively focused on the opposition between German Faith and a shallow, external, frozen Christianity as it frequently showed itself at the time.[16] The realization that this was the distinction that Hauer worked with shattered the woman. She wanted to shout out, she wrote, that what he described as behavior of a German Faithler was in fact exactly the way a true Christian thought, felt, and acted. There was no opposition there. She understood the distinctions between the two faiths vis-à-vis the question of salvation and guilt, but not with respect to their perceptions of reality. Likewise she did not see that Christians made external laws (commandments) the measure of their actions. After all, there lies within the Bible the power to grapple with every current reality of life and to penetrate it with its timeless, universally valid, and irresistible richness of life. She saw no reason why Christianity should not and could not engage itself, especially now, with the question of race and of National Socialism, and she was astonished that especially Hauer should have observed Christianity from without, thus having remained without the gates. According to her, the Christianity he described from the outside did not have its source in Christ.[17]

This last observation is very important, because it denied Hauer's claim that he understood religion from within religion. In fact, of course, Hauer's positional knowledge was much narrower, and showed up the "inverse intolerance" that characterizes postmodernism to this day. The fact is that he only understood other religions from the position of his German faith, so that denigration, as we shall see later, was inevitable. Two other Christian concepts that Hauer and his followers rejected were mentioned in Hiller's letter, namely, salvation and guilt. Why do those of German Faith object to these? The answer is simple. They go against the social Darwinism and anti-Semitism that were an essential part of German Faith.

On 19 February 1934 Hauer wrote back to remind Hanna Hiller, the wife of a cleric, that he first encountered Christianity within the Christian community and had always emphasized his respect for people whom he knew within that fold. "I don't belong to those who fight Christianity as such. I distinguish, as I made clear in my first and second talk, between the religious primal phenomenon, that is, the truly living faith or the really ruling religious powers as we also find them in Jesus and the psychology [*Seelentum*] that is the culture of a religion.[18] For example, we can affirm the primal force in Jesus. The religious culture within which Jesus is wrapped and that especially weighs down the history of his church, we have to, or at least I have to, reject. That is what I fight against."[19] So what has Hauer really said? He only accepts that Jesus was someone who had an experience with the primal force. Everything else about Christianity he rejects because it is Jewish. It means, of course, that he rejects Christianity even while he denies doing so. And why does he reject it? Because it is a foreign religious culture and psychology.

The two interpretive tools used by practitioners of a German Faith were a subtle form of Social Darwinism and anti-Semitism, and this with respect to salvation, original sin, fear, guilt, and so on. In the October 1934 issue of *Deutscher Glaube*, Hauer published an anonymous letter about the problem of Christian upbringing that is an example of this. The letter, said to have been written in 1930 and therefore deliberately chosen for the points it makes, objects to the notion of original sin because "it robs us of our happy trust in our inborn godly power" and "makes us afraid" (Anonymous 1934: 453). But what the writer really objected to was the following: "Because of original sin we are said to be fundamentally bad, needing salvation and we are to let ourselves be saved by the messiah of the Jews" (ibid.: 453).

In the letter writer's view, Christianity inspires *Angst*, where Social Darwinists celebrate the fact that life is hard. Seeing German Faith as based on Darwinism, he argues that "fear of life" must be rejected, but not the hardness of it. After all, argued the writer, "whoever made the world the way it is, with its undeniable hardness, has also given us the sense of heroism with which we can enjoy life's battle, where we win and lose, have joy and suffering, pain and delight, the will to live and preparedness to die" (ibid.: 454). "We do not need the picture of yearning for a battle-free and workless happiness that is born of Oriental feeling; we do not need it for ourselves and least of all for our youths, whose power is only developing" (ibid.: 454). "It is therefore not right to educate our youth purely for infinite goodness" as Jesus did in the expectation of an immediate cataclysmic change to a life of the chosen in total harmony without suffering. Above all, argued the letter writer, we must not force our youth into the straitjacket of a worldview that is foreign in its conceptions of time, race, and nation.

German Faith in Hauer's journal[20]

In January 1934 Hauer started his new journal, *German Faith* (*Deutscher Glaube*). His Introduction, written in a narrative style, lays out the basic themes: oneness, wholeness, and one's being part of these as well as of the community of secret powers. "In one's soul," Hauer wrote, "one hears whispers as if the ancestors awoke to bring us ancient knowledge for our new faith and creativity" (1934b: 1). "Then a message from a foreign land reached our forefathers," continued Hauer, "the message of Christ, the God above all gods. A hard battle ensued, and when Christ won, our forefathers struggled hard to make the foreign faith their own, even to create new art and songs and wisdom for it. But when the *Volk* came to, it discovered with great pain how far removed its soul was from the foreign faith. And once Meister Eckhart made them aware of how far they had strayed, they experienced a great relief. And so the German soul returned to itself; because it began to divine that with the foreign world of faith [*Glaubenswelt*] much harm had befallen them" (1934b: 1).

"Their soul," he argued, "had become impoverished and they fell into unbelief so that the doors and gates were opened to all powers of destruction. But it was not yet time for the demise of the German *Volk*. Its original will burst forth [*aufwallte sein Urwille*]; a high wave out of the life that carries all things lifted the *Volk* up, so that it became a unitary *Volk* willing to be led to a new Reich, life, and creativity" (ibid.). "But the *Volk*'s will to the Reich finds its foundation and fulfillment only in a new faith," he continued, "a faith born of the depth of our German being, able to lead to a new future, since the old, the Christian one that lasted a thousand years, is nearing its end. Our people's original volition created its own new forms of religious life for thousands of years" (1934b: 2). The time had come to leave Christianity "so that from the immediate faith that awoke within us out of the high and rich heritage of the Germanic-*deutschen* thought world may emerge the German Faith" (ibid.: 2).

"To this end, fate, whose obedient instruments we are, has bequeathed upon us a community of German Faith. What that fate's highest goal is, we do not know. Only this one thing we know: we must obey it. And if we obey, then what will come will be great" (ibid.: 3).

"So we start the new path for our journal. It is to be the unmediated expression of the movement of German Faith and of the community in which it is grounded. Struggle, opposition and resistance will not deter us. German faith and a heroic attitude belong together, for which battle and tragedy are a sine qua non" (ibid.: 3; Günther 1935a).

An article in which Hauer addressed the question that was often put to him—namely, can a faith be German or any other nationality?—followed the introduction. "Can one connect faith with the name of a *Volk*?" he asked (1934c: 3). "Is this not a return to a 'national religion'—one that has been overcome everywhere in the course of history? There was a Persian, a Greek, and an Israelite religion. Today we still have a Jewish religion. If they are to mean something, faith and religion cross all boundaries; that at least is what Christianity, Buddhism, Islam, the so-called world religions teach" (ibid.: 3).

Hauer answered the above questions by first distinguishing between the words *Glaube* (faith) and *Religion* (religion). He rejected the idea of a German religion (*Deutschreligion*), because "religion is related to the thought of systems, customs, and conceptions, which one can have and practice without being seized by them in the depth of one's being" (ibid.: 4). By contrast, "faith is a central movement of life [*Lebensbewegung*]; it is a strong willed affirmation of the last reality [*letzter Wirklichkeit*],[21] with which a person is connected from the depth of his soul" (ibid.: 4). By German Faith, therefore, "we mean that religious attitude that is most clearly and powerfully expressed in the great figures of the German history of faith. This attitude does not belong only to the German *Volk*; it breaks through in all Germanic peoples, because it belongs to the Nordic race" (ibid.: 4).

The *Edda* and the Icelandic sagas are as much witnesses to German Faith as are Meister Eckhart, Goethe and Nietzsche (ibid.: 4). To underline this point, Hauer quoted from the *Edda* and then from Eckhart. Important to us, however, is not so much the similarity between them, but Hauer's approval of what he regarded as the morality of German Faith. Eckhart states the following, wrote Hauer, "A good human being is to make his will so much like the godly will, until he wants what God wants: if, therefore, God wants that somehow I sinned, then I must not want that somehow I had not committed the sin. That is true repentance" (quoted in Hauer 1934c: 4).

To Hauer, Eckhart's words were important because he saw in them the same recognition of the "beyond good and evil" of God, as in Nietzsche's work by that title. In that work, argued Hauer, "Nietzsche freed himself of being subject to traditional moral judgments and penetrated to the knowledge of a beyond all this to the eternal life ground [*Lebensgrund*], whose power and laws are superhuman [*übermenschlich*] and removed from the usual moral arrangements" (ibid.: 5). "While the detailed thoughts of Edda, Eckhart, and Nietzsche are different," he continued, "they share the same basic attitude that is determined by the same blood-like and psychological-intellectual substance" (ibid.: 5).

"This basic religious attitude," however, "extends beyond the territory (*Raum*) of Germanic peoples; it rules the whole of the Indo-Germanic world. This is not surprising because, despite racial mixing and changes over thousands of years, the Nordic blood reigned supreme" (ibid.: 5). Within the Indo-Aryan domain, argued Hauer, one finds therefore the same recognition of beyond good and evil. Hauer gave many other examples to make his point and then concluded, "Here the racial substance breaks through to a religious attitude that contradicts the absolutism of Christianity" (ibid.: 5).

Hauer then described similarities between the Buddhist emperor Ashoka, the old Indian Upanishads, Feuerbach, and so forth, all to underline the close kinship between the peoples of Indo-Germanic tongue and culture that have lived for thousands of years in Eurasia (ibid.: 7). Consequently, concluded Hauer, "one can safely talk about an Indo-Germanic Faith and contrast it with the Israelite-Jewish-Christian one that was born and formed in the Near-Asian-Semitic space" (ibid.: 7). And it is not saying too much, he continued, "when we claim that the battle between these two faith-worlds, the Near-Asian-Semitic-Christian and the Indo-Germanic ones, is the real topic of religious world history" (ibid.: 7).

According to Hauer, "… it is in the German *Volk* that the Indo-Germanic Faith took on exemplary form for the West" (ibid.: 7). "No other people of the Indo-Germanic West had a Siegfried, an Eckhart, a Frederick the Great, a Goethe, a Hegel and Kant, a Hölderlin, a Nietzsche, a Beethoven and Wagner" (ibid.: 7). "German Faith is therefore a symbolic word for the whole Indo-Germanic world in so far as it is still a determinant of the Nordic attitude today" (ibid.: 8).

In the first issue of *Deutscher Glaube*, January 1934, three of the most important leaders of the *Führerrat* gave their views of what the religion of the German Faith Movement was. They were Ernst Bergmann, Professor of Philosophy at the University of Leipzig and leader of the *Nationalkirche*; Graf Ernst zu Reventlow, editor of the *Reichswart*, the news journal that was the first mouthpiece of the German Faith Movement; and Hermann Mandel, Professor of Theology at Kiel and leader of *The Friends of the ADGB*.[22]

Ernst Bergmann, in an article entitled "Work and Religion," worked with the analogy that "just as the unemployed have to be put to work, so the unchurched have to be given an authentic, real, living religion" (Bergmann 1934: 11). His sense of what religion is he got from Schleiermacher, who argued "that a person with religion is someone who has no holy scripture but could make one himself. Here we have a criterion. A religious seeker who left the church, for example, has religion" (ibid.). Such an individual, Bergmann says, "searches for a reality-religion, a religion of life, a religion of home [*Heimatsreligion*], a religion of blood and soil, within which quivers the heritage of our ancestors [*Ahnenerbe*]" (ibid.: 11). Contrary to Christians, wrote Bergmann, "We German Faithlers are of the opinion that the Christian sin, guilt, and repentance feelings are not religious feelings of our German nature" (ibid.: 12). "A *Volk* that wants to renew itself cannot do so through the idea of salvation." Rather, argued Bergmann, "it must realize its renewal as coming from the psychological center of its own religion" (ibid.: 12).

Connecting religion with work again toward the end of his article, Bergmann wrote, "For religion is work, not surrender, not a passive letting that happen to us that presumed administrators of the healing grace [*Heilsgnade*] bring down from the world beyond. Furthermore, the German, the godly free and godly happy human being, wants to fight for his welfare himself ... Fight honors us, not grace" (ibid.: 14–15). According to Bergmann, Christianity is no longer our religion nor is it the religion of "a time that thinks in race-biological terms" (ibid.: 15). "Those who would give our youths the Christian religion of salvation and original sin give them stones instead of bread: bread is a heroic German faith and a heroic ethics" (ibid.: 15).

In his article "Luther and German Faith," Graf Ernst zu Reventlow argued that, "we, the German Faith Movement, have no point of connection with Luther, for we have no sense of a relationship to the Bible as a godly holy book, nor to Christ as a Messiah-Savior" (Reventlow 1934: 17). What interested Reventlow was Hess's edict about freedom of conscience. The Catholic objection, that the conscience can err and does err, he dismissed as something that the Catholic Church must say since it insists on being the measure of human error. Here he found a point of connection with Luther, who argued that, objectively speaking, conscience does err, but the measure of whether it did so or not was "good faith." In this sense, argued Reventlow, "we can accept Luther's: 'Sin bravely, believe more bravely!' That is the faith that at its root is one with Kant's 'good will'" (ibid.: 22), only we must go a step further and "become who we are" (ibid.: 22).

Finally, the first issue of 1934 contained also Hermann Mandel's article, "Theses of German Reform" (1934: 24–31). Space does not allow discussing all sixty of them, especially since they only say in other words what Hauer, Bergmann, and Reventlow have already said. Among them are the following. "We do not believe in a past revelation taught through historical documents ... rather we believe in God's continuing revelation as it speaks to us through the world and life" (ibid.: 24). Mandel also did not believe that "the eternal ground of all things was only revealed to Israel and Judah but that it is revealed in a special way to each *Volk* and being" (ibid.: 24). It is a point also made by Hauer and, indeed, all members of the German Faith Movement. "We do not regard our ancestors as heathens in the denigrating biblical-Christian sense, but (with Tacitus) as penetrated with divine reverence ... for their ancestors whom they took to be the natural children of an eternal power" (ibid.: 25). Paganism should never have been destroyed, argued Mandel, "since its practices, which trusted in eternal powers, were more natural than the practices of law-abiding Jews and Paul's religion of law" (ibid.: 25).

Like Hauer, Mandel avowed German mysticism and German idealism. He also avowed a God "who is an all-penetrating power of being, not a creator who created the world out of nothing, but a god who organically penetrates the world" (ibid.: 25). The human being too is an organic whole in which body and soul are one. Importantly, Mandel wrote, "faith in the belief that race determines the life of soul and spirit is not a superstitious belief in blood [*Blutaberglaube*] and materialism, but a natural consequence of an organic worldview" (ibid.: 26).

Mandel, who at this time was still a member of the church, hated Christianity, denied the divinity of Christ, and opposed most of the Church's 1932 rulings. He had a knack for finding, taking out of context, and criticizing statements like this one, "that the newborn child of the most noble Germanic descent with the best racial qualities of intellect and body is as subject to eternal damnation as is the hereditarily handicapped half-breed of two degenerate races" (ibid.: 27). The statement was meant to make clear in no uncertain terms that the church opposed racism. Mandel chose it because he knew that it would horrify his readers, whose religion was based on the modern race principle, not archaic language.

"The Pauline-Augustinian-Reformed teachings about original sin" Mandel considered "to be insulting to the ethical and moral feeling of the Germanic race." In line with Party thinking, he affirmed Christianity only, if at all, within the framework of racial specificity and a non-dogmatic reality-religion (namely his own) as he saw it defined in Paragraph 24 of the Party Program. It guaranteed "the freedom of all religious confessions within the state provided they do not offend against the ethical and moral feeling of the

Germanic race." It also affirmed that "the Party fights against the Jewish-materialistic spirit within and outside of us and is convinced that a permanent healing of our *Volk* can only come from within and on the basis: common good before own good" (Peters 1998: 625).

In February 1934, in the second issue of *Deutscher Glaube*, Hauer published an article, "*Wesen und Ziel der Deutschen Glaubensbewegung*" (The Nature and Goal of the German Faith Movement). Here he reminded readers again, "the German Faith Movement is not a creation of today" (1934d: 49). "It existed in hiding after the defeat of Charles the Great and the victory of the Church until it surfaced again first with Eckhart and then with Frederick the Great, Goethe, Hölderlin, Fichte, Lagarde, and Nietzsche. The end of the eighteenth century brought with it a strong yearning for the sources of a specific faith. And inspired by Klopstock's fascination for the important figures of a Nordic-Germanic past, researchers, writers and artists brought the religious heritage of our pagan ancestors to light" (ibid.: 49).

"The German Faith Movement has today become a movement that has penetrated the whole of our *Volk*," Hauer wrote (ibid.: 49). "The Hess edict that guarantees freedom of conscience is not a liberalistic charter for individualism without responsibility but with religious indifference. Rather it is the right to serve the *Volk* and *Reich* in line with the necessity of our own faith and conscience and a Germanic-*deutsch* state" (ibid.: 50). And, as if he had not made his movement's support of National Socialism explicit enough, he added, "This was done with an unshakable trust in the *Führer* of the German *Reich*" (ibid.: 50).

"By German Faith we mean being grasped in our central being by a last reality and by trustingly saying yes to the demands of the eternal" (ibid.: 52). Unlike Mandel, Hauer avoided the word God and talked instead about eternal or last reality. "One can say this of any faith," Hauer continued, "but each faith has its own form" (ibid.: 52). This form "is the expression of a specific psychology and culture that, according to our convictions, has its roots in our racial design. That is why we emphasize the racial basis also of religious life" (ibid.: 52).

If someone asked us, said Hauer, "what the objective power is before which we bow down, who the religious leader is whom we obey, then we answer: precisely that religious primal will of the German *Volk* that revealed itself to all the great figures throughout the history of our *Volk*'s German faith" (ibid.: 54).

Just how ambivalent the concept of primal will is, we discover when Hauer tells us that "if we have the courage to obey" this *Urwille*, "we shall discover what unlimited richness of restorative forces are hidden in the lives and works of those great people and were given us during the course of our history" (ibid.: 54). What then is the *Urwille*? Often it was described as an inner prompting that intended to be obeyed, but then again it was said to be the expression of great Germanic thinkers' thoughts that, however, "we internalized in ourselves, and as a *Volk*, over the course of history" (ibid.: 54). "It is here that we find revelation and this revelation will heal and make the *Volk* strong for great becoming and creating in the future" (ibid.: 54). Finally, Hauer affirmed, "A life from the power of German faith will become the fulfillment of the deepest yearning of the Third Reich" (ibid.: 54). In no uncertain terms, Hauer asserted that Hitler's *Reich* and German Faith had the same source and were mutually reinforcing.

Hauer summed up in point form what he called the "concrete content" of German Faith as follows (ibid.: 55–6):

1 We believe in the *Volk*'s religious *Urwille* that has revealed itself in the great harbingers and persons of German being and life. To the *Urwille* as our only *Führer* who works within our own soul we are unconditionally bound.

2 We believe that this leadership will return us to our welfare; that the primal force will help us to find the truth that is valid for us and let us live it out.

3 The great figures of the history of German faith we regard as our prophets to whose leadership we entrust ourselves.

4 For us there is no higher revelation of the eternal reality than that found within German space and coming from the German soul.

5 The religious *Urwille* is the will of eternal reality that comes to us in the form of a faith [*Glaubensform*] that suits our being.

6 We believe that the presence of the eternal reality in the world-all, in history and in our own soul is there without end. We reject that God revealed himself only to one *Volk*. If we love Germans and German space it is because God meets us here as nowhere else.

7 The world and the history of our *Volk* and the speaking depth of our own soul is as much the word of the last reality, as is a prophetic saying. To an open heart, a flower, a stone, a cloud bear witness to the eternal.

8 We struggle that the form-giving will, which pushes us to a brave and authentic life, fulfill itself through us.

9 The world is our *Heimat* [home] that is nearer to heaven than any paradise. Battle and tragedy are the eternal law of human beings and the world. We affirm life with all its tragedies as a fate toward which obedience is the highest fortune and most blissful peace.

10 What our eternal fate is we accept calmly from the will that carries all, knowing that no being can disintegrate into nothing.

What do these innocuous statements really say? Seemingly not much. The *Urwille* that reveals "itself" on German space and through German history, soul, prophets, and nature will usher in a this-worldly welfare. It can do so only if its adherents accept these revelations as their eternal fate, submit to the eternal law of battle and tragedy that is part of it, and lead brave and authentic lives. Authenticity and bravery are achieved by fighting for things German and against things foreign, especially the imposed absolutism of the church. These words mean very little, unless one understands the deep and persistent influence on Hauer of Hinduism, especially the *Bhagavad Gita*. Even the language—"eternal fate," "eternal law," "battle and tragedy"— has its source in the *Bhagavad Gita*.

How German is Hauer's faith?

At the time of writing the above article for his followers, Hauer was just finishing his book, *Eine indo-arische Metaphysik des Kampfes und der Tat: die Bhagavad-Gita in neuer Sicht* (An Indo-Aryan Metaphysics of Battle and Deed: the *Bhagavad Gita* from a New Perspective). By the new perspective Hauer meant to convey "the basic thoughts of the *Gita* from the perspective of the German generation that is fighting for the organization of all of *völkisch* life out of the deepest foundations" (Hauer 1934a: vi). Two years earlier, as if writing about Germany, he said, "In India today we are experiencing the breakthrough of *völkisch* powers, a being grasped by the reality of nation that arises out of the unity of space, blood, and spirit and that constrains all into one community. It is a heartfelt power that shapes anew the idea of *Reich* in spirit and will in the young generation" (Hauer 1932a: 36).

The first thing about the Gita that is important to all of Hauer's thinking is what he calls *Spannung* (tension), specifically, between the two life poles of Indo-Germanic being, namely, the self-communion (*Einkehr*) with the creative depth of the soul and the world, on one hand, and the turning toward (*Hinkehr*) a life of deed and battle, on the other (1934a: 3). These are the two sides of India; but as we saw earlier, they are also the two sides of Germany. If Hauer's language in the above points is deliberately neutral in tone, it is so because it bridges analogous poles of German Faith, namely, that of communion with the *Urwille*'s revelations about eternal fate and that of action in the world through brave or heroic deeds.

Since Hauer abjures Christianity and especially any ideas of its influence on Indo-Germanic life, he argues that the familiarity between Indian and Germanic thought has to do with the fact that Aryans moved into India in the third century before Christ, where they maintained the purity of their Nordic blood for some time (ibid.: 1). The proof of this he sees as established by three things: (1) the fact that the Indo-Aryan language, Sanskrit, is Indo-Germanic; (2) the fact that research in comparative religions has shown that the oldest religious traditions of Old India point to an *urindogermanische Zeit* (primal-Indo-Germanic times); and (3) the fact that the racial traits of Indo-Aryans link them historically with the Nordic traits of Indo-Germanics. Hauer sees his argument supported by Hans F. K. Günther's study, *The Nordic Race among the Indo-Germanics of Asia* (1934) . He also refers to research of von Eickstedt, Wilhelm von Humboldt, and Schlegel, among others (ibid.: 3).

According to Hauer, the *Bhagavad Gita* is a revelation that comes to the warrior from the teacher of wisdom, Krishna, who is the embodiment of the god Vishnu. It is a philosophical dialogue on the occasion of a looming civil war that requires of the warrior that he kill people related to him (ibid.: 4).

This war is *Schicksal* (fate or destiny). It is taken to be a dispensation of providence from which there can be no escape. Given this inevitability, questions about the cause of the war or the possibility of its prevention are irrelevant and cannot be raised. Only one question is possible. What stand does the human being take toward this unavoidable event—how does he meet his fate? One of the main motifs of the *Bhagavad Gita* is visible here, namely, the conflict between the duty of the warrior who must fight for honor and "*Reich*" and the guilt that he will inevitably incur because he must kill those of his own blood. According to Hauer, this is a tragic motif that is also found in heroic Germanic sagas (ibid.: 4). Two powerful armies confront one another in a war of extinction (ibid.).

The importance of this philosophical problem to Hauer's mind is that no reasonable answer is possible. Precisely because this happening goes against all reason, one of Hauer's favorite themes, and yet is unavoidable so that the human being has only one choice—namely, how to face it—he discovers the reasons for the deed and the nature and goal of the battle. In this happening, said Hauer, life shows its true being. And it does not make sense in accordance with any faculty of reason. Attempts to give meaning to life by fitting it into a schema according to which bad deeds are punished, good ones rewarded, are seen as dishonoring the reality of life. The latter is beyond good and evil. It is precisely the uncanny darkness of life that forces the courageous to show reverence for the superhuman majesty of life (ibid.: 5). Unlike Western Christian tendencies that try to make sense of life and happenings, the *Bhagavad Gita* calls the human being to uncover the deed that is required of him and therefore actively master the puzzle of life.

All attempts, Hauer emphasizes, to master life through thought and in terms of an ethical or other sort of schema merely hinders initiative to act. The Indo-Aryan of Old India had a good sense of questions that were useless. Thus questions about the sense of life, about the why of the world or being, about freedom of choice, were never important. It would paralyze the power to act. The Indo-Aryan knew that life and battle are always tragic. But tragedy makes the hero. And this tragic-heroic attitude, which is so much a part of Hauer's German Faith, penetrated the *Bhagavad Gita*.

Hauer then translates some telling passages of conversation. They start with the warrior Arjuna's expression of heart-rending sorrow and horror as he looks at those he is to kill in battle. But Krishna ignores Arjuna's lamentation. The fight is determined. And because Krishna knows that the burden of tragedy can be unbearable, he gives Arjuna insight into the secrets of life. The world of necessity is but one side of being. The human being as he is pulled into the tragic catastrophe is not the whole of the human being. Beyond or above him is something that remains untouched by the burden of tragedy, untouched by sword and death (ibid.: 8). And so Krishna says: "... the wise neither mourn the living nor the dead ... There was never a time at which I was not, nor you, nor those kings, nor will any of us in future ever not be" (ibid.: 8). (See here Hauer's point 10 above.) "... He, to whom pain and joy mean the same, is ready for deathlessness." (ibid.: 9). And Krishna continues:

> He who thinks that one kills or is killed errs on both counts, for that one does not kill, nor will he ever be killed.
>
> He will not be born, nor will he ever die. He did not become, nor will he ever be nothing. He is unborn, perpetually eternal, *uranfänglich* [there from the beginning], how can this "human being" still effect killing? Whom does he kill?

Hauer explains that the mysterious "human being"(*purusha*) is the inner-most hidden human essence (*der Mensch an sich*) that lives beyond all empir-ical humanness in the depth of the soul and is in its final nature like God (ibid.: 9). The concept *purusha* comes from Yoga (Hauer 1932a: 9).

According to Hauer, what is being taught here is the fact that the historical-empirical fate of the human being, including death in battle, is not necessarily the end, but is rather a mere minor episode in the never-ending series of developments and changes that a human being experiences on his paths through many births. This perspective turns death into but a fateful moment (*Augenblicksschicksal*). Death loses its finality. And the fighter, who must kill, is therefore not a destroyer of human life; he is merely the performing organ of the happening in the course of the world (ibid.: 10). For life in itself, so it is revealed to Arjuna, is not extinguished through his act. That is how the hideous becomes bearable. The guilt, that fate forced him to incur, is not a guilt of eternity, but merely one of temporality (ibid.: 10).

Not only is the relativism of death and guilt that Hauer discovered in the *Bhagavad Gita* very much in tune with Ludwig Klages' postmodernism.[23] The philosophy of the *Bhagavad Gita*, worked out by Hauer in the early 1930s, anticipated justification of the deeds committed by the Nazi regime. This becomes particularly obvious in Hauer's discussion of the guilt-afflicted tragedy of human activity and the mastery of this tragedy through battle and deed (Hauer 1934a: 13).

According to Hauer, the Christian approach to morality in terms of the either–or of a good or bad deed is superficial (ibid.: 14). The Indo-Aryan came to the early realization that we can understand an ethical decision in depth only when we hit upon the inescapable contradiction between duty and duty. Here an ethical code no longer works. In these decisions we discover the general tragedy of human activity and the realization that there is no such thing as a deed that is only good. Rather the tragedy of human activity is found precisely in the recognition that each deed, if seen in light of the whole, carries guilt within it, that is, that each deed has a tragic interior (ibid.: 14). In obedience to one demand, no matter how good the intention, the human being offends against another that is just as important. In other words, human beings cannot live other than in the painful tension of this contradiction. "As is stated in the eighteenth chapter of the Bhagavad-Gita: Everything done by the human being is afflicted with guilt (*sadosha*), like fire with smoke" (ibid.: 15).

   While Hauer wrote this a decade and a half after the First World War, it is like a prophecy that would apply, or be needed, after the Second. Surely no better justification could be found to steer past accusations of atrocities. According to Hauer's apologist Dierks, he used just these thoughts in an address that he gave to the Marine Physicians Academy in Tübingen on 2 February 1945, at a time when the end was clearly in sight, where he said: "We stand by our *Schicksal* [fate]" (Dierks 1986: 330). Continued Dierks, "he could only accept what happened as fate, not very differently from the conclusion of the First World War." After he left Christianity, wrote Dierks, "he became aware of a deeper intertwining of fate and guilt. He worked out the problem in 1934 on the text of the Bhagavad-Gita" (see Hauer 1934a), ideas that Hauer took over unchanged in the republication of the book in 1958 (see Hauer 1958). "From the situation early in 1945, when the question of individual guilt was as yet understood neither by him nor by millions of other Germans, the words of chapter XVIII of the Bhagavad-Gita accompanied him—words that created, for the unavoidable guilt-entanglement, a parabolic image: 'Everything done by the human being is afflicted with guilt (*sadosha*), like fire with smoke'" (Dierks 1986: 331). Dierks was a Nazi herself, who joined the New Right in the 1950s. Consequently she did not demand, as she might have, that Hauer should have used his *Bhagavad Gita* teachings years earlier to take a stand in the conflict between his duty as professor and religious leader for human freedom and the guilt that he would have incurred because he opposed the Nazis who were of his blood.

   Hauer's German Faith was deeply influenced by a combination of Platonism (going beyond the limits of empirical reality) and Hinduism. The latter is the source of his monism, his qualified non-dualism, his radical relativism and, above all, the absence of moral and ethical constraints from any source other than that which comes from "within" a person through the primal force and the expressions of the wisdom of the specific *Volk*.

   The influence of Hindu religion on Hauer is mentioned frequently. In his article "*Skizzen aus meinem Leben*," in the January 1935 issue of *Deutscher Glaube*, Hauer wrote, "I did not find Christ in India, however, but Indo-

Aryan wisdom, that is, it found me" (1935: 9). And then he explained further, "Just as the Edda[24] once touched me in my youth, like the sound of a distant home [*Heimat*], so my heart was grasped by India, that is, above all by the old Indo-Aryan India" (ibid.).

Earlier, in a letter to Dr Walter Schliffke, who worked with the *Bhagavad Gita*, Hauer wrote, "I am glad that the Bhagavad-Gita gave you so much. I too have received much from her [the Bhagavad-Gita] and she accompanies me almost daily. One finds within it the deepest wisdom for action and life." In this letter he also mentioned that he had just completed his work, *Eine indo-arische Metaphysik des Kampfes und der Tat* (An Indo-Aryan Metaphysics of Battle and Deed) to be published by Kohlhammer. Curious too were his next comments: "Your thoughts spoke to me. They are not meant for the public, but they show all the same that Indo-Aryan being also lit a flame in you. I know of course that one cannot simply take over Indo-Aryanism into our culture, but I am convinced that its wisdom will show us the way to the profound depth of our own German soul."[25]

On 23 May and 21 June 1934 Hauer received two letters from Ernst Schulze, who was the private secretary to Tridandi Swami B. H. Bon in London, England. The Swami, who according to Schulze represented the largest religious orthodox Brahmin organization in India with 42 centers, wanted Hauer's help with the publication in Germany of his English translation of the *Gita* from the theistic Bhakti-religion perspective. Apparently, the Swami had great sympathies for "the new Germany of Adolf Hitler." He had formed his positive impressions during a visit to Berlin. Now he was eagerly learning German and kept emphasizing that he thought the German people were "the most suited of all Western peoples for an understanding of the Indo-Aryan religions." When, therefore, the Swami asked Schulze for advice about whom to approach in Germany, "I remembered your name immediately, since you are working with such great enthusiasm for the renewal of the German Faith."[26]

On 21 June 1934 Schulze wrote Hauer again. He knew from the *Völkischer Beobachter* and the *Reichswart*, which were sent regularly to him in London, that Hauer was very busy with the German Faith Movement. But he wanted to know whether his dry rendering of the Swami's English translation into German was worthy of publication. In this letter Schulze also explains that he went to England only because of his private studies and earnest searching for the theistic primeval religion (*Urreligion*) that the Aryan Indian and Aryans of the West have in common. Now he has spent a quarter of a year with the Swami in London and can say "with full awareness that the religion that the Swami was sent to bring the West is closer to the Aryan sensitivity than Jewish theology and groundless asphalt-Atheism."[27]

In his reply on 28 June 1934 Hauer mentioned that he too had contact with Indians in Germany. A Professor Sircar from Calcutta had recently given a talk about Indian mysticism that was well received. Then Hauer gave practical advice, namely, that a translation from the English into German would suit no one. The translation had to be direct from Sanskrit into German, and indeed he and some of his students had been working on just such a translation, and here they would find the Swami's English translation helpful. If the Swami knew German, Hauer could invite him to Germany for talks. Hauer pointed out that he had some influence as a member of the *indischen Ausschuss der Deutschen Akademie* (Indian Committee of the German Academy). "As you know, for years I have worked to further communication between Aryan India and Germany, and I am convinced that the new Germany, especially now through the German Faith Movement, whose goal it is to make the Aryan Faith in Germany effective again, will have much understanding for India and vice versa."[28]

Hauer's Indian teachings were severely criticized by Mathilde Ludendorff (1877–1966). The daughter of a Lutheran minister, Mathilde Ludendorff received her PhD in neurology, despised Christianity and the occult, and founded her own new religion called *Gotterkenntnis* (God Knowledge). It was a science-based religion that combined notions of race-inheritance, belief, justice, culture and economy. Since it underpinned the metapolitics of her third husband, Erich Ludendorff, it was adopted by his 100,000 followers in the *Tannenbergbund*. Mathilde and Erich Ludendorff were fanatical anti-Semites and *völkisch*, although not members of the Nazi party. While the Ludendorff tendencies had nothing to recommend them, Mathilde made some interesting criticisms of Hauer's most academic work, *Der Yoga als Heilweg* (Yoga as Therapy, 1932b). She thought that his work was neither critical nor objective (1933: 50). She also objected to his tendency to coin many new words (*Wortneubildung*) that supposedly enhanced profundity.

One of the reasons why Mathilde Ludendorff treated Hauer's work with such contempt has to do with her belief, apparently based on the work of her father Bernhard Spiess, that not only the New Testament but also the Old Testament are based on distorted Indian beliefs, especially those of Krishna and Buddha. Ludendorff claims that her father was a Sanskrit and cuneiform scholar,[29] and it is he who taught her that neither Old nor New Testament are the products of Jewish minds but of the minds of Indians, Syrians, Sumerians, and Persians (1931: 133, 140). Jewish evangelists and Jews of the Old Testament copied and distorted Indian and other Aryan sources (ibid.: 133). She spends several pages reviewing Krishna and Matthew parables that talk about the same theme but evidence very different moralities and deeds (ibid.: 140–62). Regarding God, for example, Ludendorff argues that the author of the five books of Moses took over a God concept that is basically Indian but changed it into a Jewish race-God (ibid.: 164).

Hauer was aware of Ludendorff's criticism. And while he in turn criticized her inability to understand his empathetic method, he recognized that her criticism (and in 1936 that of her husband) endangered his own metapolitical ambitions. In his next major book (1934e), therefore, while he continued with his Indo-Germanic or Indo-Aryan arguments, he shifted to emphasize the Germanic-*deutsch* part of it. He explained the latter as a specific Germanic expression of common, ancient underlying beliefs that were Indo-Aryan (ibid.: 177). Like his *Indo-Aryan Metaphysics* (1934a), so his *Deutsche Gottschau* (The German View of God, 1934e) was a popular and metapolitical work.

Chapter 6

The Germanic-*deutsch* leg of Hauer's German Faith

Klages, biocentrism and the pre-modern

Hauer's German Faith stood on two legs: that of Hinduism, especially the *Bhagavad Gita*, *Upanishad*s, and Yoga; and that of Germanic thought, especially the *Edda*, Eckhart, and the writing of any "heretical" German philosophical and literary figures, particularly the Romantics. We also saw that Hauer's conception of religion was layered: a universal experiential layer at the bottom, giving rise to culturally specific expressions on top.

Hauer and other founders of religions and/or literary circles of the 1920s were not original thinkers. Rather they radicalized selectively ideas from Herder and other Romantics and achieved a sense of newness by coining words, often ones impossible to translate. Thus Hauer's universal experiential layer giving rise to culturally specific expressions is but a modification, one could say distortion, of Herder's early homogeneous pre-*Volk* condition followed by a great diversity of *Volk* cultures, a diversity that was the result of historical rather than biological development (Malefijt 1974: 100, 102). But where Herder, although he admired the poetry of diverse peoples, used reason and analysis to present his social philosophy, Ludwig Klages and those who were inspired by him, including Hauer, reverted to metaphysical thinking and used religion to interpret religion, and worldview to deconstruct science. While time and duration played into their thinking, they preferred to bypass history and focus on pre- and post-history. Given the greater emphasis on biology at the time, they substituted the metaphysical notion of biocentrism for the science-based one of logocentrism.

It was the fashion of the time to reject modernism, which was associated with rationalism, materialism, cosmopolitanism, and—thanks to Houston Stewart Chamberlain—with Jews. Instead, the tendency was to hark back to the pre-modern and prehistorical. The aim was not, however, to dwell on the past for its own sake, but to adapt past things deemed to be authentic to current times, that is, to the post-modern.

About history, Klages said, for example, after a very long period of "ahistory" and prehistory, the history of humankind is but a short break,

6.1 Ludwig Klages, philosopher, co-founder of the German Graphology Society

6.2 Houston Steward Chamberlain, inspired by Nazi ideology

barely an interim, since it is unlikely that this history will last more than one to two thousand years (1929b: 766, 767–8). In places he talked about the post-historical humankind, or post-history, analogous to the post-modern (*nachgeschichtliche Menschheit*) (ibid.: 767). Like Spengler, and numerous other post-historians, Klages saw himself and his compatriots as being the "last of the Mohicans" (*letzte Mohikaner*). He anticipated an apocalypse (ibid.: 768).

More than Spengler, Ludwig Klages was at the forefront of this tendency. He was inspired by Johann Jakob Bachofen's (1815–1887) work on the importance of symbols, rather than concepts, during antiquity, and he postulated, before Hauer, a unique pagan culture that was increasingly threatened and destroyed by modern rationalism and logocentrism. The latter he referred to as rational or scientific thought (*Geist*), and he saw it as the adversary of symbolic or metaphysical thought (*Seele*) (Klages 1932: 1301).[1] It is important to understand that to Klages a symbol is not only a sign of something unseen; rather, each symbol *is* what it means; it *is* its meaning. It is metonymic and thus has psychic power. To put it in the tortuous language of Klages, "the essences or souls, with which the symbol is connected by being one of its revelatory forms, are … so to speak cosmic characters and therefore reach far beyond the playroom of mere comments that one may make about one's own nature" (ibid.: 1274). In simple words, symbols used by one's ancestors in antiquity had the power to impact and steer people today.

Aschheim (1992: 82) points out that Klages saw Nietzsche as one of the martyrs of paganism who broke down the church walls. Nietzsche's fervor of life became an irrational *Lebensphilosophie* to Klages (ibid.: 80). "The rational spirit of science is only an expression of the same rational spirit that called into life the modern state and modern capitalism ..." and it will probably not last longer than the rational spirit of scholasticism of the Middle Ages (Klages 1929a: 128, 130). In fact, wrote Klages, several things entered the world stage together: the ideal of free civic self-government; incorporation of Roman law; "Protestantism" of every kind; ideas of expansion and progress; calculated self-interest; and a discovery-based science (ibid.: 128). Not unlike Hauer, Klages thought that this Jewish Geist destroyed organicism and the cosmic dimension.

Metaphysical knowledge, not the assumed impartiality of the "search for truth," enables us to grasp the essential reality of things, including our dual nature: a bearer of reason and a bearer of life. But reason, living within the world of happening, is a stranger (ibid.: 129). Klages offers this formula: the historical human being is doubly constrained—either to tie up life in reason or to loosen and undo reason in life. The first leads to the practice of knowing through facts and their relationships; it is a straight path up the ivory tower of science in the eternal pursuit of knowledge. The second leads into a labyrinth with uncountable paths and directions that ultimately meet, however, at one and the same midpoint, namely, at that reality whose being can only be experienced. "The former is progressive and logocentric, the latter contemplative and biocentric. If we look at the pursuit of knowledge of the whole of historical humankind, we find from the beginning among the most diverse peoples overemphasis on logocentric intellectuality over a biocentric one; but we have only led with the former within Christianity until its exclusion" (ibid.: 130).[2]

Now these distinctions between logos and life, logocentrism and biocentrism, science and metaphysics, the ivory tower or the labyrinth, and so forth, we find also in Hauer and in numerous street philosophers and religious founders in Germany of the time. Privileging metaphysics above science played into the hands of Nazis in two ways: first, it justified Nazi tendencies to interpret scientific research in terms of the *völkisch*, National Socialistic and organic worldview; second, those who saw themselves grasped by an essential, that is absolute, eternal reality applied a radical relativism and amoralism to all else.

Opposed to the "concept-bound" modern human being, Klages (1932: 1251), following his interpretation of Bachofen, postulated "image-bound" prehistorical human beings called "Pelasgians."[3] It is a fact of prehistory, says Klages, that the Pelasgian consciousness is the force behind mythology and the fact that there is such a thing as depth of soul or inner depth (*Innerlichkeit*). Here is the basis of experience. According to Klages, experience rests on the process of having spiritual inner experiences brought about by absorbed heeding of images (*schauen*) that puts one in touch with the Pelasgian consciousness because it is the force behind the images of myths, poetry, and legends (in which the heeder is absorbed). "Images and only images grasp the soul" (ibid.: 1254).

More than anyone else, Klages' thinking explains why religion, philosophy, literature, sagas, epics, and poetry were all "sacred" means of furthering National Socialism. They were all part of what he called the "reality of *Dichtung*," which—being more than simply poetry—refers to works of, and talent for, language art.[4] Language artists (*Dichter*) are an almost extinct group of people who with the use of language practices dating back to primeval times represent (in powerful images) the soul-like content of experiences rather than telling them. The aim of *Dichtung* is to "grasp the language-sensitive hearer" (ibid.: 1255). The language art of all tribes, in all times, including the songs of peoples, confirm in Klages' thinking that people are grasped solely and exclusively by images that come to life when an understanding listener takes in the words. Language art emancipates the soul of a word and it does so through inspired (or spiritualized) word usage that in turn has the power to spiritualize the listener (ibid.: 1255).

While Klages' work reminds one of Herder, who thought that humankind's humanity was best discovered by looking at the oral and written literature of a people, especially their poetry, Herder's thinking is not what Klages' is, namely, metaphysical. To Herder, poetry and literature were language "monuments" that preserved the psychology of a people. While Herder assigned a special role to the poet, namely, that of an educator or evangelist who, given his gifts of insight could see or discern the "preordained plan" of the world, he does not go in for mysticism nor abandon empiricism.

To make his point about the power of images, Klages quotes a poem about the sea by the German poet Lenau. He does so in order to show that what appears to the inner eye through this poetic use of "sea" is "real only as an image"; "it has nothing of the reality of the object named sea" (ibid.: 1256). The objective sea can be found in a specific place. But the "sea" conjured up by the language artist cannot be found anywhere nor anytime except in a good hour when reading the poem, and there never a second time as in the first. Reason fails to grasp the poeticized "sea", since, to gain insight, one has to abjure all reasoning activity; one is without reason (*entgeistet*), and is surrendered to being grasped by the image that the poet or seer has freed of its thingness (ibid.: 1256).

According to Klages, if the faith of modern man is word-based, that of Pelasgians and of peoples of nature (*Naturvölker*) is image-based. Image-faith is knowable not through concepts, but only through symbols. Symbolic thought or image-faith (*Bilderglaube*) was hegemonic among Pelasgians and indigenes, not a faith in reason and the reality of things, although of course Pelasgians and primitives reasoned.

Although Klages used ideas of anthropologists such as Bachofen and Edward Burnett Tylor (ibid.: 1293–4), he changed them to meet his own ends. "We use the name Pelasgianism," argued Klages, not only because Bachofen did not reject it, but also because the Romantics used it to designate "three very different human groups ... that think in symbols" (ibid.: 1258). One group, says Klages, "consists of authentic language artists [*Dichter*] among all peoples and times in so far as these *Dichter* were not so much personalities as they were the receiving organs of language-capable waves [*sprachfähiger Wellen*] of the soul" (ibid.: 1258). The second group "consists of the ahistorical [*aussergeschichtlichen*] peoples of nature, if not of the present, then of the most recent past" (ibid.). The third group "consists of prehistorical [*vorgeschichtlichen*] ancestors, above all European peoples of education [*Bildungsvölker*], whose nature is unlocked through images of gods, cults, symbols, mysteries and myths" (ibid.). The tone-setting group is the third; it is the measure for the rest. But there is something that all three groups have in common, namely, the use of elementary symbols (ibid.: 1260).

Klages laments that the *Monon des Geistes* replaced the *Theion der Seele*. This is so because "the victorious monotheism of the Israelite prophets ... unleashed an unbounded hate of godliness itself into this world" (ibid.: 1266). It used its "vampire-like will to power to curse all idolatry [*Götzendienst*]" (ibid.). To let the reader "hear the deadly hate," Klages uses Duhm's rendition of a conversation between Amos and Hosea (ibid.: 1267). "Who could mistake," Klages asks, "that the opposition between mono-god-thinking [*Eingötterei*] and multi-god-thinking [*Vielgötterei*] is but dressed in elevated speech to hide the real opposition, namely, that between the naked will to destroy [*nackten Zerstörungswillen*] and the image-pregnant soul [*bilderträchtigen Seele*]."

The opposition between rational scientific thought and symbolic metaphysical thought has been juxtaposed not only with the usual dislike of things Western, but importantly also with anti-Semitism. Having arrived here, therefore, it is appropriate to delve into Hauer's representation of German Faith.

The German beholder

In the Preface, which is dated December 1934, of his book, *Deutsche Gottschau: Grundzüge eines Deutschen Glaubens* (1934e),[5] Hauer tells us that the book was written for the *Volk*, not for theologians and philosophers of religion. For academics he would soon publish another book, *Religion und Rasse* (1934e: i; 1938). The title of the book, said Hauer, is to reflect that of the ninth chapter, *Germanisch-deutsche Gottschau* (Germanic-German God Contemplation) (1934e: 197–224). And because he uses the word "God," which he usually does not, and wants to affirm that this faith is in fact Germanic-German, he explains, "that faith always has to do with the last reality [*letzter Wirklichkeit*], with 'God'" (ibid.). Having been criticized by Mathilde Ludendorff because his religion is Indian and occult, he goes out of his way to emphasize, at least in the first pages, its Germanic origin. Finally, to ward off criticisms from theologians, he argues that "more important than systematics," or dogma, "was the living expression of that, which I carry within myself as religious experience and conviction" (ibid.).

The aim of the book is also, he writes, to show the principal characteristics of a German Faith. To do this, numerous credentials from the Germanic-*deutschen* history of faith are presented. This is not done to prove a dogmatic authenticity of German faith, argues Hauer. His Faith does not have Holy Scriptures to which it is bound. Rather, "the documents and credentials of the inner history of our *Volk* are an important proof that through the centuries there was no shortage of seers and prophets for our specific [*arteigenen*] Faith" (ibid.: i–ii). Hauer sees here the unlimited wealth that was withheld from the younger generation at great cost.[6]

The aim is not, however, to look only to the past, Hauer tells his readers. German Faith remakes itself continuously; it is alive to the times in accordance with the latter's needs (ibid.: ii). "The reason for its birth is always the same: the German soul grasped by 'God' [*gottergriffene Seele*]" (ibid.: ii).

The pressure for a German Faith has powerfully affected the new Germany and especially the younger generation, argues Hauer. Nothing will be able to deaden this impulse. The determination of this perseverance gives us the confidence "that what is making itself known here is not the small will of individuals or groups, but the eternal creative will of the German *Volk*. Only this creative will can bring about the inner foundation of the Third Reich with which German Faith is organically connected. We stand and fall with the Third Reich" (ibid.: ii).

In the Prologue of the book Hauer defines both faith generally and German Faith specifically. Thus he writes, "We are fighters for a faith against all non-faith. Faith is not holding something to be true. Faith is life, power, and security in one's innermost being. Eternal Reality meets us in our Faith. Faith is surrender to the will of this Reality; it is creating and fighting in accordance with its Must; it is knowledge of its victory. Faith is trust in the power that resides within the heart, and the heart is where the creative god unites with the upright and sacrificial person" (ibid.: 1). Faith, wrote Hauer, "is mastering the task with which God's rule has confronted us" (ibid.: 1).

As usual, Hauer argues that religious confessions and trust in dogma have ruined faith. The German Faith Movement, however, will return faith to its position of honor by imbuing it once again with life and love. "Within us presses the power of new emotion [*Ergriffenheit*], creative life from the holy depth of our *Volk*, from which all great things emerged on German soil," wrote Hauer dramatically (ibid.: 1).

The Preface and Prologue define a political ethos in religious terms. It is a politics of battle (*Kampf*) that Hauer preached. The *Kampf* would be against things foreign, especially Jews. The two most important defining qualities of the ethos were obedience and surrender to what he called alternatively Eternal Reality, the inner Must, or the will of this Reality. For all practical purposes followers were encouraged to follow their heart, even though Hauer knew from hundreds of letters and conversations that their hearts were stirred by Nazism and anti-Semitism.

Some readers might argue that Hauer's ruminations are at best ridiculous and at worst have little to do with practice. Such a conclusion is wrong. Minimally, Hauer used his beliefs to justify actions and outcomes. We see this, for example, in the correspondence between C. F. Lemcke, first-leader of the *Gemeinschaft Deutscher Erkenntnis* (Society for German Knowledge), a splinter group from Ludendorff's *Tannenbergbund*, and Hauer on the occasion of the 1934 Scharzfeld conference. At this conference, all *Bünde* and religious groups gave up their distinct identities and attitudes in order to become one unitary German Faith Community (*Deutsche Glaubensgemeinschaft*). In his May letters of 1934, Hauer insisted that the union occurred "organically."

Answering Hauer, Lemcke disagreed, arguing that the Scharzfeld results were orchestrated. Finally, after the war, in the late 1940s and 1950s, when it was in Hauer's interest to make himself the victim of Nazi persecution, a third version emerged, shaped by Hauer himself through the historian Hans Buchheim.[7] Buchheim (1953: 186) argued that, while Hauer himself had been pushed onto a more radical course, he felt uncomfortable with the Scharzfeld events because they did not agree with his ideal picture of a religious community. Furthermore, Hauer led Buchheim to believe that Heydrich was the force that led Hauer's movement in the radical anti-Christian and, later, "*areligious* political direction" (ibid.: 185, 191). How untrue Buchheim's claims are we shall see in the correspondence below and in a later section that deals with Hauer's letters to Werner Best.

While Lemcke, in discussing the 1934 Scharzfeld conference, praised Hauer, he explained that he and his followers had to leave the conference because the coordination (*Gleichschaltung*) of all communities (*Gemeinschaften*) into a unitary German Faith Community meant that the latter was no longer a community of fate that, however, respected different styles and expressions of experiences and ways of being (*arteigene Schicksalsgemeinde*).[8] He could not, therefore, fulfill his task. He understood, however, that Hauer now had what must have made him totally happy: "the 'totalitarian Faith', as Hitler has the 'totalitarian state'!"[9] "The play of free and unbound powers in the now unitary German Faith Movement stops," continued Lemcke, "and the claim to unlimited authority [*Totalitätsanspruch*] of unseen powers for the German Faith Movement is the first mistaken consequence [*Folgeunrichtigkeit*] of the new German life of faith."[10] And, despite these people's dislike for Christianity, Lemcke too ended his letter with Luther's famous words: "*Hier stehe ich, ich kann nicht anders,*

Gott helfe mir, Heil" (Here I stand; I cannot do otherwise, so help me God). Only, Lemcke added the infamous "*Heil.*"[11]

Hauer's answer was prompt and to the point. "At stake is the issue [*Die Sache*]. And here we have to be clear: the time to discuss how we might want to organize ourselves is gone. It is the hour of decision. What happened in Scharzfeld was not the decision of the Board of Leaders nor was it the force of my will; rather it was the whole original breakthrough [*ursprüngliche Ausbruch*] of the people's will [*Volkswille*] in the German Faith Movement."[12] Hauer assured Lemcke that he did not push for his leadership; the decision came from the *Urwille* (original will) of the community. "What became," continued Hauer, "grew organically from a Must, a Necessity [*Muss*] that I had to heed as much as the next man." In other words, the German Faith Community is the expression of the authentic *Urwille*.

On 30 May 1934 Hauer wrote Lemcke again. "I still don't understand why the great happening unleashed such bitter disappointment in you. Nor do I understand your objections. Everyone was most happy about the Union. That the small *Bünde* were a hindrance was clear. That no one other than me was ready and qualified to lead was also clear. Therefore, what happened in Scharzfeld was something entirely organic [*ein durchaus Organisches*]." What really was his objection, he asked.[13]

Lemcke answered Hauer that he left the conference early (on 21 May) because "an unrestrained, emotional, raging, repulsive mob tried to force their will upon responsible leaders. It was behavior that one observed with repugnance even at political meetings."[14] And, he continued, "The happenings of the 21st, 5th were not in the least organic." Indeed, Lemcke repeated what he wrote previously, that Hauer "has his 'totalitarian' faith, as Hitler has the 'totalitarian' state."[15] After all, he continued, "the inner political situation of the *Reich* makes it clear that the dissolution of all groups, associations and parties did not result in what we thought was desirable."

On 14 June 1934 Hauer wrote Lemcke another letter. He emphasized again that the Scharzfeld events were entirely organic, not forced, and that the time for *Bünde* was over. In this letter, Hauer also pointed out that actually he knew nothing about Lemcke's group; he had not seen any publications; nor was he aware of any significant activities. All the same, and no doubt because Hauer needed numbers, he wrote Lemcke that a position in the leadership was available should he affirm positively the German Faith Community.[16]

In a June 1934 letter to Hauer (the day is not given), three leaders of the *Gemeinschaft Deutscher Erkenntnis* spelled out what their expectations of the conference had been and why they were disappointed. While the seven-page letter was tedious, some points were important. For example, they thought that they shared two important goals with the German Faith Movement when it was an umbrella group: (1) they were all united in their common rejection of Christianity, and (2) they wanted Hitler's state to recognize all groups under the German Faith umbrella as German pagans.[17] It also suited them that the German Faith Movement, which supported the fundamental freedom of the individual, rejected any spiritual restraint and use of power as incompatible with a German sense of God (*deutscher Art Gotterfühlens*). Given these commonalities, they were prepared to cooperate for the unity of a great gathering of non-Christians striving for a German Faith that was only, however, in its beginnings.[18] Above all, they were first and foremost responsible to their 10,000 members who had broken with Ludendorff's *Tannenbergbund*.[19]

Then they learned with some astonishment that the *Bünde*, including theirs, were to be dissolved so that henceforth "only individual German pagans could become members." What they found particularly objectionable was that "a young national comrade [*Volksgenosse*] interrupted Hauer's talk and demanded that the Board of Leaders be dissolved, that all groups disappear, and that Hauer be made their sole *Führer*."[20] Given all the hoopla, and since their freedom and absolute right to self-determination had been stolen by an irresponsible mob, it was clear that there was nothing left to do but leave. In their movement, they wrote Hauer, "… only leaders carry responsibility."[21] All the same, they declared themselves prepared, as a distinct group, to fight alongside Hauer's movement against the oppression from Christian churches.[22]

On 2 July 1934 Hauer sent back another long, firm letter. He objected to their characterization of the Scharzfeld meeting as hijacked by an unruly mob of "wire-pullers." Contradicting what he said in his letter of 28 May 1934 that it was not a decision of the Board of Leaders, he now argued that the dissolution of the *Bünde* had already been decided upon in February by the *Führerrat* and in response to many letters from *Bünde* leaders asking for just this dissolution. If their group was taken by surprise at the turn of events, it could only be because they had never participated.[23] What Hauer did not quite tell these men, however, was that the founding of the unitary German Faith Community occurred not only with the prior approval of the *Führerrat*, as he now admitted, but also with the coordination of Rudolf Hess, and the two *SS-Führer* Heinrich Himmler and Reinhard Heydrich (Kratz 1994: 298).[24] For the continuation of the free religious as a separate *Bund* within the GFM (the only permitted exception), Hauer too received Himmler's agreement (ibid.: 298). Indeed, it is quite clear from Hauer's letters that he did not do anything important without consulting Himmler or other SS leaders.

Hauer's Nazi book

"The German Faith Movement of today," writes Hauer in his book that attempts to capture the essence of National Socialism (1934e: 4) "is a phase of a several-centuries-old battle between the Near-Eastern-Semitic and the

6.3 Hans F. K. Günther,
social anthropologist and raceologist
in Jena, Berlin, and Freiburg

Indo-Germanic world. Only in terms of this relationship can the historical meaning of the German Faith movement be clearly understood." It is important to recognize that this battle has three forms: a biological-racial one, a political-economic form, and a worldview-religious one. While the complexity of these forms often hides just what the battle is all about, a closer look reveals that the two worlds are determined to be world historical antagonists. And the "geo-biological basis" for the fateful opposition between these two worlds is "the difference of Race and Space" (ibid.: 4). While Hauer concedes, following his friend Günther's (1934) thinking that Indo-Germanic peoples, like all people, are racially mixed, both agree that the Nordic race was especially effective (Hauer 1934e: 6).

Neither space nor time permits translating Hauer's argument word for word. His *Deutsche Gottschau* (1934e) is at any rate merely an overtly political, that is, a Nazi version of what he has said and written elsewhere. What he does here, and even that is not new, is to appropriate the thoughts of German or Germanic literary figures into the Indo-Germanic tradition. That goes for Plato, Kant, Goethe, Fichte, Arndt, Hölderlin, and Eckhart, among numerous others. How the appropriation is done is common to all National Socialist ideologues, indeed, fascists. As we shall see below, Payne (2002) following Emilio Gentile explains it well. At any rate, Hauer writes about

Eckhart, "His rhetorical figures and images are often Christian. But the content of his teachings about the root of human religious psychology [*Seelengrund im Menschen*][25] is absolutely non-Christian and purely Indo-Germanic" (Hauer 1934e: 185). Furthermore, Eckhart thought in these terms because he abjured abstraction. Instead, Eckhart was immersed in the immediacy of reality and from this perspective beheld (*schaut*) truth, because he was entirely alive to the here and now (ibid.: 185).

The ninth chapter of Hauer's *Deutsche Gottschau* is a masterful seduction of the mind. The chapter starts with his exposition of the Nordic mythos of *Ragnarök* about the twilight of the gods (*Götterdämmerung*) and the peculiarly *Ur*-Nordic sense of the tragic (ibid.: 199). As one would expect, the Nordic mythos is eventually linked to the primordial Indo-Germanic faith world.

What is most important to Hauer, of course, is to underline the total difference (*grundverschiedene*) of German Faith from Christianity. The evidence that the lineage of thought as represented by Eckhart, Goethe, German Idealism and so forth survived as a distinct German Faith in the midst of Christendom is not enough. Hauer looks for another source. And this source, he thinks, is found in the fact that ancestral Germans affirmed as self-evident truth the fundamental ideas of the Indo-Germanic realm while they rejected instinctively Christianity (ibid.: 208). The source is therefore a race-related (*arteigene*) experience of God. Here Hauer uses the word *Gotterfahrung*, with which he implies that, because our natures are not receptive to everything, we can only accept from another that which is already alive in us (ibid.: 209). His assertion sits on the meaning of *er-fahren* (he-driving to), which means to gain inner knowledge of something by oneself driving to it and taking possession of it. This in turn means, says Hauer, gaining actual consciousness of a reality that is already there (ibid.: 209).

Hauer argues that the root of every faith is an objective ultimate reality and a human subject who experiences it, is grasped by it, and affirms it (ibid.: 225). The distinction is between a primeval phenomenon and specific religious cultures. Hauer analyzes ten primeval phenomena and for each at least two different religious cultures. For example, he argues that the first primeval phenomenon is faith. But faith is always culturally expressed. While faith is never in conflict with a specific cultural form, the religious culture of one people is always in opposition to, and maybe downright lethal to, another (ibid.: 227).

Neither time nor space allows listing each phenomenon with its varied cultural expressions. What is important to point out, however, is that Hauer always worked with but two opposed forms; one from the Near-Eastern Semitic faith world, the other from the Indo-Germanic one. Of these the former was always ugly, the latter beautiful. In the end, the reader who remembers what Nietzsche did with Islam becomes aware that

Hauer used the Indo-Germanic faith world as a wishful picture of religion that was used to effect in the reader the rejection of its opposite. The impulse was the same as when Hauer worked behind the scenes to remove a Jew or Christian from a university post. Yet Hauer did not regard himself as anti-Semitic. Nor did all of his followers, even when some joined because they hoped he was. Can one live a lie not knowing that one is doing so? I think the answer is yes. And the implied deed can be performed explicitly by someone else.

Chapter 7

Organizational help from *Wehrwolf*[1] and the SS

Groups and numbers

During the conference of 29–30 July 1933 at the Wartburg near Eisenach, many German faith groups joined what became known as the *Working Community of the German Faith Movement* (ADGB). For the sake of brevity, we shall simply refer to it as the German Faith Movement, although it did not drop the "Working Community" designation until the Scharzfeld conference in 1934.[2] Among the groups that joined were: Hauer's Friends of the Coming Community (FKG); Dr Kramer's and Carl Peter's League of Free Religious Communities (BFG); Dr Pick's and Professor Drews' Association of Free Religious Communities (VFG); the *Rig-Kreis* of Hessberg, Wesemeyer and Groh; the German Faith Community (DGG); the Nordic-Religious Working Community (NRA) of Norbert Seibertz, director of the regional superior court; and W. Schloz's Eagles and Falcons (AF). Smaller groups included: C. F. Lemcke's Community of German Cognition (GDE); O. Michel's German-religious League (DRB); the Working Circle for Biocentric Research (AfBF) of Deubel, Eggert-Schröder and Kern; and many others. The AfBF, although led by Deubel and others, was focused on the works of the graphologist and *völkisch* psychologist Ludwig Klages. The Germanists Bernhard Kummer and Professor Neckel also attended the conference, as did the race psychologist Ludwig Ferdinand Clauss. Further prominent figures included Fr. W. Prinz zur Lippe of the Young-Nordic League (JNB) and Professor Schultze-Naumburg. Paul Schultze-Naumburg (1869–1949) was an architect and leader of the state universities for architecture and educational art in Weimar. In 1932 he was also a Member of Parliament for the Nazi party. Excepting the free religious ones (*freireligiöse*), all groups were National Socialists or National Socialistic in their orientation.[3]

The internal organization of the ADGB consisted of Hauer as its *Führer* and a Board of Leaders (*Führerrat*) whose function was advisory. Two-thirds of the Board members were Nazis. They included the *Reichswart* editor Reventlow, the race ideologist Hans F. K. Günther, the propagandist Dr von Leers, the Germanist Professor and first Director of *Ahnenerbe* SS Hermann

Wirth, the radical Nazi philosopher and religious leader Ernst Bergmann, and many others. Right from the beginning, therefore, Hauer cultivated Nazi contacts, including ones with the Nazi Minister of the Interior Wilhelm Frick (1897–1946),[4] the Nazi Reichskommissar Dr August Jäger,[5] and the SS-*Obergruppenführer*[6] Werner Best (1903–1989)[7] (Bartsch 1938: 51). The composition of the *Führerrat* and ADGB would change over the years as different individuals and groups joined and departed, but the thrust of it would be to become ever more crassly anti-Christian and pro-Nazi.

No one knows the exact size of the membership. In answer to the German Christian Manfred Boge's question about how many registered members the ADGB had,[8] Hauer answered about 200,000.[9] Hauer also mentioned that important leaders of the NSDAP were members—Reventlow, Dr von Leers, Wirth, and an important leader of the SS—but that he did not want to mention other individual names except to say that the Hitler Youth leader Baldur von Schirach did "not officially" belong to them. "We have many more supporters of course," wrote Hauer, "they will join (officially) as soon as we have (state) recognition." Regarding Boge's rather hostile question about Hitler's religion, Hauer answered that he did not know the religious attitude of the chancellor. "But I do not believe that you can count him among the Christians." Hauer also mentioned "many farmers and workers are followers who long for a German Faith even more intensely than the intellectuals."[10]

On 15 January 1934 Boge replied somewhat aggressively to Hauer that really leading personalities of the NSDAP such as Hitler, Hess, Göring, Goebbels, Feder,[11] Frick, Röhm, Seldte,[12] Rosenberg, and so on, did not belong to the ADGB. Did Hauer not see this as an unfavorable omen? And tauntingly, Boge then continued that in Silesia church attendance was increasing mightily, as did giving so that new churches could be built again.[13] There was no further reply from Hauer for the moment. We know, however, from Hauer's correspondence that at least Hess and Frick were favorably inclined toward the movement, and most likely also Feder, Seldte, and Bormann. Rosenberg was like-minded but followed his own ambitions.[14] Apparently Goebbels, a "non-believing Christian" who cynically remained "officially" in the Catholic Church, opposed the German Faith Movement. After all, he believed his own propaganda, namely that one needed no religion other than National Socialism.[15] He called the German Faith Movement a "Nordic pagan religion sponsored by Alfred Rosenberg (1893–1946), Martin Bormann (1900–1945)[16] and Professor J. W. Hauer" (Bramsted 1965: 8).

The actual number of German Faith believers, including those who classified themselves as *gottgläubig* and, for example, those who belonged to the Ludendorff movement, among others, is not known. Opportunism, secretiveness, and deceit played into this numbers game. According to Bartsch, who calculated his figures from memberships mentioned in the journal

Durchbruch, the number of registered ADGB members was about 10,000 in the summer of 1936 and 39,542 in January 1937. These figures did not include the 60,000 to 70,000 *freireligiöse* who were members of the ADGB from 1933. Reventlow, the editor of *Reichswart*, mentioned that about 2½ million people declared themselves to be followers in 1935. In that year too, the movement referred to itself as a "movement of millions" (*Millionenbewegung*) (Bartsch 1938: 68).

A large membership increase occurred after the Sport Palace meeting in Berlin on 26 April 1935. Because the crowd filled the Sport Palace even after its 20,000 seats were occupied, it had to be closed by the police. Apparently vigorous propaganda preceded the meeting, with as many as 90 talks per month being given all over Germany (ibid.: 68). The topics were provocative, such as "can a German be a Christian," "German morality without Christianity," "German Faith, not Bible nor *Edda*," and so on (ibid.). Bartsch calculated that 12 million people were reached in various meetings within the nine-month period preceding the Sport Palace rally. Given large attendances, the figure is plausible. Furthermore, were we to include the popular literature that was read in those days—books that sold millions of copies and propagated similar ideas—an audience of 12 million is too small. It is unlikely to have included the millions of schoolchildren and university students who were supplied with this literature.

Help from *Wehrwolf*

Whatever the actual figures may have been, Hauer had the problem of organizing the German Faith Movement into district and local groups in the various cities, towns, and villages (Bartsch 1938: 68, 70). Here too an energetic Nazi came to his aid.

On 24 October 1933, high-school teacher (*Studienrat*) Kloppe, who was also editor of the journal *Wehrwolf*, wrote Hauer congratulating him for having brought the various fighters for a German Faith under one movement. He wanted to join Hauer's cause, rope in old comrades, and win over several thousand young, energetic and disciplined lads from all over the country as helpers.[17] At the time Kloppe was the *Reichsführer* of the *Wehrwolf*, one of the fighting *Bünde* that were now in liquidation because they had joined the Hitler Youth.

Hauer enthusiastically welcomed Kloppe to the ADGB, especially since the *Wehrwolf* had been a *Bund* of fighters, and "a fighting spirit" is what they needed in their battle for state recognition. Having just returned from negotiations with Hess in Berlin, Hauer anticipated a hard, if not unfavorable, battle.[18]

In the meantime, Kloppe had already begun to canvass in support of the ADGB. Many of his comrades, he wrote, "reported on difficulties that you have, including the influence on women, and so on."[19] Difficulties could be overcome, thought Kloppe, if individual members did not stand alone but found themselves in a circle of like-minded friends who together could overcome the tenacity found in some localities. Kloppe thought that they should organize into regional leaderships (*Gauleitungen*) analogous to the NSDAP.[20] He also suggested that Hauer appoint him as his honorary organizational leader quickly because the mood of the youths was favorably inclined toward the ADGB.[21]

Hauer's so-called influence over women requires some clarification. The *Köngener Bund* that preceded the ADGB had a large following of women. As I pointed out in another chapter, Hauer was a guru-like figure, and some prominent women (from the poet Anna Schieber, to the democrat Gertrude Bäumer, to Marianne Weber) gave him their loyalty for different periods of time. In this respect, Hauer's *Bund* went against the notions of *völkisch* theoreticians. Like Hauer, the latter saw the *Bund* as the driving force behind a "higher development" of youths. It was to occur only, however, at the express exclusion of women from exclusive male groups (*Männergruppen*) (Nanko 1998: 75). According to Nanko, Hauer's position fell in with that of a small group of matriarchy researchers such as Herman Wirth, Bernhard Kummer, and Sophie Rogge-Börner (ibid.: 75). The inspiration behind this trend was, of course, Ludwig Klages. Wirth, Kummer, and Rogge-Börner belonged to the German Faith Movement at times and/or continued to work with Hauer on his journal *Deutscher Glaube*.

In his reply to Kloppe on 14 November 1933 Hauer did not address the issue of women, but admitted that the organizational work had been slow owing to his illness as well as his visits to the Reich Ministry of the Interior and Hess in Berlin. He agreed, therefore, to the informal appointment of Kloppe, although he told him that it would have to be confirmed by the Board. Hauer pointed out that in Halle, which was Kloppe's hometown, the ADGB already had a number of members including a young academic named Werner Hülle, who assisted a Professor Hahne. "Hülle is a long member of my closer community, is thoroughly *deutschgläubig*, and a National Socialist for years" wrote Hauer.[22] Hülle and the National Socialists Ernst Krieck, Friedrich Hielscher, and Paul Krannhals spoke at the Kassel *Tagung* that was planned for 1932 but took place from 1 to 7 January 1933 (Nanko 1993: 80, 94). Other participants were the *völkisch* poet Georg Stammler, the Quaker Elsbeth Krukenberg, the Democrat Gertrud Bäumer, the *völkisch* Catholic priest Nikolaus Ehlen, and the Jewish scholar and Zionist Martin Buber (Nanko 1998: 94). On 30 January 1933 Hitler took power, and on 29–30 July 1933 the ADGB was founded.

In his November 1933 letter, Hauer pictured Kloppe's work as consisting of finding appropriate regional leaders or checking out ones suggested by Hauer who would then, if Kloppe thought they were worth it, appoint them formally and oblige them to do their duty. In all of this, Kloppe was to work closely with Hauer's manager Paul Zapp.[23]

Kloppe's first job was to check out Dr Julius Deussen of Leipzig, who was suggested by Flurschütz as a *Gauleiter*. Hauer emphasized that the search for leaders was to be done through confidential persons and correspondence or personal meeting. Thereupon Kloppe was to characterize the individual, and Hauer would take it from there. Hauer also suggested that Kloppe reign in the *Wehrwolf* sisters, since Frau Dr Scola with her sisterhood (*Schwesternschaft*) had already declared her willingness to help the ADGB.[24]

In his reply to Hauer dated 17 November 1933, Kloppe agreed to be an informal organizational leader until the Board confirmed him. In the meantime his only concern was to apply the organizational experience that he had garnered from having been a *Wehrwolf* leader. He suggested that he work quietly or secretly (*im stillen*) so that no difficulties should arise from the fact that the former *Wehrwolf* leader was suddenly appearing in a publicly prominent position.[25]

Kloppe thought that the organization of the ADGB should be built in a fashion analogous to the NSDAP, namely, into Regions, Circles, and so on. Hauer should confirm the Regional and Circle leaders once he found them agreeable. Thereafter, starting in the spring of 1934, Kloppe suggested that conferences be organized for Regional and Circle leaders so that Hauer could get to know the men personally and validate their status. Finally, Kloppe suggested that he and Zapp should plan how to raise money and other practicalities.[26]

Hauer agreed with Kloppe's plan and mentioned that he had received a letter from Friedrich Wilhelm Goddemeyer, who was the Deputy Head Propaganda Leader (*Hauptschulungsleiter*) of the SS. Like Kloppe, Goddemeyer wanted to work secretly for the ADGB within the Bureau of Race and Settlement. Hauer wanted Kloppe to contact Goddemeyer.[27]

Because Goddemeyer's letter is important, it is worthwhile describing it in more detail. Goddemeyer informed Hauer that he knew of his movement from the *Reichswart* and from Professor Günther, whose student he had been for the last ten years.[28] Goddemeyer joined the NSDAP in 1923 and was now the Deputy Head Propaganda Leader for the Bureau of Race and Settlement within the SS, Section XVII in Münster, Westphalia. Through frequent visits of Dr Rechenbach, said Goddemeyer, he had heard a lot about the ADGB and now wanted to join it. "For years now I have developed the worldview consequences from a combination of my biological knowledge and the National Socialistic idea. I come to my non-Christian, *völkisch* and Germanic faith outlook on life, therefore, from the natural science perspective."[29] In his position, it was in his interest that all Propaganda Leaders have the correct worldview. In the building of their Section he was particularly keen to ensure that none of the Propaganda Leaders, as well as none of the other co-workers of the Bureau of Race and Settlement, were Christians. He would see to it as well that the non-Christian Propaganda Leaders, the co-workers and his old acquaintances in the Party would join the ADGB. He thought it most important that like-thinking people be organized within one tightly knit organization.

"In the propaganda business itself that has within its purview the SS formations, on the one hand, and country youths, on the other, I shall not tolerate—for that matter I am not allowed to—anyone trying to mix biological knowledge with Christian ideas in any form whatsoever ... I am well aware, however, that I am not allowed to trumpet this goal" since they lived there in a very conservative church-dominated part of the world. "We don't want to persuade, but to convince."[30]

Being assured of gaining many followers among the SS and, with Goddemeyer's and Kloppe's cooperation, also among youths in the country, Hauer told Kloppe that he was most anxious to start university groups. To that end he was giving a public lecture that he hoped would widen his group. But the organization of university groups was to be done systematically and thus to be part of Kloppe's job. Furthermore, wrote Hauer, he had been approached by the Hitler Youth to ask Kloppe to organize youth groups within it. Here the former *Köngener Bund* Youth leader Dannemann could help.[31]

Kloppe confirmed what he thought Hauer expressed in his letters to him, namely, that the leadership (*Führung*) must be supported by a strong organization. To that end he made three suggestions. First, he told Hauer that of the former *Wehrwölfe*, with whom he had a ten-year relationship, 80 percent were *Sturmführer* in the SA and were in charge of a considerable part of the youth. The majority of these *Sturmführer* answered his letters and confirmed that young people longed for a new faith; what was needed was a point of attraction. And that point of attraction had to be a *Führer*. Kloppe would therefore take over the organization of the fighting troops and would "represent the Ernst Röhm of the German Faith Movement."[32]

The way he saw it, each regional leader who was under the spiritual guidance of Hauer was to have a team who prepared meetings, passed out leaflets, and generally saw to it that the literature of the German Faith Movement was distributed among the people. Second, Kloppe suggested that the women's organization of the DGB be entirely separate from the men's to avoid gossip. Here Frau Dr Scola was to take over, because she had many years experience of organizing women. Finally, he reminded Hauer that it was the link to workers that had prompted him to write Hauer. Sixty percent of the *Wehrwolf* consisted of artisans and workers and thirty percent were farmers. "Especially among the farmers we must win ground," wrote Kloppe, "and since the *Wehrwolf* had most of its groups in villages, we have good points of connection." Ludendorff had most of his support in Schleswig-Holstein, which was also a farming area. Finally, Kloppe mentioned that the Minister of Science, Art, and Public Education had called him to Potsdam, where he was to be made director of education of the model school that was to revolutionize the educational system. Nevertheless, he would still find time for Hauer's work. And then he ended his letter with one last suggestion, namely, that they end their correspondence with the "*Sieg-Heil*" greeting as was practiced by the NSDAP.[33]

Hauer agreed with Kloppe's characterization of his organizational work as Ernst Röhm-like.[34] But he did not yet want a separate women's organization. Rather, he thought that Frau Dr Scola should gather women's groups on the quiet (*in der Stille*). What he particularly wanted her to do was to find women and girls who could work in the Hitler Youth.

Then he told Kloppe that he had just given a talk about the German Faith Movement in Stuttgart. He thought the talk would become programmatic for Württemberg. The most important people of the government and the National Socialist Press were present. "The National Socialistic Press will open itself to the movement and that is an important step forward," reported Hauer. He also informed Kloppe that their press officer for Württemberg would be Mr Drewitz, who was the second editor of the *NS-Kurier*. Drewitz was thoroughly supportive of the DGB and had even won his boss over.[35]

After Hauer had had a discussion about organization with his assistant Paul Zapp, he wrote Kloppe again, this time advising some caution. He now distinguished two phases of organization. The present phase consisted primarily of gathering followers, forming internal structures, and advertising. It was in the following phase that a tight organization was to be built that would span Germany in order to let the thrust of the German Faith Movement have its full impact. For this second phase Hauer wanted the Board's approval and a critical and tightly organized mass of people. In addition, for the organization of the second phase he wanted a plan from Kloppe that would include fees and finances, and he wanted to work closely with him.[36]

Hauer also advised caution vis-à-vis youth activities. He informed Kloppe that he had negotiated with leaders of the Hitler Youth who belonged to the ADGB:

> We agreed that I first get in touch with the *Reich* Youth Leader, Baldur von Schirach. As you know, the *Reichsführer* wants to avoid the penetration into the Hitler Youth of any cross-organizations. Our organization would count as a kind of confessional organization. And it is possible that the *Reich* Youth Leader might consider it trouble and act accordingly.[37]

Since that had to be avoided at all costs, Hauer's youth leaders suggested gathering loose groups through personal contacts and introducing them to the DGB at times of celebration. Importantly, Hauer advised against naming a *Reich* youth leader of specifically the German Faith Movement. Later, he thought, when it became clear to everyone that the German Faith was, in fact, the religious foundation for the National Socialist movement, things would be different.[38]

In the matter of finding proper leaders for regions, towns, and so on, Hauer distinguished between what is possible for a political organization and a religious movement. A political organization can build up a machine that functions independently. By contrast, in a religious movement this is not possible; the machine must be closely bound up with the spiritual leadership. It meant that regional leaders must know that Hauer personally, in the name of the ADGB leadership, appointed them and deposed them. The greatest care was needed and, as an example, Hauer mentioned that they had just installed a Württemberg leader, Wilhelm Schloz, whom he had known personally for many years.[39]

Hauer also answered Kloppe's criticism of Hauer's writing. Kloppe must have suggested that someone else write the flyers because Hauer wrote too high-mindedly. Hauer insisted, however, that he could also write simply. Since the ADGB was becoming a popular movement, Hauer thought it good to write plainly. While he himself would write the flyer, *What does the German Faith Movement want?*, he was willing to let someone else write a flyer on the topic, *The German Faith Movement as answer to the yearnings of German Youths*. As for a flyer on the topic, *The German Faith Movement and Women*, he preferred to leave it or perhaps have Frau Dr Scola work on it. The important thing was, said Hauer, that anything written in the name of the ADGB had to be approved by him. Finally, he mentioned that his journal *Deutscher Glaube* would start January 1934. Hauer ended the letter, as requested by Kloppe previously, with a "*Sieg-Heil* and the watchword: forward and forward again!"[40]

By the time Kloppe answered, around 4 December, he was in Potsdam. He reported having met Reventlow and finding that they were more or less in agreement about matters pertaining to the ADGB. He also reported on the situation in Berlin. "The Führer will leave us freedom of faith in Germany; what he does not want is a war of faith [*Glaubenskampf*] that might disturb the hard-won unity. Regarding the question of state recognition, several leaders answered that it was impossible to recognize a small group of but a few thousand members, since it meant incurring the wrath of the churches. They would want to see proof that the German Faith Movement had such a large echo in the German *Volk* that it could not be ignored."[41] Kloppe set himself the goal to fulfill that condition.

In this letter too Kloppe discussed the matter of fees, about which there was some disagreement between him and Hauer. Kloppe insisted that all should pay fees and that this would be important for state recognition. He was willing, however, to allow reduced rates for SA and SS members and would write this into the bylaws. Above all, he wanted a free hand in matters of organization, and asked Hauer to give him three months to see the results. On all other matters he was in agreement with Hauer's suggestions. Kloppe was most eager to make Hauer's journal *Deutscher Glaube* obligatory for all leaders. It would become the main journal, said Kloppe, making all others secondary.[42]

On 7 December 1933 Hauer affirmed that Kloppe should move forward with his organizational tasks. "Without doubt," wrote Hauer, "the times are right. In all of Germany people ask about the ADGB and what it means. People are open. In six months perhaps something else will grasp their attention. The church struggle has also opened people's ears to our ideas and points them in our direction. Before this favorable condition changes, we must have organizations in each city and region that can then, when the wind changes, work quietly in the background."[43]

Regarding fees, Hauer agreed that he did not want shirkers. He told Kloppe, however, that he received truly shocking letters especially from teachers, but also preachers, who had lost their jobs and most of their pensions because of their faith. He suspected that there were dozens, perhaps hundreds, of such people. From them no fees could be demanded: his conscience would not allow it. Hauer also cautioned Kloppe regarding his eagerness to make *Deutscher Glaube* obligatory reading for all leaders. "It would arouse suspicion," wrote Hauer, "that I am using the organization for my own benefit."[44] "If the journal is to become the mouthpiece, it must do so of its own accord and because of its quality."

Regarding a meeting between the two men, Hauer mentioned that, while he would go to the mountains over Christmas, he would be in Tübingen until the eighteenth because the Hitler Youth had asked him to give a talk during their Christmas celebrations. He ended his letter, as Kloppe requested, with "*Sieg-Heil!*"

With Hermann Claasen of Berlin-Zehlendorf, Hauer discussed Claasen's suggestion of creating a general gathering point for the ADGB in Berlin. Hauer thought that Claasen should cooperate closely with Arthur Lahn, *Führer* of the Nordungen and with a Dr Jöckel who was to be added to the *Führerrat* of the ADGB.[45] Finally, Hauer mentioned having just received a card from Kloppe. It said the following: "To the *Führer* of the German Faith! The first three SA-troops (*SA-Stürme*) for the German Faith Movement. *Sieg-Heil!* Signed, Fritz Kloppe, Joachim Blessing, and W. Lindermann." Kloppe "moves fast," commented Hauer, "and I hope he is the right man."[46] He wanted Claasen to contact Kloppe immediately.

By 23 December 1933, however, Hauer had received contradictory reports about Kloppe; especially, unfavorable remarks about his moral qualities. Hauer mentioned his disappointment in a footnote of a letter to Reventlow (in Nanko 1993: 325). In 1934 Kloppe found another group to organize.

SS help in Stuttgart

In the meantime, Hauer also had to reorganize the free religious (BdF), consisting of about 140 congregations and between 60,000 and 70,000 adult members. To help with this task Hauer pulled in the poet Georg Stammler (1872–1948).[47] Stammler was to look after congregations in the Freiburg area, for which he would be given a small honorarium. Furthermore, Hauer promised to use him in his Leadership School (*Führerschule*) that he planned to open in November, and to make him, as representative of the news journal *Deutsche Richtwochen*, a member of the *Führerrat*.[48] Hauer's offer followed a letter from Stammler in which we learn that he was closely associated with the *Wandervogel*,[49] had been on the Board of Wilhelm Schloz's Eagles and Falcons (AF), and taught now and then at a university. Because his name comes up after the Second World War, it is of interest to note that Stengel von Rutkowski, also on Hauer's *Führerrat*, held a position in the Bureau of Race not only of the SS but also of the AF.[50]

Lower-ranking SS were also eager to help Hauer get his movement off the ground. Thus on 7 May 1934, SS-*Sturmführer*[51] Erich Spaarmann told Hauer that he had won the Heidelberg professor Dr Hirt, an anatomist, for their cause. He pointed out that Hirt, "who was also the main indoctrination leader of Spaarmann's 32nd SS-*Standarte*,[52] has very great influence on young students as well as on the SS men in his units. Once he really gives himself over to our cause we shall have won a very active coworker and worthy human being." Furthermore, reported Spaarmann, he had won over another SS-*Sturmführer* from Mannheim who was also an indoctrination leader and has great influence over a large circle of people. "In this manner I shall recruit men throughout the *Reich* who are capable in their own right of building large cells."[53]

Spaarmann was not happy, however, with the local Stuttgart community of the German Faith Movement. He thought them unimpressive. They gave the impression of belonging to an old men's club (*Herrenclub*), he told Hauer, "Men who are to be the primary fighters for the German Faith Movement have to look differently." He told Hauer that he could not, however, lead the local community because he still had too much to do at the SS; he could, however, be useful to the movement throughout the *Reich*.[54]

Hauer was delighted with Spaarmann's help. While he wrote Spaarmann on 11 May 1934 that his criticism of the Stuttgart DGB community was a bit sharp, he understood it. "That's why I hope to win youths," said Hauer. He also encouraged Spaarmann to meet Hauer's Stuttgart man, Dr Gerhard Schmidt, who would impress him positively. He was sorry that Spaarmann could not also lead the local DGB community, "since the people we attract have much to do with those who lead."[55]

Spaarmann obviously did make the effort to meet Dr Gerhard Schmidt, because on 31 May 1934 the latter wrote Hauer that he had "just met an SS-*Führer* who heads the indoctrination work in the south, whose name is Sparmann [*sic*] and who lives in an SS home." Schmidt thought that Spaarmann could take over the leadership of the Stuttgart community and wanted Hauer to talk with him. He also suggested that Hauer speak with a Miss Poerschke and with Dr and Mrs Duvernoy about the matter and that Wilhelm Schloz and Spaarmann meet.[56]

After the Scharzfeld conference, Schmidt wrote Hauer again. By this time Schmidt had met with the Stuttgart leaders Poerschke, Silgrat, Rothermund, Schloz, and Stockmeyer to discuss the leadership of the Stuttgart commu-nity.[57] Apparently, Stockmeyer knew his own inadequacies and was willing to step aside. Without another leader, however, they kept him on. He himself, reported Schmidt, could not take on the local community because he had more than enough work with students. "Sadly, we met rather stiff resistance from student leaders against the DGB. I have not even received permission to leave, cost free, copies of *Deutscher Glaube* in the reading room of the student union, and the leader of the student body made derogatory remarks about our student circle. Even my suggestions that I invite Graf Reventlow or Professor Günther for talks was rejected by the organization bureau with the excuse that it did not fit the times."[58] Leaders seemed to be frustrated with the religious battles generally, continued Schmidt, because they saw them as making the *Volk* restless. What was certain, said Schmidt, was that among students as well as in the community they had more problems there than elsewhere in the country. Perhaps, people were spoiled by Hauer's talks. "Many are 'interested,' but to work for the cause or join the movement … here many Swabians are slow to decide …"[59]

Puzzled by the student body leadership, Hauer wanted to know what was behind it: "I do not think it impossible that the Member of the High Consis-tory, Pressel, has his hand in the game. Naturally, we do not want to give in here."[60]

Indeed, Wilhelm Pressel (1895–1986) was very popular with students in the years 1933–1934. He argued that it was the students who "pushed" him toward National Socialism. Whatever the truth, in the spring of 1933 Pressel brought hundreds of his Protestant ministers to the Faith Movement of German Christians (GGDC), the wing of the church most supported by Hitler (Wischnath 1998: 303–4). Already in August 1933, however, he was one of the leaders who seceded from the German Christians and, within Württemberg, became a bitter opponent of National Socialism (ibid.: 299). Then in January 1934 he was assigned the dual task of maintaining ties with the Confessional Church, whose synod meetings he attended, on the one hand, and toning down the radicalization of the German Christians, on the other. Hauer, who was well informed about internal church affairs, would have known this and seen Pressel as one of his enemies.

"Most immediately," continued Hauer to Schmidt, "we need to know whether Christian journals are found in the reading room of the university cafeteria. If they are, we must insist that our journal *Deutscher Glaube* be placed there too. Perhaps you should discuss the matter with Dr Keller of the Ministry of Religious Affairs (*Kultministerium*). I can tell you, strictly confi-dentially, that Dr Keller, speaker for university affairs, stands with us. But no one is to know this, lest it make his position in the Ministry impossible. The churches would be up in arms against him without letup. It is good that you should know this. But keep it to yourself. Perhaps he can advise you what to do."[61]

The secrecy surrounding Erich Keller (1894–1977) helps explain why he was regarded as being insincere and untrustworthy by many students as well as being a spy for the Party. He was in fact one of the first hundred of 18,000 preachers to become a member of the NSDAP in 1930. In July 1933 Christian Mergenthaler (1884–1980) called Keller to the Ministry of Religious Affairs. He put him in charge of university affairs and to work on the Ministry's dream of starting a university for teacher training in line with a National Socialistic worldview. Keller worked with Hauer and Rosenberg's ideas and, like them, opposed Aryanism to Semitism, was very anti-Semitic, and taught Nordic myths and legends, and various aspects of the National Socialistic worldview (Jooss 1998: 295). Hauer, Mergenthaler and Keller consulted frequently on all sorts of matters, but especially on matters of religious education, conferences, and students. After denazification and various court cases in which Keller fought to reduce his sentence from "political incrimination" (*belastet*) to "fellow traveler" (*Mitläufer*), he worked with Hauer again in the latter's right-wing Working Community for free Research of Relgion and Philosophy (AfFRP) and later, 1956, in the creation of the Free Academy (FA). These organizations were gathering points for former Nazi intellectuals and academics including Margarethe Dierks, who wrote a thorough but sanitized biography of Hauer.

In the same 1934 letter, to encourage Schmidt further, Hauer mentioned yet another Nazi who was on their side. It was the leader of the guild (*Gilde*) in Stuttgart, Mr Drewitz, whose brother was the second editor of the NS-Courier (*NS-Kurier*). Spiritually, they were on Hauer's side. Hauer suggested that Schmidt make contact with him. Admonishing Schmidt to persevere, Hauer reminded him that difficulties "make us more willing to sacrifice" and help us become "a fighting community." It was also becoming clearer, said Hauer, that Swabians were not good soil for their movement, but hopefully Wilhelm Schloz could change that, as could Spaarmann if he could be won over for Stuttgart.[62]

Women

Some months earlier in 1933, Hauer received a letter from Frau Dr Scola, who brought her 300 members of the women's movement called The German Woman, formerly of the *Wehrwolf*, to the ADGB.[63] Since the *Wehrwolf* had disappeared within the Hitler Youth, Scola's group reverted to calling themselves The Sacrificial Group of League Sisters of German Combat Soldiers (*Die Opfergruppe der Bundesschwestern deutscher Sturmsoldaten*). They had a peculiar task; one, however, similar to Hauer's. They saw as their "particular responsibility working for a specifically German Faith in God [*artgemässen deutschen Gottglauben*], wrestling for the totally new within the German soul," something that they were assigned to do by their *Reich* leader. "For years, this struggle against things foreign, the shaping of the new, fills our weekly evening work." These women, argued Scola, formed a *Volksgemeinschaft* in the truest sense of the word, "for we are simple women with no more than public school education, who for this very reason are proof that the new German God-Faith that emerged again out of the indestructible ancestral heritage [*Ahnengut*] has its starting point in the simple soul."[64] She further underlined her like-mindedness with the Hauer people by mentioning that, following the advice of Bernhard Kummer, with whom she corresponded, she had joined the board of Carl Friedrich Lemcke's GDE. Lemcke's group had split off from Ludendorff's *Tannenbergbund*. Kummer as well as Lemcke's group, it will be remembered, were already part of the German Faith Movement.

Hauer interpreted her interest in the DGB as the work of organic laws: "Never before in my life did I have the sense of standing under a fate that out of necessity consummates itself from the basic powers of our German soul."[65] Despite the inevitable workings of the destiny that Hauer described here, and despite his belief that the ADGB could no longer be overlooked by the Ministry of the Interior and the Deputy Chancellor of the Reich, Hauer anticipated a long fight for state recognition and welcomed these women combatants.[66] Unlike men inquirers about membership, these women were not offered anything. They were to think for themselves about how to organize their fight for the faith.

Intellectuals, writers, and media

When Dr Werner Hülle, who would become an editor of *Deutscher Glaube* in 1936, asked Hauer about the wisdom of letting Kloppe organize the German Faith Movement, Hauer answered, "If we are unwilling to allow danger we cannot risk anything." He also pointed out that he "had to risk putting men in positions dozens of times because of the many inquiries from people everywhere about organizing various groups."[67] With Hülle too he discussed roping in more theologians and philosophers to help with their work. They had the theologians Mandel of Kiel and the *Privatdozent* Dr Kurt Leese of Hamburg. They also had the philosopher Fritz Berger, author of a book about Herder, in their fold. Hauer suggested that Hülle recruit more.[68]

In matters of organization, as in all other things pertaining to the German Faith Movement and his academic life, Hauer cooperated deliberately and carefully with Nazis. His *Bünde* work and contacts from the 1920s paid off. Many of the people who were once in the *Bünde* were now in the SA, SS, and the Hitler Youth. We see here that he had sections of the SS, SA, and Hitler Youth behind him. Editors of the *NS-Kurier*, of the Nazi journals *Wille und Macht* and *Sturmtrupp*—the latter two under the supervision of Gotthart Ammerlahn, chief editor of the National Socialistic Youth Press—all supported Hauer and the ADGB.[69] So did the editor-in-chief Kurt Herwarth Ball of the journal and press called *Hammer*.[70] It was music to Hauer's ears to hear Ball affirm that religious renewal was absolutely necessary and that it was absurd to have National Socialistic Christian ministers affirm the Aryan Paragraph in all aspects of their lives, while continuing to base their teaching and preaching on the Biblical God.[71] A similar attitude was expressed by a twenty-four-year-old Hans Riemann, owner of the National Book Distribution for Nordic and Völkisch Literature, who wrote Hauer 6 November 1933 from Aachen. He informed Hauer that he had grown up in *völkisch* groups and had been a member of the NSDAP since 1929. Since he could not abide Christianity, he was eager to start a group for the German Faith Movement in Aachen. While he was too young to be its leader, he would have no difficulty finding one through his business contacts. The task would not be easy, he warned Hauer, because "Aachen swarms with Jesuits."[72] Werner Bänsch of the Silesian Radio was also eager to help out.[73]

Hauer also brought Nationalistic and National Socialistic writers and poets into his movement, or they found their own way to him. I mentioned Georg Stammler earlier. A letter too arrived from Georg Fuhrmann, who wrote under the pseudonym Egbert Falk.[74] A more important and colorful arrival was Curt von Trützschler (full name Baron Curt Trützschler von Falkenstein), apparently from a highly respected old aristocratic Weimar family. He was known as one of the renowned writers and poet-philosophers in Dresden who had talked or corresponded, over several decades, with the most famous men of Germany about religious, life-philosophical and national economic problems. Among them were Siegfried Wagner (1869–1930), who called Hitler "a splendid man" in 1923 and whose wife Winifred was a passionate Nazi and Hitler supporter (Wagner 1999: 70–1); Friedrich Lienhard (1865–1929), editor of Weimar's national-conservative *Türmer*, through which he spread his syncretistic beliefs consisting of a combination of Old Germanic, Greek, and racial-*völkisch* tendencies; Henry Thode author of the *Ring des Frangipani*; Rudolf Eucken (1846–1926), a life philosopher (*Lebensphilosoph*) from Jena who founded the Rudolf Eucken *Bund*, which was against naturalism, a social-eudemonistic ethic,[75] and against clerical Christianity; Hans von Wolzogen (1848–1938) who was made editor by Richard Wagner of the *Bayreuther Blätter*, in which he perpetuated Wagner's anti-Semitic, nationalistic, and Christian-Idealistic thoughts. Wolzogen was the grandson of the famous architect Karl Friedrich Schinkel.

Trützschler further corresponded with Alexander von Gleichen-Russwurm (1865–1947), a vague irrationalist and mystic who at one point belonged to the Münchener literary salon frequented also by Heinrich Mann and Friedrich Lienhard, among many others. Further correspondents included Viktor Blüthgens (1844–1920), a youth writer from Berlin who edited *Gartenlaube* and *Deutsche Monatsschrift*, and Werner von Siemens.[76]

Trützschler first wrote Hauer on 4 June 1934 to tell him that the Nordic, Germanic, and German Faithlers, as well as the free religious wanted him [Trützschler] to be the leader of Dresden's local DGB community. He accepted and asked Hauer to approve his appointment as soon as possible so that they could go to work forcefully.[77] Trützschler included a newspaper clipping with information about himself.[78] Describing himself he wrote, "I am a captain, have three war medals, am a member of the *Reich* writers association [*Reichsschriftstellerverband*], the *Deutschen Arbeitsfront*,[79] and also the War Victims Association [*Kriegsopferverband*]. Know the *Führer* personally."[80] The included "newspaper clipping gives information about me," he continued. "Furthermore so can National Education Minister Jacksen as well as Minister Council Florey of Saxony's Economic Ministry and generally all top Dresdner." Trützschler claimed that the simple people, the middle classes, as well as the intellectual community loved him, so that he had influence everywhere. He promised, "We shall recruit thousands of members, directly and through public talks. All Dresdner and convinced Germans look forward to your lecture on the 15th of this month." In a P.S. he told Hauer that he had carefully studied six of Hauer's writings, has absorbed them, and "now radiates Hauer's spirit, making firm propaganda!"[81]

Some years later Kolbenheyer and others would become involved. Furthermore, the names of intellectuals such as Mandel, Leese, Berger, Clauss, Günther, Hülle, Bergmann, Kühn, Wirth, von Leers, and many others, are now familiar. Only in matters of women was Hauer cautious, not because they were not willing to join, but because he was ridiculed by some Nazis for having too many of them under his influence. Regarding the matter of women, Hauer also received an unpleasant letter from Karl Dehne reminding him that only a year or so ago he had totally supported the worldview of Mathilde Ludendorff in a talk given before students and others in Tübingen. Dehne objected to Hauer's about-face and to his notion of a German Faith.[82] But on this topic, more will be said later.

Chapter 8

Hauer and the war of attrition against Christianity

Introduction

By 1933 religion in Germany was muddled. There were three major forces at play: the Catholic Church, the Protestant Church, and the diverse groups of German faithlers, *völkisch*, and free religious. With the *Reich* Concordat passed in Cabinet on 14 July and signed in Rome on 20 July, the Catholic Church ceased to be part of the religious confusion. Not so the Protestant Church. It was gravely divided into various factions from the Young Reformers, who wanted an independent church but one unconditionally loyal to the state, to the *Deutsche Christen*, who had no use for the Old and New Testaments and made Jesus a fellow Aryan.

In April 1933 Martin Niemöller founded the Pastors' Emergency League in opposition to the *Deutsche Christen*, who wanted to enforce a clause in the church that would expel converted Jews including "their children and grandchildren from the Protestant clergy" (Bergen 1996: 34). At the time his brother Wilhelm was a member of the Nazi party as well as a sympathizer of the *Deutsche Christen* (ibid.: 13). He would later join Martin Niemöller and leave the *Deutsche Christen* in the care of extreme politico-religious radicals such as Joachim Hossenfelder, Reinhold Krause, and the Thuringian Julius Leutheuser.

Joachim Hossenfelder became *Reich* leader of the Faith Movement of *Deutsche Christen*. He supported entirely the National Socialist worldview demands for a "positive Christianity" that would join in the fight against Marxists, Jews, world citizens, and freemasons (Zipfel 1965: 29–36). He called for purity of race and protection of the Volk against degeneration. The views of Dr Reinhold Krause, who would become the *Gauobmann* of the Faith Movement of *Deutsche Christen* in Greater Berlin, were if anything more radical than those of his close colleague Hossenfelder. Krause was for coordination, fanatically anti-Semitic, and wanted the Aryan paragraph applied to the church. Ideologically, he was a follower of Rosenberg's *völkisch* religion and empathetic to Hauer's views. During the Sport Palace speech that Krause gave on 13 November 1933 before an audience of

20,000, he "proclaimed that 'a new feeling for the homeland' must arise in the church and the first step towards it was 'liberation from everything un-German in worship and the confession: liberation from the Old Testament with its Jewish morality of rewards, these tales of cattle-traders and pimps'" (Scholder 1988: 552–3).

Hauer was a keen observer of the church struggle, but before we look at his response to it, two things must be mentioned. Zipfel (1965: 32) points out that, while Hitler's henchmen continued to cajole the Protestant Church into doing their bidding, Hitler's own views had already changed. Apparently Rauschning cited a Hitler talk given on 7 April 1933, in which the latter said: "With the confessions, whether this one or that one, it's all the same. They have no future. At least not for Germans. ... Nothing will prevent me from eradicating totally, root and branch, all Christianity in Germany. ... A German Church, a German Christianity, it is all rubbish ... One is either Christian or German ..." (ibid.: 32). This did not prevent Hitler, however, from giving a radio talk that same year on the night before the 23 July Protestant church elections, urging people to vote *Deutsche Christen* because they "stood self-aware on the same ground as the National Socialist state" (ibid.: 36). Few people knew the view that Rauschning recorded; many will have heard Hitler on the radio and during the elections felt the full force of party support.

How then did Hauer respond to the *Deutsche Christen*? His attitude was ambivalent. On the one hand, he thought it was the epitome of hypocrisy that non-Christians, which most *Deutsche Christen* were, should lead the church. He knew that Hossenfelder had totally politicized Protestantism; that he considered the propaganda points of the NSDAP about marriage, family, race, *Volk*, state, and the authorities to be Christian goals (Zipfel 1965: 35). But on the other hand, this broadening of the Church to make room for believers in things German rather than in Jewish Christianity was precisely what he wanted. How deeply shocked was he then, when he learned in June that the new church constitution that was to become law (*Reichsgesetz*) in July remained rather traditional. Instead of attacking the central tenets of Christianity, the *Deutsche Christen*, led by Hitler's confidant Ludwig Müller (1883–1945), attacked the organization of the church thereby forcing it to be responsive to the *Führer*-principle. Believing Christians, like the *Reichsbischof* Bodelschwingh (1877–1946)[1] and the General Superintendent of the Kurmark Otto Dibelius (1980–1967) were squeezed out and their positions taken over by the National Socialists Müller and Hossenfelder respectively (Zipfel 1965: 34; Conway 1968: 11, 34).

Months before these events, Hauer responded swiftly to Nazi takeover in January, and coordination (*Gleichschaltung*) and the enabling act (*Ermächtigungsgesetz*) in March. He did so by first handing over the *Köngener* Youth to the Hitler Youth and then calling a meeting of the Tübingen chapter of the adult *Köngener* on 7 May 1933.[2] At this meeting it was decided that Hauer would not give the *Köngener Bund* to the *Deutsche Christen* and their National Socialist *Reich* Church as the spirit of coordination might demand. Instead, he suggested trying again to gather the Youth Movement, *Bünde*, *völkisch*, and free religious under one roof and to fight for religious tolerance and recognition as a separate religious body parallel to the church (Cancik 1982: 176; Scholder 1988: 526). This he did by organizing the Wartburg conference for 29 and 30 July of that year.[3]

Hauer also reacted swiftly to the rumor in June that there would be a new Evangelical (Protestant) Church Constitution, which, as indicated above, would leave the Reformation Confession untouched.[4] This was the moment to confront the Protestant Church with its utter hypocrisy and its consequent two options. To that end Hauer rushed off an open letter addressed to the Protestant Church Commission and the *Reich* Leadership of the *Deutsche Christen* (Hauer 1933a). In it he wrote that he was puzzled that the church did not consider the needs of those who, on the basis of their convictions, were no longer bound to that Confession nor to the Old and New Testament as the measuring rod of their lives and beliefs (ibid.: 4). It was deceitful for the church to remain tied to the Old and New Testaments when many members and clerics did not believe in them or in the traditional presentation of Jesus.

Then Hauer defined the first option. Were the church honest, he argued, it would take the final step in the liberal direction and make room for all those others who simply had faith. He was thinking of people of German faith "to whom God reveals himself through the great figures of German history, within German space, and through German destiny." Only a church that accepts German faith is "pure protestant-German in its attitude" (ibid.: 6).

Knowing that the church would not accept further liberalization, Hauer mentioned the second option. He would take the difficult step and demand a gathering in order to create a German Faith Community (*Deutsche Glaubensgemeinschaft*). "We are planning this step in full awareness of our responsibility. *Wir können nicht anders*" (ibid.: 9).[5]

Then Hauer explained how he would clean up Germany's religious confusion. He envisioned an umbrella group which he tentatively called Religious Working Community of the German Nation (*Religiöse Arbeitsgemeinschaft Deutscher Nation*) that would subsume three bodies: the Catholic Church, the Protestant Church with its Protestant free churches and sects, and the German Faith Community. The three bodies would work together in matters concerning *Volk* and state, from religious education to national celebrations (ibid.: 9).

Having completed the open letter, Hauer instructed his assistant Paul Zapp to take it directly to the proper authorities and to ask for a quick reply.[6] In the meantime, the open letter was printed as a pamphlet entitled *Constitutional Change or Revolution of the Church*, and sold (Hauer 1933a). In the letter to Zapp, Hauer mentioned that two other pamphlets were being prepared to help the breakthrough of the German revolution. One was enti-tled *Where are the German intellectuals? (Wo bleibt die deutsche Intel-ligenz?)*. It was also published in 1933. The other pamphlet, then still a thought, was called *A Christian or a German State? (Christlicher oder deutscher Staat?)*. It expressed Hitler's assertion mentioned above, that one is either Christian or German, but not both. Together the pamphlets explained where Hauer stood vis-à-vis church and National Socialism, namely, for the latter and against the former.[7]

While in Berlin with the open letter, Zapp was to contact various people. They included Gregor Strasser, who supported Hossenfelder's *Deutsche Christen*, favored a German form of socialism, and was an SA man and a superb organizer.[8] He was also to contact Ernst Graf zu Reventlow (1869–1943). A fanatical National Socialist, he was the founding editor of the *Reichswart*, severe critic of the Weimar Republic, and defender of equal rights for German non-Christians (Scholder 1988: 451). Reventlow was initially sympathetic toward Strasser's view of German socialism, but then shifted to Hitler's position and became a member of the Reichstag for the National Socialist party. In his *Reichswart* on 11 June he had already published an article defending a community of faith with full rights parallel to the Christian Churches but not part of them (ibid.: 451). These men Hauer wanted at his side at the Wartburg conference. And indeed Reventlow became coleader of the Working Community of the German Faith Movement.[9]

Hauer was especially anxious that Zapp contact Kleo Pleyer (1898–1942), leader of the BF, who looked after the invitations to the Wartburg confer-ence. According to Hauer, "several very important personalities" had warned against extending an invitation to Erich Ludendorff to attend the conference. The problem was said to be Ludendorff's wife, Mathilde, who was a religious leader in her own right and had an intense dislike of what she called Hauer's occult views.[10] By not inviting Ludendorff, Kleo Pleyer was "to avoid an error."[11]

At around this time too came a report from a *Köngener* that Bernhard Rust (1883–1945), member of the NSDAP since 1925 and then State Commissioner in the Prussian Ministry for Science, Art, and Popular Educa-tion (*Volksbildung*), had taken away the right of representatives of the Protestant Church to speak in the name of God. Apparently, Rust said that the idea was not to justify oneself in the name of the "concept of God, which was uncontrollable, but to justify oneself in the name of that within which God was controllably revealed, namely the voice of the *Volk* and its history."[12] The *Köngener* man wrote this excited letter because he thought that now was the time to strike at the church and make demands for the Germanic-*deutsch* soul.

This is of course what Hauer had done. But if Hauer expected a quick reply from the Protestant Church, he was mistaken. None came. We only learn from his assistant Herbert Grabert November 9, 1933 what the Church

Commission and *Reich* Leadership of the *Deutsche Christen* thought of the open letter. While they respected Hauer's having been a missionary and a Protestant theologian, they could not work with him because of his paganism and the suggestion that he would create a "new religion."[13]

Grabert, Hauer, and the *Deutsche Christen*

Like many young Germans of the time, Herbert Grabert (1901–1978) found his politics through religion, and after the mid-twenties with Hauer's guidance.[14] Having spent a year in the Youth Movement, he studied history of religions in Tübingen and theology in Berlin from 1922 to 1926. He passed his first theological examination in 1927 while also qualifying as a sports teacher. Before completing his PhD with Hauer in 1928, he assisted Kretschmar and colleagues with clinical psychiatric work. This background rather than philology, one of Hauer's specialties, informed his PhD thesis, "A Comparative Study of the Psychology of Mystics and Psychopaths" (Junginger 1999: 114).

A follower of Hauer's anti-Christian thought even before he worked with him, Grabert nevertheless entered the Protestant theological seminary in Soest (Westphalia) to become a pastor. When inner conflicts sabotaged his studies, Hauer appealed to Otto, who helped a financially strapped Grabert by making him editor of *Christian World* (*Christliche Welt*). This suited Hauer because in that position and the Berlin location, Grabert would be Hauer's eyes and ears. The situation changed in late 1933, when an esti- mated 60,000 free religious joined the ADGB. Hauer now made a deal with a publishing friend Rühle (of Kohlhammer) to publish the journal *KG* and, given the prospects of sales to many members, to pay its editors honoraria. The path was clear for Grabert's move to Tübingen, where he would also do his *Habilitation* with Heinrich Frick.

On 23 October 1933, while Grabert was still in Berlin, he wrote a trium- phant letter to Hauer. "Now I am free!" he stated. "My path is clear ... I am ready to fight for the religious renewal of our *Volk*." Grabert was particu- larly overjoyed that he was freed from having to make compromises "that make one liberal in a dangerous sense because they seduce one to a forced inner reconciliation with what one has already overcome." He would have been destroyed by the compromises, continued Grabert, "had I not always seen you in the vanguard of the fight for the new, and if I had not always been able to fight for you, so that the whole world knows and says: 'Hauer is his master'."[15]

Confessing his trust and loyalty in Hauer, Grabert wrote, "you are not only the *Führer* of the religious turning (*Wende*), you are *in* the middle of it."[16] Grabert then announced his imminent official exit from the church, something he was unable to do earlier because he had to support a wife and three children.

His book about unbelief included a chapter about the dissident type. It proved how ripe his decisions were and how thoroughly conditioned by religion.[17] He promised to become a full member of the ADGB, which he called a "band of fighters" (*Kampfschar*).[18] And making himself useful immediately, he informed Hauer that he had gathered a lot of material about "the way in which the *Deutsche Christen* are trying to take the wind out of our sails." This material he sent to Reventlow, who would know what to do with it in the *Reichswart*.

On 30 October 1933 while still in Berlin, Grabert mentioned that his position within the theological faculty had become impossible. People were suspicious of his association with Hermann Mandel, a Kiel theologian who headed the Circle of Friends of the ADGB.[19] Hauer and Mandel organized this group for those who supported the ADGB but had not yet left the church because they somehow clung to Jesus, although they rejected the notion that Jesus was the Son of God. In his book *Actual Religion* (*Wirklichkeits-religion*) Mandel argues that he and his followers can only accept Christianity within the framework of a God-given racial specificity and an undogmatic religion that coincides with number 24 of the NS Party Program. As in point 24, for Mandel the measure of all things was "the life of the *Volk*" and "the feeling of morality [*das Moralgefühl*]" (see Mandel 1934: 29).

Grabert argued, therefore, that his closeness to Mandel—who furthermore gave his book *Unbelief* (*Der Unglaube*) summa cum laude—raised people's suspicion and opposition against him. He was glad that he escaped all this in time. He also mentioned that one of Hauer's opponents at the Wartburg conference, Dr Fuchs, who was an SPD man, was suffering from an apocalyptic mood through which "he saw the future of our *Volk* as pitch black." This man, like the "*homo politicoreligiosus*" Hans Teichmann, who also belonged to the petrified Social Democratic Party, waited for, rather than contributed to, the demise of their oppressors.[20]

As editor of *Christian World*, Grabert also sent Hauer a full report about Reinhold Krause's Sport Palace speech. He correctly saw it as the beginning of the breakdown of the DC, but was wrong about the expected resignations. Grabert expected that *Reichsbischof* Müller would be deposed immediately. Hossenfelder would then take over and invite the ADGB to join the *Reich* church. This of course did not happen and, indeed, Grabert only suggested this scenario because he did not want the ADGB in the *Reich* church.[21]

Grabert's news excited Hauer, but not in the direction of joining the German Christians. To incorporate the German Faith Movement within the realm of the church would spell its end, replied Hauer. "We must go our way alone and fight."[22]

In fact, Hossenfelder tried to hold the DC together in spite of the Sports Palace debacle. He did not succeed because Niemöller, Barth, and others of the Pastors' Emergency League demanded early on 14 November that

Ludwig Müller distance himself from Krause's views. According to Scholder (1988: 559–66) Krause was dismissed that very day, and Hossenfelder along with two other members of the Clergy Ministry resigned on 29 November 1933. Grabert was right about one thing; "the German Christians suffered a decisive defeat."[23]

To Grabert, Hauer wrote that the events surrounding the German Christians were very meaningful. He greeted the fact that the *Reichsbischof* had "ended the watered-down version of Christianity within the church." Thinking about Mandel and others, Hauer expected that they would join him. He was optimistic about the future because membership of the ADGB was increasing daily, especially with the arrival of important party people.[24]

Did any of the German Christians join the German Faith Movement as Hauer hoped? Existing correspondence affirms that some did. For example, Hauer observed Krause's German People's Church Movement, and the two had contact. On 16 January 1934 Hauer wrote him: "I have long been of the opinion that the German Christians should have left a church bound by a Confession. What brought the Faith Movement of the German Christians down is in my view the contradiction between Confession and a free German Faith."[25] Hauer hoped that the German People's Church that Krause now led would break all compromises. "That would mean a free German Faith. And if I understand your letter, you already have that. For [Rosenberg's] 'Myth of the Twentieth Century' is one of the foundations of this German Faith. For those who confess it, however, it means the end of the Christian church."[26] What remained was a new construction, argued Hauer, and the more decisively they built the new, and for the moment, next to the church the more ground they would take from it. Working within the church was impossible, said Hauer: "The *Reichsbischof* is not a *Führer*. He is fully in the hands of orthodox stalwarts."[27]

On 15 February 1934 Hauer asked Dr Reinhold Krause for information concerning the union of three groups. He meant by these Krause's German People's Church, Mandel's German Church, and the Circle of Friends of the ADGB that Mandel also led. Hauer was concerned that they sort out their respective tasks, and especially matters of organization—this because Hauer had learned from Kloppe, who once was the organizer of the ADGB, that he was now organizing Krause's movement and that he had advised some ADGB members to join the German People's Church. Kloppe obviously did not understand "that we decided in Berlin that you as inner-churchly movement and I as outer-churchly movement are working toward the same goal."[28]

Hauer was keen to unify their movements by having Mandel and Krause become co-editors of the journal *German Faith* and subsuming Krause's journal within the ADGB. Krause, Hauer and Mandel tried all kinds of unions. Finally, during the height of the German Faith Movement's growth in the summer of 1935, Krause joined the ADGB (Bartsch 1938: 74).

Members

As we saw in another chapter, more than a dozen existing groups, from the free religious to Nordic and Germanic ones, formed the ADGB. Having been nationalistic and *völkisch*, in some instances Communistic and National Socialistic, long before 1933, these groups had joined because at this time it was still believed that Hitler favored a "positive" Christianity and might, therefore, coerce "non-Christians" back into the Christian fold. Although they feared the loss of their petty leadership positions, they finally did what the *Bünde* could not do, namely, unite and fight ostensibly for "freedom of conscience" and "state recognition" as a faith beside the church.

Two other kinds of individuals were interested in the ADGB: the old church leavers, that is, free religious individuals (*Freireligiöse*) or free Protestants who ran into constant trouble with the new regime, on the one hand, and the new church leavers or National Socialists and theology students who were in constant conflict with the church, on the other. Herbert Grabert was one example of the latter. Hauer's student, later secretary and organizer, Paul Zapp (b. 1904), who joined the *Köngener* when he was 17 years old, was another (Zapp 1934).[29] In 1970 Zapp received life imprisonment for the murder of at least 13,499 people as leader of the Sonderkommando 11a and the Einsatzgruppe D. Not surprisingly, he justified his deed in terms of Hauer's and the SD's religious worldview (Junginger 1999: 140; Kwiet 2004: 257–8, 259).

Most young men who joined Hauer's ADGB were conflicted. They usually came to their intense dislike of Christianity and Jews by having read a specific set of literature or having experienced a specific influence. Thus Werner Klitsch, who (unlike others) did not give a long autobiographical sketch of himself, wrote Hauer on 5 October 1933: "As a National Socialist and opponent of Jews, it is impossible for me to continue to belong to present-day Christianity, because it is supported by the Old Testament, which is Jewish and friendly to Jewish things." He then quoted Alfred Rosenberg's *Mythus* (1930: 592): "The so-called Old Testament, as a religious book, has therefore to be abolished once and for all."[30] Klitsch supported this declaration by citing Theodor Fritsch's *Handbuch der Juden* (1923), Houston Stewart Chamberlain's *Grundlagen des neunzehnten Jahrhunderts* (1899), Julius Streicher's *Stürmer*, and Graf Ernst zu Reventlow's *Reichswart*.

Klitsch also claimed that he could no longer belong to the *Deutsche Christen*. According to Klitsch, in a recent change of heart, and as reported in the *Reichswart* (no. 37, 17 September 1933, page 1), the bishop declared that the newly organized church would retain the Old Testament.

"That's why I want to ask you," continued Klitsch, "how you stand to the Old Testament, the personality of Jesus, and the falsification of the New

Testament through Paul." And here he quoted again from the *Stürmer*, *Mythus*, and so on. "Should you be against the Old Testament and the prevailing Christianity which, at any rate, ought to be called Paulinism, then I wish to apply for membership."[31]

A point of which we cannot lose sight is that Klitsch, as of the writing of his letter, still belonged to the Church whose faith and dogma he intensely disliked and did not believe. Ideally, people who wanted to become members of the German Faith Movement were to have left the church. This demand was part of the Movement's constitution. Hauer soon learned, however, that many who joined his movement, like Hauer himself until the fall of 1933, were still church members. For a time, he gave different inquirers different answers about this requirement. Finally, he persuaded leaders of the board to suspend the ruling until the movement had won state recognition.

The Klitsch situation and others like it is very important because it throws light on a scholarly controversy. For example, Junginger (2001: 30) claims that in 1938, 75 percent of the members of the SS, NSDAP, and army were Christians. By contrast, the scholar Herbert F. Ziegler, with whom I corresponded about these figures, wrote me that his research on prewar SS officers had yielded very different figures. Using a sound sampling method, he looked at two thousand official SS personnel files under the entry "religious affiliation." On the basis of this entry he came up with the following figures: 83.6 percent of the officers from the *SS-Totenkopfverbände* (Death Head Units) claimed to be "*gottgläubig*," a general term used for *deutsch*, Nordic, or Germanic believers, among others. Of the officers from the *SS-Verfügungstruppe* (Armed SS Units), 78.9 percent claimed to be "*gottgläubig*"; and 66.7 percent of the officers from the General SS Units claimed to be "*gottgläubig*." On the average, therefore, about 76 percent of the SS were *gottgläubig;* not the same as Christian (Ziegler to Poewe, e-mail, 17 January 2001; Ziegler 1989). Apparently relying on the statistical yearbook of 1938, Junginger disagrees.

Junginger's rejection of Ziegler's figures is important because it leads him to conclude that the impact of neo-pagans (*Neuheiden*) on National Socialism is negligible and that the Church with its then 61.9 million official members exaggerated the danger that they claimed came from groups like that of Hauer. By contrast, given the six hundred thousand Christians who "paganized" or "Germanized" Christianity with the *Deutsche Christen* phenomenon, and the millions of readers of pagan literature who, however, officially remained within the church, one can hardly dismiss the *deutsch*, Nordic, Germanic, *Gotterkenntnis*, German Christian, and innumerable other alternative faiths, as having had no impact on National Socialism (Barnett 1992; also Lohalm 1970 for views different from Junginger).

A letter similar to Klitsch's was written to Hauer by a Pastor Misch Bergleiter from Romania.[32] Bergleiter had received a newsletter about the ADGB and wanted to become a member. But he lived in Romania, where the

German Evangelical Church maintained a German school and their *Volkstum*. While he left the active service of the church as its pastor, he led the German secondary farming school, which, given their circumstances, needed the protection of the church. What he wanted from Hauer, therefore, was literature and acknowledgment that he would do the work of the ADGB clandestinely, until it received formal recognition and equal rights from the *Führer*.

Most interesting is Bergleiter's explanation of how he came to think along *völkisch* lines. People were content with the church, he wrote, until doubt set in. This doubt was called forth and set on a firm course, said Bergleiter, through Theodor Fritsch's *Hammerschriften* and through Friedrich Andersen's and Kurd Niedlich's German Church Movement (*Deutschkirchliche Bewegung*).[33] Worth mentioning is the fact that Theodor Fritsch and Friedrich Andersen represented two of the major streams in the rabidly anti-Semitic *Schutz- und Trutz Bund*. This *Bund* systematically propagated anti-Semitism. At the same time, it opposed the traditional direction of the Christian Church and represented, in the case of Fritsch the Germanic direction, and in the case of Andersen the German Christian direction (Lohalm 1970: 172). Dr Kurd Niedlich was one of the most important pioneers of a *völkisch* Christianity. He wanted to create a church based on Germanic-Christian principles that would unite organic evangelical, catholic, and non-churchly circles. In his publications about a German religion he announced a heroic Christianity that would remove all Jewish elements from the Bible and return to religion the mythical tenderness that speaks symbolically to Germans through their fairy tales and sagas (Boge 1935: 6). Andersen too, who in the thirties led the German Church *Bund*, held with Niedlich that Christianity was not only peculiarly receptive to German *Volkstum* but was, once it was stripped of its Jewish accessories, also similar in nature (Boge 1935: 5–8).

That these streams of German folk religiosity were akin to, and linked with, both the German Christians and Hauer's German Faith Movement, hardly needs mention. But the influence on Bergleiter also came directly from the Hauer circle. Thus Bergleiter wrote "because of our study of Hans Günther, Ferdinand Clauss ... Bernhard Kummer, Herman Wirth, Ludendorff, and so on ... we long since came to the understanding that we had to find our way back to a German knowledge of God."[34] The first three individuals were on the Editorial Board of Hauer's journal, *Deutscher Glaube*. Only the Ludendorffs were competitors and enemies of Hauer's ADGB. But they shared a common thought-world.

In his reply, Hauer informed Bergleiter that he had read his letter at the ADGB's *Führer* convention in Berlin and that Bergleiter was accepted as a fellow combatant in their cause.[35] Bergleiter was enthusiastic about his acceptance and, having read Hauer's open letter to the *Deutsche Christen*, he agreed that the ADGB was but the continuation of Luther's Reformation. He

8.1 Rudolf Hess, 1933

then informed Hauer about their Bishop Glondys's opposition, which, however, Bergleiter considered as being "nothing other than a renewed attack against the *völkisch* renewal movement of National Socialism ... and a rejection of the *Deutsch*-Germanic faith foundation."[36] Hess's decree he assessed correctly as mere toleration, arguing that full equal rights were needed.[37]

On 21 October 1933, Hauer received a confidential letter from Heinz Bischoff, who had obviously looked for work with the ADGB but was just called to work as vicar in the administration of the Protestant Church of his land in order to handle press questions. Just eight days earlier he had joined the ADGB. Nevertheless, both the church and Reventlow assured him that he could follow his call and retain his ADGB membership at the same time. To Hauer he reported that, indeed, ADGB views fell on fruitful ground in the Braunschweig church circles. "At present," he continued, "I have begun to give instructions and hold discussions within a small circle of young, interested people to clarify what the relevant basic foundations of religious work are ... All the rest must grow."[38]

It was not unusual that Hauer would ask someone not to join or rejoin the church. As above, this involved young theologians who were desperate for a job. Thus Hauer wrote Dr Karl Küssner, an old acquaintance from *Köngener Bund* times, that he would try to find Küssner a position in the ADGB's Leadership School that was to start in November. Alternatively, he would make him the main speaker of the 10,000- to 12,000-strong former free religious *Bund*, which was now in the ADGB. This *Bund* was in trouble with the security police because the former speaker, whom Küssner or a National Socialist would replace, was a communist.[39]

While Hauer accepted the membership of Bischoff despite his church involvement, he categorically rejected that of Manfred Boge:

> Membership of a 'Christian' in the ADGB is not possible for the simple reason that we are fighting for recognition of our rights as a non-Christian community beside Christian ones. ... Negotiations with the regime require that we draw a straight line. To create some kind of relationship of the ADGB to Christians, however, we formed the Circle of Friends of the ADGB that is led by Mandel of Kiel who is a professor of theology.[40]

A similar answer was given to Pastor Gubalke, who complained of having been harassed in some way by the church. This man wanted to know Hauer's position with regard to Jesus; no doubt because, like many non-Christians in the church, he still saw something of value in that world figure. Hauer replied that the ADGB did not recognize a "Lord" except in the sense of an "eternal one" who is not called God. Personally, continued Hauer, "Jesus is a brother and comrade in the fight for a free faith ... but in the form of a German Faith." With respect to Christ, "I am a free man. I am also free to decide against his word and commands when they do not mesh with my sense of inner necessity (*inneren Muss*)."[41] Regarding Gubalke's complaint about harassment (*Drangsalierung*), Hauer referred him to Reventlow, who collected and published such cases. Otherwise, Gubalke was advised to join the Circle of Friends led by Mandel.

Hauer also advised a teacher named Aufrecht who, like Gubalke, continued to feel something for Jesus to join the Circle of Friends. To him too he mentioned receiving many inquiries about the ADGB, which had become quite simply "a large movement that swept through the German *Volk*." Picturing himself as having answered "the call of the time," Hauer described himself as being finished with Christianity and Church.[42]

Easily accepted and acceptable was a Mrs Marie Seeger. Not only had she left the church officially, but she also found the competition, Ludendorff's *Tannenbergbund*, lacking. "I read with the deepest inner agreement," she wrote, "Rosenberg's book *Mythus des 20. Jahrhunderts* and the book of Graf Reventlow *Für Christen, Nichtchristen und Antichristen*."[43]

To a Gustav Schütt from Düsseldorf, a National socialist who had gathered a small group of people around him who were interested in the ADGB, Hauer wrote: "Daily I receive letters from young Party members who indicate that they are relieved that the coercion to follow church and/or Confession is over. Within the National Socialist party the path is now open for the

German Faith Movement."[44] He assured Schütt that especially Hess accepted the movement as a reality and promised it space in the Third Reich. The difficult fight (*Kampf*) ahead was that with the church, wrote Hauer, but he was pleased to see that young National Socialists in particular were ready to take up that fight. He then mentioned that there were a number of ADGB members in the Düsseldorf area who needed to be consolidated. Schütt should take on that task, and to help him Hauer would send material and speak there in future.[45]

Hauer also received letters from editors of journals who felt that their contributions had been ignored. One such letter came from Alfred Miller, editor of *Sign of the Flame* (*Flammenzeichen*). Miller authored books and articles typical of that time, "The Degeneration of Peoples under the Cross" or "Christian totalitarianism, the greatest danger to German Unity." To Hauer he voiced his frustration that his journal had been ignored. In the process, he mentioned that he was a friend of Reventlow and read his *Reichswart*. He once worked on Theodor Fritsch's *Hammer*.[46] He had discussions with Loerzer who was then the *Reich* leader of the German Christians. He rejected the request of Dr Fuchs, a dentist who was bishop of the German Community, to let *Flammenzeichen* become the organ of that community. He opposed the dogma of the Ludendorff movement, to which he had once belonged.[47] Hauer replied two days later, saying that the *Reichswart* had become the official organ of the German Faith Movement, but that he would make a greater effort to mention *Flammenzeichen* in future talks.[48]

On 15 November 1933 Hauer received another letter from a young pastor named Fluhrer who was alienated from the church that, however, educated and employed him and paid his salary. Fluhrer wanted to leave the church if Hauer could help him. "As of today," wrote Fluhrer heroically, "I feel released from my ordination vow and have won back the freedom of transaction with the church. Were they to remove me from my office, I should be proud to have made this sacrifice for the sake of my free German conscience."[49] Attached to the letter was a long autobiographical statement that described his life as a fatherless soldier in World War I. Despite grave doubts, he let himself be persuaded by his economically destitute mother and an uncle to study theology after the war and become a pastor. Like so many other young Germans, his choice of readings, *Bünde*, and trying other denominations and religions led him to the German Faith Movement and National Socialism.

Already during the war, Fluhrer disliked the Christian sense of sin. Reading Stefan George made him lose any sympathy for the "theology of the cross" and taking a course in philosophy made him doubt Christianity altogether. His inner conflicts were put to rest temporarily when, after the war, he joined the volunteer units to help put down the 1919 revolts that led to the creation of a socialist republic in Bavaria. When this was over in August of that year, however, his inner conflicts returned full force. "Study of philosophy taught me to think," he wrote, "and one Christian faith proposition after the other sank into dust."[50] While he wanted to switch to philology, his mother and uncle pressed him to study theology in Erlangen. In the meantime, the family's financial fortune disappeared altogether.

He read Stefan George and briefly joined and left a fraternity. Then he learned about the free Protestant theologian Johannes Müller (1864–1949), who ran a sanctuary at Schloß Elmau and whose doctrine, which he expounded in his journal called *Grüne Blätter*,[51] was "stop worrying and start living." Then inflation came and the Kapp *putsch*[52] with its street fights and shattering scenes. Fluhrer was part of these and, being penniless, joined volunteer groups where, at least, he was fed. But the strain was too much, and in the winter semester 1920–1921 he suffered a nervous breakdown. While he returned to his studies again a year later, he took no joy in them. He found some relief attending the services of the free religious because they taught primarily classical and modern literature. *Faust* became his German bible, because he taught "feeling is everything."[53] At the same time, he also tried various denominations including Catholics, Adventists, Methodists, Jehovah's Witnesses (*Ernste Bibelgesellen*), Quakers, *Christengemeinschaft*, and others.

The revelation that would guide his future was brought on by none other than Nietzsche, whose poem *From High Mountains (Aus Hohen Bergen)* pointed Fluhrer straight to "the glorious *Führer* Adolf Hitler," to whom he had but one thing to say: "free the path for our German Faith." He signed the letter, "*Heil Deutschglaube!*" (Hail German Faith).

Another man eager to cooperate with the ADGB was the medical doctor Hans Brenke. Because he had not officially left the church, he sent Hauer a letter on 18 November 1933 to confirm that he was an accepted member. What prevented his leaving the church earlier, he wrote, was the *November-republik*.[54] He was now, however, prepared to do so, if Hauer thought it to be strategic.[55] In his response to Brenke, Hauer commented first on the included copy of a letter that Brenke had sent to Reventlow concerning the *Deutsche Christen* and the Hess decree. "It can only be good that the Christian Church finally decided to remember its true Christianity so that the half-decided can finally decide and come over to us," wrote Hauer.[56] Regarding the official leaving of the church, Hauer wrote, "today I consider it almost a duty that we leave the church officially and through our example effect the decision." Then he told Brenke that, although worried about losing his university post, he himself left the church in the early fall before the Hess decree.[57]

To a Lieutenant von Kunowski, who asked Hauer about the ADGB, he answered that the ADGB was simply an effort to bring together all those of German Faith in the Third Reich. The intent was, explained Hauer, to let the ADGB grow organically into a large community of those professing a German Faith. In the meantime, a group made available speakers, teachers, and others who conducted rituals, consecrations, and funerals.[58] Hauer was particularly keen to have such ceremonies performed in the army to break the Christian monopoly, and to that end, he wrote von Kunowski, he had in mind building a Leadership School in Tübingen.

Although he was invited, Alfred Rosenberg did not attend the Wartburg conference, nor did he seem to answer Hauer's letters. This did not prevent Hauer, however, from writing Alfred Rosenberg whenever an opportunity presented itself. On 23 November 1933, Hauer wrote Rosenberg that he had read with great joy Rosenberg's article about "the National Socialistic worldview" in the *Völkischer Beobachter* of 18 October. He took Rosenberg's words as a sign that they had finally overcome the danger of being subjected to religious intolerance from "members of denominations and reactionaries." He continued, "The church was well on the way to making the National Socialist state its minion to be used (one could now say) for its own dark purposes."[59] Writing almost like an informer, Hauer continued:

> I have just now again heard the talk given by the local full professor of church history, Rückert, about "Luther as a German," in which great emphasis was put on the notion that Lutheranism was closely related to National Socialism. It is noticeable, however, that this relationship was only discovered after National Socialism achieved its victory and even then not right away, but only after it was noticed that the National Socialist victory would be maintained.[60]

As a sign of belonging to the same fighting community, continued Hauer, he included a small pamphlet that he hoped Rosenberg would find the time to read. Then he mentioned his regrets at not having seen Rosenberg at the conference. "But I understood your motives thoroughly. It was necessary that those who held politically towering positions withheld their attendance at that time." And then Hauer pointed to the fact that the ADGB had already gained historical importance if only because it was the excuse for the Hess decree. It looked as if their movement, Hauer wrote Rosenberg, could become a People's Movement. Especially young National Socialists enrolled daily and people in the party who held important posts in educational service, in the SA, SS, and so forth.[61]

On 29 November 1933 Hauer received a confidential letter from a 26-year-old city curate named Rudolf Scheuer. Writing in an autobiographical style, Scheuer reported that he completed his university finals in theology and was ordained in 1932. Since then he had been a country pastor for eleven months and was then moved to Frankfurt where he served as curate in the old main church of the city. His disillusionment with Christianity started with the liberal theology of Professor Freiherr von Gall, a student of Wellhausen, as well as Gogarten and Friedrich Karl Schumann. His secret love was the mysticism of Eckhart, and his favorite subject German theology

(*Theologia Deutsch*). While he had no interest in Barth, he considered liberal theology to be a distortion.[62]

As with Fluhrer and Hauer himself, Scheuer's doubts about Christianity started before his studies in various youth groups (*Bünde*). He had belonged to a youth *Bund* in the early 1920s and then joined the German Boy Scouts, which was taken over by the Hitler Youth. While he still had close ties with his friends in the Hitler Youth he became a member of the NSDAP and the SA. Even before he became a member of the NSDAP, he was beaten up by Communists and suffered from a serious head wound.[63]

Apparently, Scheuer was interested in Hauer's *Köngener* for years. More importantly, in university he read Günther's *Rassenkunde* (1930). Since then he had been grasped by a fascination with the possibility of a relationship between religion and race and a race-determined Christianity. "I never really felt comfortable within Christianity even though I come from a Christian family," he wrote.[64] Then in August 1933, he read about Hauer's journal *KG*. Since then he had read every issue that contained articles by Hauer, and begun to make inquiries about the German Faith Movement. He had heard Hauer speak about India and had read Hauer's book *The Religions* (*Die Religionen*). He was further fascinated, wrote Scheuer, by the history of Germanic religion, psychology, and generally themes dealing with *völkisch* religion. To him Christianity was finished and he wanted to be part of the new spiritual breakthrough. In short, he wanted to leave the church and serve the new, but he saw no possibility, unless Hauer could offer him one.[65]

A month later, Hauer sent back a short answer: if Scheuer felt at one with the basic attitude of the German Faith Movement, the possibility of work existed, if not now then in the future. They were in the process of building local groups and communities in which people could be employed. In the meantime, Scheuer was to become clear, whether or not he was free from a church-linked and dogmatic Christianity and stood so much in the grasp of the must or power (*Muss*) of a free German faith that he could dedicate himself bravely and loyally to their cause, and this from a deep sense of inner conviction.[66]

On 30 November 1933, Hauer received a letter from Dr Erika Emeriti, who despite her PhD was still a student[67] and a reader of von Reventlow's *Reichswart*.[68] She informed Hauer in terms of her "world view" she no longer had anything in common with the church or with Christianity. Hence she had joined the NSDAP two years ago—"officially, I still belong to the church."[69] She led a group of National Socialist women students and was at the same time the district indoctrination leader (*Kreisschulungsleiterin*). "Regarding political indoctrination," she taught that "National Socialism and Christianity are incompatible ... many share this *viewpoint*!"[70]

Hauer agreed that Christianity could not be the religious foundation of National Socialism. To him it was ludicrous that Protestantism should be fixated on the Old Testament when the German people stood in the middle of a big *völkisch* departure. "It is heartening to see with what an assured instinct this is felt by young National Socialists who come to us in swarms [*Scharen*]. Letters like yours arrive from all over Germany."[71]

Hauer then encouraged her to recruit groups at the University of Bonn for the ADGB. To others he bragged that the ADGB already included young Party members who worked in the SS Bureau of Race and Settlement, for example, Lothar Stengel von Rutkowski and Heim Schröder. Their radicalism and anti-Semitism did not seem to worry him.[72]

Conclusion

The post-World War I German environment, like post-war situations generally, consisted of hunger, impoverished youths, and *Bünde*. Where the *Bünde* left off, the ADGB and *Deutsche Christen* picked up to prepare a liberal path that led straight to National Socialism—and beyond, if we think of the neo-pagan New Right today. The path was made smooth by numerous fraudulent professors and theologians who thought it more important to work for immediate relevance than to think, observe, and restrain. Together they encouraged hardness in an already hardened youth.

Chapter 9

Werner Best

Hauer's contact in the SS

Best and the war youth generation

Hauer was involved with the SS from the beginning, and it was the SS too that three years later demanded his resignation from the movement. Hauer's worldview and that of the SS were ideologically compatible. But Hauer's personality and his personal charisma were not. Himmler, Heydrich and Wüst eventually opposed Hauer. Nevertheless, students from his Aryan Institute were hired by the SS, although they were routinely subjected to sharp and critical observation.[1] What they lacked was a *Führernatur*, a combination of hardness, sobriety, and comradeship. But like the SS, they had learned from Hauer to approach their research and work from a worldview perspective.

Matters dealing with teaching German faith and doing propaganda for the German Faith Movement, Hauer discussed personally with *SS-Reichführer* Himmler.[2] Police matters, especially where the free religious were concerned, he discussed personally or in letters with Dr Werner Best. Werner Best also received Hauer's ideas about Catholicism and Zionism. At the time, Best was the president of the police of the Land of Hessen. Their interaction declined after Best moved to Berlin to work with the Gestapo.

Karl Rudolf Werner Best was born on 10 July 1903 in Darmstadt, where his father was a postal inspector. His father fought on the Western front, and was wounded and died in the fall of 1914. Thereupon his mother moved with her two sons to her hometown near Mainz, where Best attended high school until he graduated in 1921 (Herbert 1996: 42).

Importantly, Herbert (1996: 43–4) points out that Werner Best, unlike Hauer, was very much part of the "youth of the war generation," that is, they were born between 1900 and 1910, too young to be at the front but old enough to remember the war and its effects. Because that generation, including Best, held important posts in the SS, it is worth describing their characteristics. Herbert relied especially on Günther Gründel's (1932) publication for his insights.

According to the latter, the young men were referred to as the "war youth generation" (*Kriegsjugendgeneration*). They did not experience the front but

9.1 Werner Best, Hauer's contact in the SS

they were deeply affected by shifting news and especially defeat, which was accompanied by hunger, deprivation, poverty and destitution. This generation witnessed the complete breakdown of the world of their fathers and all that it meant (Herbert 1996: 43). Old values were overthrown or reevaluated, and with it came the development of the child's soul for the larger whole and, generally, for *völkisch* and collective experiences. As well, the usual class differences between workers and intellectuals softened. Witnesses of that time remembered that *Volk*, *Nation* and evil enemies (*böse Feinde*) were living concepts in these young minds. Especially Prussian and Rhineland youths who had direct contact with the enemy after the war had a deep sense of "home." Their love of country and postwar experience was radical. They knew on whom to blame their collective impoverishment and loss of privileged career prospects, something that is also echoed in the lives of Heinrich Himmler (1900–1945), Reinhard Heydrich (1904–1942), and their somewhat older compatriot Joseph Goebbels (1897–1945).[3]

The war youth generation tended to be hard, sober, strong-willed and—unlike Goebbels—reticent. In their battle for existence, meaning, and success, they learned to be in control of the weapons and methods of war. The danger of their peculiarities lay in the combination of what they understood to be love of truth, simplicity, seriousness, taciturnity, reticence, rough coldness combined with a frequently reiterated emphasis on relevance (*Sachlichkeit*), objectivity and reason. Even after the war, they could not see that their exaggerated sense of relevance sabotaged truth and objectivity. Dropping differences of opinion and attitude for the sake of relevance was a favorite demand made even by Hauer and his followers. It had the effect of enforcing conformity. They rejected "verbal altruism," "verbal moralism," and "verbal patriotism," preferring to be thought unfeeling instead. Hauer, Himmler and Best saw justification of these in the *Bhagavad Gita*, as was shown in a previous chapter. In short, the generational life style that Best helped create and Hauer fleshed out consisted of coldness, hardness, radicalism, and an exaggerated sense of relevance (Herbert 1996: 44).

According to Leggewie (1998: 114), unlike the common run of Nazis, Best developed a higher legitimacy of the political police, which he saw as a physician at work on the body of the German nation (*Volkskörper*). While many intellectuals in the SS belonged to its research body called "*Ahnenerbe*," Werner Best was involved with police and security functions. He received his law degree in 1928 and initially served as a judge. In 1930, he joined the Nazi party and one year later the SS. As stated above, his contact with Hauer was closest between 1933 and 1934, when he was President of the Police for the state of Hessen (*Landespolizeipräsident*). At the time he lived in Stuttgart, but later he was transferred to München.

Werner Best defended the *völkisch*-organic worldview that he regarded as the core of National Socialism even after 1945 (Leggewie 1998: 114). In the 1950s, he tried unsuccessfully to return to politics. His plan, however, to reinstate former members of the NS and SS within their professions and society and to achieve a general amnesty for them succeeded (ibid.: 212, 302). Werner Best died in 1989.

The free religious

Hauer's letters to Best dealt primarily, but not exclusively, with problems of the free religious.[4] These people renamed themselves the League of German Faith Communities (BGDG) and became part of the German Faith Movement in 1933. Problems involved mainly accusations by petty local officials that some free religious were Marxists or Communists. Of interest to us is how Hauer handled and discussed these cases and how he made himself useful to the SS.

Already in 1933 Best became a member of the Board of the ADGB at the request of *SS-Reichsführer* Heinrich Himmler.[5] That Himmler had a great interest in Hauer's German Faith Movement is not surprising. He was already interested in Indian philosophy and Buddhism in the 1920s, especially in the Kshatriyas, "the noble warrior caste of the Aryans who conquered and ruled India some 1700 years before Christ" (Padfield 2001a: 90). He wanted the SS to be "at once a secret police and warrior elite." Through Hesse's *Siddhartha*, but especially Hauer's books, Himmler became fascinated by the idea of cultivating the value of ruthlessly detaching himself from passion (ibid.: 91). Believing like Hauer, in the "Aryan ancestry of the Germanic race," he knew the Hindu doctrine of Karma and collected quotations from "the Hindu Vedas and Bhagavad-Gita" (ibid.: 92). When, in 1936, Himmler quoted the words spoken by Lord Krishna to a warrior, Arjuna, he was surely relying on Hauer's *Eine indo-arische Metaphysik des Kampfes und der Tat: Die Bhagavadgita in neuer Sicht mit Übersetzungen* (An Indo-Aryan Metaphysics about War and Deed: a New Perspective on the Bhagavad-Gita with Translations) published in 1934 (ibid.: 60).

Himmler determined that Best should be the mediator between himself and the German Faith Movement.[6] Not only did Best play an important role in bringing the ADGB and SS together; by the end of 1933 he had already gone a long way to ease the activities of the free religious in Nürnberg, Baden, and elsewhere (Nanko 1993: 168, 190). But petty problems continued.

Thus Hauer wrote Werner Best about a piece of writing that had fallen into the hands of the secret police and that made some sort of accusation against the business office of the free religious in Leipzig. "It seems to be the work of a malevolent person," wrote Hauer.[7] He suspected foul play for several reasons. First, the note came from the Catholic section of town and Catholics wished the *Bund* harm. Second, Hauer suspected this mischief to have been done by someone who had been expelled from the group and who wanted to achieve two purposes, to harm the *Bund* and to attack the regime. Third, Hauer thought it possible that the malevolent person was part of a conspiracy involving church organisations that were in the habit of denouncing the free religious for godlessness (*Gottlosigkeit*) and therefore for Bolshevism.

It should not be surprising that Hauer's main suspicion fell on Christians. While he gave direct expression of his hate for Christianity infrequently in his letters, it was very real. As Kratz (1994: 299) reminds us, during Hauer meetings against Christianity and Jewry, even when SA- and SS-Christians objected, they were brutally beaten down; and in the Rhineland, when German Faithlers denounced Christian youths, the latter were picked up by the Gestapo.

Hauer wanted Best to look seriously into the Leipzig matter because those who wanted to destroy the German Faith Movement, he argued, tended to focus on the free religious *Bund* precisely because this group now had a firm core and was well organized. He reckoned that this was the reason why denunciations were sent to the *Reich* Ministry of the Interior, headed by Wilhelm Frick (1877–1946). Hauer suggested that Best deal directly with the treasurer in Leipzig, Carl Peter.

Hauer also sought Best's approval for putting a temporary head in the Nürnberg free religious community, which had also been searched by the secret police and cleared, so that the youth initiation ceremonies could continue. He wanted to assign a well-known student to the post, one who was also a convinced National Socialist. Hauer pointed out that, if there were ever Communists in the free religious fold, the Communist party removed them since the *Bund* consisted of believers. It was, however, the case that many free religious formerly belonged to the SPD, were active within it, and were primarily proletarians.[8]

When new religious competitors irritated the ADGB, Hauer informed Best of their irrelevance. This applied to Artur Dinter (1876–1948), who talked at the German People's Church (Weiß 1999). Until it was banned, Dinter's journal and movement were called Spirit-Christianity (*Geistchristentum*). As Hauer understood it, the goal of this movement was to restore the pure teachings of the Savior. It was as good a religious or political goal as any. Unfortunately, Dinter's polemic was not only directed against the church, but also against various communities within the German Faith Movement. Hauer actually considered taking him to court.

To Hauer it was dangerous that Dinter talked "about the ADGB today as an 'anti-Christian Godlessness-Movement' in order to push us into the godlessness movement of the formerly bolshevist type."[9] Furthermore, he was merely venting his anger about his rejection by the Board of the ADGB. Dinter had been refused, explained Hauer, because "the ADGB is a non-Church movement," whereas he stood for a kind of Christianity. Furthermore, the behavior of Dinter at the Wartburg in 1933 was unseemly. Hauer had to make a special effort, for example, to prevent Graf Reventlow from leaving the meeting. Since then Dinter had persecuted the ADGB with insults. Because Dinter's extremism against the church did not suit the Nazis in the early years, Dinter was removed as regional leader in Thüringen in 1925 and removed from the Party in 1928. As of Hauer's writing, he was still publisher of the extremely anti-Semitic monthly journal *Geistchristentum* (Dohnke 1999: 902–3).

On 27 February 1934 Hauer informed Werner Best briefly that he would be in Nürnberg on 4 March to give a talk. That afternoon he would travel to München, where he wanted to look in on the Gestapo, as well as the Cult Ministry and Ministry of the Interior. If possible, he wrote, he would like to speak with Rosenberg.[10] Apparently, Best could arrange that for him. He would then return to Stuttgart to give talks on Thursday and Friday and to have lunch with the undersecretary (*Ministerialdirektor*) Dill on Saturday. Hauer hoped that he could also meet Best in Stuttgart. Whether this meeting happened is not known.

After returning from the various meetings with the political police in München, Hauer reported back to Best. He had wanted to speak with Best about important things concerning the Bavarian communities. This having failed, he would now answer Best's letters.[11] Best wanted information about a lecture given by a Professor Linhardt, apparently to Catholic students. Hauer knew nothing about it, but would have his assistant Paul Zapp check into it. Regarding Best's question about Dr Paul Krannhals,[12] Hauer offered the following information. Paul Krannhals and his wife belonged to the

Friends of the Coming Community, which was also led by Hauer. Krannhals had participated in conferences and given papers. He was the author, according to Hauer, "of the great work," *Organic World View 1928* (*Organische Weltanschauung*).[13] He also worked very hard for the German Faith Movement.

Krannhals "is a German-speaking Balt, was once captured by the Bolshevists but escaped.—His wife, Juga Krannhals-Russell is a poetess of the German-faith type, but with a strong inclination toward Christ. She works hard for the mutual understanding of religions," reported Hauer. Then he told Best that Juga K.-R. once wrote a report about the 1933 Kassel meeting of the KG that gave offence because she was impressed with the speaker, Martin Buber, who talked about Israelitism [*Israelitentum*]."[14] But, said Hauer, "this is a purely religious matter with her. Her German-faith mentality and her confession to the Third Reich are untouchable."[15] Religion, in other words, had nothing to do with anti-Semitism.

Hauer could not give Best any information about a Dr Heinz Kurz nor about a Freiherr von Aufsess, except that the latter had asked for material about the movement.

Hauer was able to give some information about a Director Lothar Binhöffer (sometimes spelled Bonhöffer), namely, that he belonged to the Nordic-Religious Working Community. According to Hauer, this community had about 130 members who joined the ADGB at the Wartburg, "but, seen from my perspective, it has always tried through numerous intrigues to break the ADGB up. Because their leader wrote a very misleading article in their publication, I asked him to leave the Board of Leaders."[16] This he did and took some of his people with him. "Since then he [Dr Seibertz] and Dr Kusserow have tried any means to damage the ADGB ... they practice very nonfactual criticisms. The reason seems to be that; on the one hand, they think that they have to protect paganism, which is thoroughly unnecessary since I protect it." On the other hand, said Hauer, "there are personal reasons" for their enmity. "The Nordic-Religious Working Community tried some years before the Wartburg (1933) to do what we did, namely, bring together the whole German Faith Movement. They did not succeed for the simple reason that they had no leader of caliber. Neither Seibertz nor Kusserow is that. This fact of their failure and my success they have never forgiven me. That is the sole and deepest reason for their polemic." Having talked to Bonhöffer and others, continued Hauer, he had the impression that they regretted the Seibertz and Kusserow line. Bonhöffer was a religious German-faith oriented person, "although of a specific monomaniacal tendency" that is common among "most Nordic-Religious Community members."[17]

In the final analysis, thought Hauer, the group would never be more than a sect. "Within my community, which is determined by future-oriented leadership, they might have achieved something. By themselves they are insignificant and, to the extent that they cannot accommodate themselves, they will become troublemakers, as is the case with Seibertz and Kusserow."[18]

Friedrich Steves, Hauer told Best, was a Hitler Youth leader somewhere in München. "He is 43 years old, and a pioneer fighter for the Germanic faith."[19] To that end, "he belonged to the GGG[20] of Fahrenkrog and to the *Nordungen*, both of which belong to the ADGB." According to Hauer, Steves was a stalwart fighter, which was why Hauer made him a local leader in München, and he had been a National Socialist for years. Consequently, so Hauer, "he is unconditionally reliable."[21]

> "Regarding my application to the Bavarian police, I want to add this. The political police have ruled that since Stahl resigned and a totally reliable Party member was put at the head of the community, the Nürnberger Community [another free religious group], should be returned its complete freedom of activities. Police Inspector Bergler himself read the decree to me. It means that the secular confirmation at youth [*Jugendweihe*] can be taken up again. I would appreciate it, if you could check that the governmental police organs act in accordance with the decree."[22]

Hauer told Best that in Bavaria a number of communities were handicapped. The community in Schweinfurt was totally forbidden. The speaker for the political police asked that Hauer make an application to the authorities for this Bavarian, as well as for the Palatinate communities, so as to clear them. This Hauer did. He also had included two other documents which showed that the *Bund der Freireligiösen*, formerly *Volksbund für Geistesfreiheit*, and now *Bund der Gemeinde eines Deutschen Glaubens*, was not politically active but left politics a matter of personal choice. Hauer also answered the Marxist charge that was usually leveled against the free religious. He told Best that seventy to eighty percent of the free religious were proletarians. It should not surprise any one, therefore, if some of them had been Marxists. After all, the same was true for the church. Just recently he had spoken before 1,300 people of primarily the Nürnberger Gemeinde. Afterwards, he had conversations with some of them and he noticed that not only were "these people ready and willing to be led to the *Volk* and faith, but they had already confessed themselves to the Third Reich and its *Führer*, perhaps even before the revolution."[23]

Hauer wanted to make two other general remarks, he told Werner Best. First, he "observed that the proletarians, even ones who were once Marxists, converted to the Third Reich far more sincerely and quickly than did those intellectuals who had not belonged to the movement before the revolution." Hauer ascribed this new loyalty of the workers to the fact that "they saw that the regime was serious about social justice and fought against joblessness, things that the Marxists once hoped for." Furthermore, argued Hauer, "I am convinced that precisely those workers, who are being converted to the

Third Reich by a single-minded leadership, will become the unswerving fighters for this *Reich* and can be relied upon by the *Führer* of the *Reich*."[24] Hauer thought it essential for the continued existence of the Third Reich that "former Marxists should be led concentrically from the religious and *Volk*-like perspective.[25] And no community and leadership could do this better than the Working Community of the German Faith Movement. In a very special way, they have the task to see to it that those former Marxists will not get bogged down religiously and politically so as to become susceptible to secret political propaganda that would make them dangerous to the Third Reich. Those Marxists who submit to our leadership will notice soon enough that their deepest longing finds its fulfillment in us."[26]

Usefulness of the free religious for the fight against Catholicism

Hauer worked hard to be personally useful to the SS. But he also pointed out the usefulness of his Movement, and here of the free religious, to the SS. "The origin of this community is the fight led by a German-faith man against the nonsense of the holy robe (of Christ) in Trier [*des Rockes zu Trier*] in the year 1843.[27] In that year a Catholic priest of German type dared the unthinkable. He wrote an open letter to the Archbishop of Trier against the robe nonsense, in that he denounced this un-German practice and instead stood up for what he called a German-Catholicism, that is, a faith born of a German-nature."

He was excommunicated, explained Hauer, "and that is how he started the large movement that in time became the main part of what are now the free religious." These communities transformed themselves many times, said Hauer. "They did not of course remain untouched by the free thinker movement and the like. How could it be otherwise? Above all, they did not have a meaningful *Führer*. But the good old substance is still there today and has asserted itself. And they have one thing to their credit; namely, they fought unswervingly against reactions from the church, especially those that came from the Catholic side. Frequently, their fight took the form of propaganda for church-leaving, which angers some ministries today, because it is feared that we could kindle such a movement again." However, "the movement went in the direction that we affirm, namely, the direction that would break the power of especially the Catholic Church in Germany."[28]

Then came Hauer's old refrain, "you know, of course, that I make a distinction between authentic Catholic faith, that is, between people who are genuinely concerned about the Gospel and that form of Christianity, and the church that plays with power politics, the form that is represented today by the Pope and the whole apparatus that he sets in motion against us." He observed all this recently in Austria, wrote Hauer. "And so I am of the opinion that we have to do all in our power to resist especially this attack, which is being prepared secretly and with unheard-of power, by opposing it with an unshakable front of our own."[29] And building up to a climax, Hauer continued, "This front can no longer be the Protestant church. It is divided within, without leadership, and has returned to the tradition of a confession. It will not be long before it will fall apart. The building of a free church has already begun secretly; I have exact information about that. *The only bulwark that can oppose this onslaught of Roman power politics is the German Faith Movement.* On us rests the responsibility to pre-prepare the spiritual and religious fighting troop that can absorb the shove and finally knock down the attack."[30]

Continuing the above argument, Hauer wrote, "In this movement as a whole, the free religious are an essential part. They are spread across the whole of Germany. And in this one point, namely, the fight against reaction and claims to power of the church, they have been unshakable from 1843 to this day. They have an excellent organization; and they have trained fighters who have dared to act for their belief. They have submitted to my leadership and therefore indicated their will to march in the direction that I call."[31] Consequently, Hauer suggested that all should be done to ensure their complete freedom of movement under his leadership "so that we are not unprepared." The religious and *völkisch* fighting troops, although untrained and unarmed, would not be surprised by an attack from the Catholics. "It may just be that the fate of the Third Reich hangs on our preparedness." And with emphasis he continued, "for this much is clear: the Catholic Church has not reconciled itself with the Third Reich and will not be able to reconcile itself with it. A battle is unavoidable. It will come sooner or later. And this fight cannot be led with political means alone. That's why the *Führer* of the *Reich* needs us. ... We live from the same root-power and have the same goal: the Third Reich. The clearer we are about the fact that the German Faith Movement alone will resist and knock off the attack, the more effective should be the care taken that this movement finds its form."[32]

And then Hauer argued again for the freedom of movement of the various communities. Best was not only to present Hauer's view to Himmler, but was also to work quietly (*in der Stille*) to benefit their case. He asked particularly that Best persuade a local brigade leader to work with the political police for the freedom of the Bavarian and Palatinate communities. "Because Bavaria is the access gate of that Roman might, strong guards need to be established here." And Hauer would help. "I am prepared to put absolutely reliable people in positions of leadership both in Bavaria and the Palatinate." He would make an unerring party member the regional leader, who would be under the "immediate direction" of Hauer and would look after the communities.[33]

Hauer wanted Best to act immediately, since the communities suffered from their insecure status. Furthermore, argued Hauer, "both the Protestant and the Catholic Churches do all in their power to cast suspicion on the communities and the ADGB, because they know how dangerous we will become to their claims of power." He wanted Best to inform him immediately of any suspicions cast on them, especially after he discovered just what distortions about them were being circulated in the Cult Ministry. Hauer apparently spent four hours sorting out this mess with the Director of the Ministry, Mezgar.[34]

Hauer on Jews and Zionism

When Hauer conveyed his views to Werner Best on the so-called Jewish problem, the book that would change Nazi thinking about Jews (Wirsing 1942) had not yet been published. The general thinking was still informed by Rosenberg's 1922 publication on Zionism. Apparently, Rosenberg tried to uncover the reasons for the movement and came to the conclusion, one shared by most anti-Semites at the time, that it did not make sense to fight Zionism because it countered assimilation. The idea that all of Jewry would be absorbed by a Jewish state found favor, until it was realized that the state was to be Palestine (and not, for example, Uganda, as Joseph Chamberlain had suggested in 1903). Then the calculations began and it was recognized that Palestine would probably not even be able to absorb one-third of world Jewry. Why then was the Jewish Agency in Tel Aviv so keen on Palestine? Giselher Wirsing provided the answer in 1938, and it is still popular in extreme Right circles today: The plan was to turn Palestine into the Vatican of a world Jewry that would, however, continue to enhance its political and economic power in Western Europe and the United States.[35]

Writing in 1934, Hauer told Best about his long tour through the Orient in 1928. One of his goals was the thorough study of Jewry (*Judentums*), especially Zionism. On the basis of his observations, Hauer concluded that Zionism alone offered a possible organic solution to the Jewish problem and one not harmful to Germans. According to Hauer, Zionists wanted to be nothing other than Jews. They were probably the most active and strongest party in world Jewry. In Hauer's opinion, Zionist leaders would be prepared for a peaceable understanding with the Third Reich. Thinking of his Workweeks during the *Bünde* phase, Hauer reported that "over the last two to three years I have tried to find National Socialists willing to engage in conversations with leading Zionists for the purpose of finding a solution to the Jewish problem, without angering world Jewry. That cleansing the German *Volk* of Jewish elements, especially in the leading classes, was necessary forced itself upon me from year to year through my observations of academic life and of different German universities, especially also through my observations within literature, art, and so on. I therefore made a firm effort at this university and tried already in 1929 to prevent a professor coming here who was a baptized Christian but was of Jewish descent.

Unfortunately, I did not succeed then. The documentary evidence of my battle can be found in the files of the philosophical faculty."[36]

Hauer claimed that he had to take up the fight against Jewry forcefully. And then he talked about Professor Krieck's attendance at the conference where Martin Buber also spoke. Hauer acted with the hope that the Work-week example would have an effect and that such discussions would be carried upward into authoritative positions. He wanted to avoid the heavy shock to German world trade caused by world Jewry. Unfortunately, this did not succeed, with the result that foreign trade was more or less ruined. "Naturally, I dare not claim that had we followed the path of discussion, as I intended, we would have succeeded and not drawn the enmity of world Jewry upon ourselves. But I can tell you confidentially that only recently an outstanding Zionist leader approached me with the question whether a new discussion were possible, because a number of leading Zionists were not in agreement with the attitude of world Jewry toward German trade."[37]

To the question how Zionists could possibly be interested in the hostile position toward Jews of the Third Reich, Hauer had a simple answer. From his worldview perspective, Jews belonged to a foreign race that could only be treated as a foreign *Volk*, one that could never nor must ever be integrated into an Aryan *Volk*. And exactly this strengthened the position of Zionism vis-à-vis other solutions. Their aim was, after all, the return of as many Jews as possible to Palestine and to turn them into a clearly bounded people (*Volk*), with the consequence that Zionists would fight sharply the attempts of world Jewry to integrate Jews within diverse nations. Consequently and, as peculiar as it may sound, argued Hauer, "the Zionist sees his idea strengthened by the position of the Third Reich." In Hauer's opinion this fact could be exploited. "In this way, we could possibly regain our ruined export." He ended by affirming that he is "prepared to mediate at any time."[38]

Even before Hauer's letter to Best, there were of course contacts between Zionists and Nazis and, indeed, Jewish critics even asserted "that Nazism and Zionism were working hand in glove" (Laqueur 1972: 500), but as Laqueur points out, and as correspondence between Hauer and Buber showed, any "imputation of cooperation or collusion" was "pernicious nonsense" (ibid.: 500).[39] Even at the best of times Hauer saw Buber's position as that of an adversary (*Widersacher*) and his good thoughts about Buber would soon sour.

Regarding Hauer's comments on Zionism, Werner Best wanted concrete suggestions from Hauer about who would be suitable as negotiating partner. Minimally, he thought, "such contact would be of the greatest informative value."[40]

It is not known whether or not Hauer ever made concrete suggestions. But the above view even struck students as being naïve. For example, Werner Gebhard, a graduate student in philosophy told Hauer bluntly in 1935 without a solution of the Jewish problem there would be no Third Reich.[41] Furthermore, he wrote, the only motive behind the removal of Jews from Germany could be hate, not Christian love of neighbor. For Jews were hardly human but "the personification of evil in the world." In his reply Hauer agreed that the Jewish problem required a radical solution and the best thing would be if there were no Jews in Germany. He steered away from the idea, however, that every Jew should be persecuted with hate.[42]

By September of 1935, Hauer learned that the Nazi party no longer wanted his resistance activities vis-à-vis Jewish academics or the Jewish problem. In his letter to Wolfgang Goetze, an ADGB leader in Kiel, Hauer wrote that he had received an urgent warning from someone in an important position that the ADGB should stay out of quarrels with academic personalities. Furthermore, he explained, local Nazis were of the opinion that the battle against Jewry was not the task of the German Faith Movement but exclusively that of the Party.[43]

Hauer had also learned directly from the *Reich* Church Minister Kerrl that the latter saw the DGB as a peace disturber. In a meeting with Reventlow, the latter said the same. It was Hauer's view, however, that the *Führer* would thank him personally one day for the fight that the DGB fought against all confessions and that then they would know that their work was necessary, more necessary than that of anyone else. "If we don't succeed," wrote Hauer, "the Third Reich will be lost." Thrilled that 1,200 people attended the Julfest in Heilbronn, despite their current problems, Hauer wrote: "We are not a sect nor a confession, for it is already crystal clear today, we have seized the whole."[44]

But things were not well any longer between the Party and the DGB. Hauer even asked Hans F. K. Günther for help. Apparently in response to Heydrich's personal request, Hauer wrote Hitler a memorandum warning against the Hydra that is Christendom. While Günther suggested that Hauer use more sophisticated methods of persuasion toward his followers, Heydrich clearly encouraged greater radicalism (Banach 1998). In the end Hauer admitted to Günther that the young extreme National Socialists in the movement went at it hammer and tongs.[45]

By late 1935, Hauer's letters to Werner Best changed from being proactive to defending himself against various attacks from the Ludendorff movement as well as from the principal official in charge of non-Church communities and the groups of the *völkisch* movement, de Boer. Clearly, while the DGB was at the height of its popularity, was talked about, expanded organizationally, and in addition to Hauer's monthly journal, *Deutscher Glaube*, and Reventlow's *Reichswart*, published the more radical weekly *Durchbruch*, it fell out of favor with the SS (Buchheim 1953: 189). One reason was that in 1934 it was still thought by the SS that Hauer's DGB might play a useful role in the church politics of National Socialists. By October of that year, however, Hitler had lost all interest in making a place for the church in his state. Instead, the battle against clerics and, some months later, against the denominations started in earnest (Buchheim 1953: 190).

The journal *Durchbruch*, which Hauer intended to appeal to the simpler minds, was soon taken over by younger, more radical members who were thought to be under Heydrich's control.

Conclusion

On 1 April 1936 Hauer wrote Hans F. K. Günther of his decision to resign from the administration of the German Faith Movement.[46] The radicals that he helped radicalize, including Grabert, Schloz, Orlowsky, Hessberg, and many others, were beyond his control. He did not then know that Heydrich encouraged them. Günther agreed to let the radicals live out their radicalism while Hauer continue to work out his thought-world in more peace and write for a more sophisticated audience.[47] Soon Hauer negotiated with the publishers Karl Gutbrod and Georg Truckenmüller to do something thoroughly new, in line with his own radical change away from what had become a purely political fight.[48] He surrounded himself with new editors, among them Hans F. K. Günther—a friend also of Hans Grimm—and continued the spread of a German Faith even beyond 1945.

Chapter 10

The faith of the Nationalists
Narrative and the Third Reich

Allegorically speaking, God too would not be able to stand this world for
eight days if he were not a creator.
                      Reference to the conditions in Germany after World War I,
                                                   Erwin Ackerknecht[1] (1918)

At present our 'face' is so badly destroyed, as it never was for any other
peoples in similar situations, not Athens, nor Aigospotamoi and Chaer-
onea, or even France in 1871 ...
                                                       Max Weber[2] (1921)

Introduction

Germany's slow crab crawl toward democracy since 1848 came to a complete
halt in 1933. The revolutionary change that ushered in Hitler's dictatorship
took 13 years to prepare from 1919 to 1932. In the literature of nationalist
storytellers such as Hans Grimm, they came to be known as the protest years.

During these years, and as a direct response to the defeat of World War I
and the revenge-spirited Treaty of Versailles, a "new faith" was born
(Grimm 1954: 260; Keynes 1920: 56). As we already know, the key
elements of that faith were the concept of a Third Reich, the *Führer* principle and a unified *Volk*. But there was more. The faith was centered on
male privilege, male strength, male ruthlessness, and male forcefulness
(*Durchsetzungsvermögen*). A homoerotic culture was forced into existence. Women worth admiring were starkly beautiful, hard, taciturn,
described in terms of their aristocratic bearing, loyal mothers and, above
all, loyal political partners to philandering husbands married to politics
and Nazi party formations. Where they existed, a man's homosexual predilections were constrained only by the duty, if he had recognizable Nordic
qualities, to copulate with an attractive woman in order to top up the
Nordic element of an otherwise genetically mixed—some argued degenerate—population. The popular anthropologist of race, Hans F. K.
Günther (1936; 1941) wrote books and articles about the right kind of

10.1 Adolf Hitler with Göring, Goebbels, Himmler, Streicher, Frick

marriage, while in *Bünde* circles, and later in SA and SS circles, homoeroticism was rampant and homosexuality practiced.[3]

This male-focused faith became deed (*Tat*) in 1933. Carl Schmitt (1938: 614) called it a totalitarian "moment."[4] At the time of his writing, Schmitt could not have guessed how right he was. The totalitarian dictatorship lasted until 1945. With the total defeat of World War II—and this time with the determined presence of the allies in Germany, especially Britain and America —the crab walk toward democracy, based on the "other faith" as Grimm called it,[5] started again and has continued since. In this turning, first toward National Socialism and then after World War II toward democracy, the press and nationalist authors played a major role.

Because the Nazi revolution was unrelentingly brutal towards its self-defined enemy—Christianity, Marxism, and European Jews—many scholars have tried to find an explanation for what they regarded as unexplainable in the distant German past (Berlin 1999; Mosse 1981a; 1981b; Poliakov 1974). The implied assumption seems to be that something so brutal must have taken a long time to develop. Other scholars have gone even further. They explain the end result of Nazi brutality, the Holocaust, in terms of a specifically German eliminationist anti-Semitism rooted in Christianity (Goldhagen 1996, 2002; Steigmann-Gall 2003).

The evidence of this research shows that their arguments, though understandable, are wrong. These scholars have simply not researched in

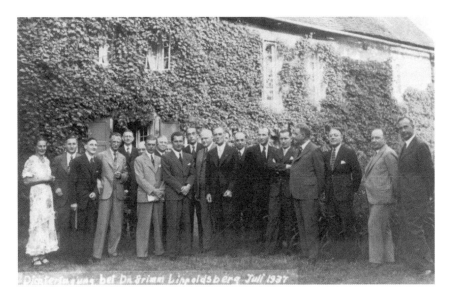

10.2 Hans Grimm, Conference of Nationalist Poets

handwritten documents and similar sources the specific slant that National Socialists forced upon politics, namely, that of privileging and worshiping male force and ruthlessness in the context of a new political religion.

The sanctification of politics and the privileging of male ruthlessness was supported by specific publishing firms and nationalist authors who, through countless well-organized and well-attended public events throughout the 1920s and early 1930s, created a large following for their starkly new romantic worldview. As Schulze (1998: 220) points out: "Of the thirty-four German book titles that sold more than half a million copies between 1918 and 1933, only three were written by figures identified with Weimar culture." They were Kästner, Remarque, and Thomas Mann. By contrast, the favored authors included Hermann Löns, Hans Carossa, Walter Flex, Hans Grimm, and Clara Viebig (ibid.: 220; Axmann 1995: 185). There were in fact several others, all of them associated with Hans Grimm and his annual conferences for nationalist poets (*Dichtertagungen*). Furthermore, Schulze does not include in this list of authors Hitler, Rosenberg, and Goebbels.

In the worldview of nationalist and National Socialist authors, Christianity was dead—rejected, overcome, ineffectual, or its symbols used and abused to make political points. Even when Jesus is mentioned, he is ideologically interpreted as a heroic warring figure (Klagges 1934). As Goebbels, who wrote a book entitled *Michael: A German Destiny in Diary Pages* (1929)[6] has his protagonist Michael proclaim after he freed himself of the

10.3 Hans Grimm and family, 1931

notion that Christ is love, "Enlightenment overcame me; I shall write a drama, Jesus Christ as hero" (1929: 52). It is after his protagonist reached this stage of secular enlightenment that Goebbels frees his venomous tongue against Jews whose "physical being" he finds "revolting" (*ein körperlicher Ekel*) (ibid.: 57). "Religion?" says Goebbels, "Naïve as you are. What has this to do with Religion or Christianity?" Speaking of Jews, he says, "He destroys us or we render him harmless, anything else is unthinkable" (ibid.: 57).

Unlike Goebbels, whose effort to turn Christianity into a secular Germanic faith was wasteful of mental and emotional energy, Grimm was an agnostic from the start, who wrote with an amazing psychological efficiency. He abhorred wasting words to express emotions that were entirely beside the point. According to Grimm, human fortunes are determined by luck, time, fate, and, above all, by the country (that is, its history and its imperial reach) into which one was born. It is the nation that sets the parameters for the individual's development of personality and character, not the other way around. Uprooted individuals and families who do not find their way back to their roots are no more than a flash in the pan, there and soon expired forever (1918a). But this formational direction of what it is to be human (*Entfaltung*) is only visible at times of crisis. And it is times following the Jameson Raid, the Anglo-Boer war, and World War I in South Africa, Namibia, and Cameroon, that Grimm writes about. His ideal was imperial England, whose countrymen he experienced personally in England and abroad. He claims that it was a

10.4 Joseph Goebbels,
Reichspropagandaminister, 1940

major shock to learn that the English, some of whose traits he idealized, insisted on being Germany's and Germans' most determined enemy.

In their letters to one another, Grimm and his cohorts expressed being for the "Third Reich," against "anti-Germanism," and indifferent to Jews. Grimm claims that he is not an anti-Semite but an a-Semite.[7]

But what is meant by "Third Reich"? Grimm, following his deceased friend Moeller van den Bruck, meant to express with it the religious hope of salvation from the grinding needs of Germans during the Versailles era – an era that robbed young Germans, especially, of the hope of developing their talents freely anywhere in the world. The contrast is with England whose people could unfold their talents in numerous colonies.

Closed off from the world, German salvation was to come, however, not from God but from the "fount of the power within the *Volk*" (Grimm 1931: 11). That is what "Third Reich" meant—a fount of power expressed by its best poets. He meant from poets and writers like him. Grimm's merciless pessimism, which he expresses in all his books, is intended to inspire people, as peculiar as it might seem to fight the fight that fate has thrown at them (Grimm 1918a, 1918b; 1926). And the fight that destiny has predetermined is one that is invariably forced upon a man by an external aggressor.[8]

The main characters (usually men) in the presence of such a confrontation have but two choices; to appropriate their (usually) lost or diminished sense of national identity and fight, or to avoid such appropriation and be but a flash in the pan facing final extinction (Grimm 1918a; 1918b). Why does he have to appropriate a seemingly lost identity? Because—unlike Britons— Germans were usually (and after 1918 always) Germans in someone else's colonies. In Grimm's experience the aggressor was invariably England, not because the English were uniquely pugnacious, but because England was an empire. It was a people with space where its young could spread their wings, while Germany, especially after Versailles when its colonies were taken from it, was a people without space and thus without prospects of development (Grimm 1926). From the British perspective, said Grimm, Germans were always unwelcome interlopers.

Two epitomizing experiences shaped Grimm's religious poetics. One was his experience of England's wars and economic ambitions in Southern Africa before he returned to Germany in 1910 to become a writer. The other was his experience of the First World War, where, as an intelligence officer, he became the unwilling witness of the disloyalty of German soldiers who were inspired by the writings of the Jew, Walter Rathenau (Grimm 1954: 92–3).

Grimm was sensitive to anti-German feelings from his early years in England (1896) and South Africa (1897–1910). There he read the *Saturday Review*, which already in 1897 discussed the necessity of war with Germany.[9] He also witnessed the Anglo-Boer war (1899–1902) and claims to have helped concentration camp victims. The English attitude toward Germany, perceived as it was as an unwelcome rival that must be eliminated,[10] shocked him to the core and he remained pathetically obsessed with English–German relations throughout his life.

Following his two epitomizing experiences, Grimm became acutely aware of any anti-Germanism. Although he rarely did so publicly, in 1931 he wrote a piece where he is pointing a finger at Jews who, in his view, are pouring "blind hate" on an "awakening soul" whose time has come (Grimm 1931: 13). What is threatening here, although in none of his writings does Grimm see it, is his unwavering determination to serve the nationalist cause, even if that means putting Hitler into power. He makes this feeling clear in 1932 in letters to Alfred Hugenberg[11] and, later, in a letter to Ilse Hess (wife of Rudolf Hess) dated 6 May 1938, "Until now I have only known one sole passion, despite some irritations (with National Socialist behaviors), namely that Germany succeed, and Germany can only succeed today if National Socialism succeeds."[12]

The writers

Few scholars have taken seriously the simple fact that a limited number of determined radical believers could do formidable damage in a relatively short period of historical time. Thus, enthralled by a specific vision and drive, by told and written stories reinforcing the fulfillment of one deed, Hitler's National Socialists were eased into government.

10.5 Erwin Guido Kolbenheyer, nationalist
writer linked to Grimm and Hauer

In the 1920s and early 1930s, behind the background of a left-liberal democracy, three political blocks vied with one another in print and deed to destroy the Republic. There was firstly the Catholic *Zentrum* party that stood for a morality linked to Rome. In the time period considered here, the left condemned its authoritarianism, the right its internationalism.

The second group—and the one that is of interest to us here—is the splintered, elitist, but highly determined and energetic nationalist block. It is from this corner of writers and publishers (Lehmann, Diederichs, Georg-Müller, Albert-Langen) that a new German nationalistic literature was developed (Günther 1935b). Ignored by the mainline press, some of them established a major publishing firm in 1931 by merging three presses into one: Georg-Müller, the Hanseatische Verlagsanstalt, and Albert-Langen. Its goal was to further German and Nordic authors and it did so with great success (Stapel 1931). The books of Ernst Jünger, Hans Grimm, Ernst Wiechert, Winnig, Binding, Blunck, Carossa, Claudius, Löns, Kolbenheyer among many others became, as noted previously, bestsellers selling tens and hundreds of thousands of copies, making several authors millionaires. These nationalists supported (apparently not without some misgivings) the NSDAP because they saw it as a tool to break down the liberal Weimar Republic.

The National Socialists were the third major block. They shared with the nationalists the determination to destroy Weimar. But where the nationalists

10.6 Nationalist author Rudolf Binding at Grimm's Lippoldsberg Conference, 1935

did not have a clear sense of what kind of government would replace the democratic republic, so long as it represented *Deutschtum*, the Nazis did. They too had their own publishers: for example, Franz Eher, München, who published the terror-inspiring *Völkischer Beobachter*, on which Adolf Hitler was listed on the masthead as "editor" until March 1933; Armanen Verlag, Leipzig; Karl Gutbrod Verlag, Stuttgart; and numerous others.

In their obsession to turn the liberal wasteland (*Leerraum*) of Weimar into a dynamic German force, *Zentrum* and the Nationalists became so preoccupied with immediate petty political maneuvers that they lost sight of both the big picture and the dirt at their feet. In the process, they conceded the necessity of a totalitarian and anti-Semitic "moment," only to find themselves faced some years later with the destruction of the Second World War and the Holocaust.

Development of the new faith:
not Christ but the Third Reich

As pointed out above, in the early 1920s radical young Germans, among them students, professors and writers, sought to overcome their doubts and despair over the dismal political, economic, intellectual and spiritual conditions of their defeated country, one they saw as "culturally occupied," by seeking salvation (*Erlösung*) through their own "German soul" (Reuth 2000: 57). What this meant varied, but the major idea had to do with

10.7 Ernst Krieck, Nazi pedagogue

encouraging young Germans to have faith, religious faith, in something called the "German *Reich* within" or the "Third Reich."[13] In other words, instead of the Word of God (a universalistic faith), the Word of the Third Reich, a local faith rooted somehow in the German soul, was propagated. The whole thrust of core Nazi radicals was to overcome what they regarded as an already secularized Christianity and replace it with a faith in the "Third Reich."

Let us look again at the example of Ernst Krieck. It will be remembered that he was Professor of Pedagogy in Frankfurt and a participant in Hauer's annual conference. Like many who emerged from the *Bünde* movement, he was fond of sitting with his students around a bonfire to celebrate the summer solstice and sermonize about the "Word of the Third Reich."[14]

At one such bewitching moment, he told his students the story about a Calabrian monk who, at a time of crisis 700 years ago, announced a word of yearning and glad tidings that was passed on by the young Franciscan movement until it became an awakening among peoples. It was not the word of Christ that was passed on, but the word of the Third Reich—by which was meant, said Krieck, a religious and political yearning for a higher sense of communal existence. But because the Word, Third Reich, was not then rooted in the solid soil of a specific *Volk* and state (as Christianity's roots were) it lost its symbolic meaning. But then in 1923,[15] the Word of the Third Reich was preached again, this time by Moeller van den Bruck (1876–1925).

Moeller understood it as a deep religious hope, but rooted it in current reality and history. The Third Reich represented yearning for salvation from despair through the fount of power that had its source in the German people (*Volkskraft*), not in an otherworldly God. Krieck ended his midsummer night's talk with a hail to the German Youth, German *Volk*, and Third Reich (Grimm 1931: 11).

Grimm wrote this piece quoting Krieck in 1931, and it was republished in 1980. Krieck's midnight ritual talk was observed by a Jewish colleague (named Jourdan), a Social Democrat and congresswoman for Frankfurt who reported it to the authorities, causing Krieck to lose his Frankfurt position. Grimm knew both Moeller and Krieck personally from Versailles days. Krieck's forced removal from his job (he was moved to another town) frustrated Grimm, who contrasted his own "a-Semitism," (not anti-Semitism) with Jewish "Anti-Germanism" and the blind hate that went with it (ibid.: 12).

Those Germans (from Hitler, to Rosenberg, to Himmler, to Heydrich, to Klagges, to Hauer, to Grimm and innumerable others) who became prominent National Socialist ideologues, even though Grimm and other nationalists like him did not become members of the party, were uniformly obsessed with overcoming Christianity and persuading other Germans to do likewise. The discomfiture with Christianity (as with Jews, even when they were "friends") is one of "the silences" or a self-imposed discretion that is an essential ingredient of Grimm's storytelling (Grimm 1918a; 1918b).[16] Grimm did not hate, perhaps because he regarded it as too direct an emotion or as incompatible with his upbringing. Curiously enough, though, he perceived that the English (and, it would seem, Jews) hated Germans.

At any rate, Nazi ideologues started from the position that Germany was in a serious crisis, as they were personally, and both nation and person had to be renewed radically. Since, however, all foreign isms (from Bolshevism, to liberalism, to capitalism, to imperialism) were contemptible because they were associated with the victors, they had to come up with something "genuinely German" and with it create a German faith put in an appropriate German form.

The crude version of this faith was the slogans that one saw splashed on cathedrals in the 1930s. For example, they said, "Germany's Youth believes only in Germany!" (*Deutschlands Jugend glaubt nur an Deutschland!*) Or "We would rather drive into hell with Rosenberg than into heaven with the Pope" (*Wir wollen lieber mit Rosenberg in die Hölle fahren, als mit dem Papst in den Himmel!*) [17]

The more sophisticated version had a different beginning and medium. To create a new faith that would grasp young radicals, writers in the nationalist fold looked to two experiences: (1) the war in the trenches and (2) the current life of the common folk. Furthermore, there were already popular (*völkisch*) ideas published about how a people fall apart (Spengler 1920; Moeller van den Bruck 1923) and how such a people, by going back to natural fundamentals like race and the religion specific to it, might raise themselves up again (Chamberlain 1899; 1916). This literature, rather than church dogma, was the measure of the worth of their interpreted experiences.

As we saw in previous chapters, Hauer's works too show that the essence of National Socialism sits on experiences and experiential knowledge. It is "experience-near" and this was the source of its persuasive power. Furthermore, personal and national experiences were fused by subsuming the former under the latter. All else was dogma to be destroyed. This kind of "experience-near" writing and the indiscriminate fusing of personal with national, religion with politics, and of the past with the present, became useful propaganda tools.

More sophisticated authors such as Grimm (1918a; 1918b) and Blunck (1936) wrote in the form of sagas or family epics. Sagas have a very anthropological look, at a time when anthropology, especially physical and psychological anthropology, was popular. Epics retained a sense of history while achieving an aesthetic distance. The reader was taken back centuries or to exotic parts of the world where Vandals and Boers on horses and oxcarts were pursued by the imperialist armies of Romans and Britons. Even the unschooled readers could tell, however, that the local (meaning German *Volk* and Nation) was good, while the global (meaning intrusive people, sometimes Romans and Britons, after 1918 Jews and Internationalism) was bad.

Grimm's concern about Jews was rarely expressed openly. But being exceedingly frustrated with Thomas Mann's wholesale condemnation of German conduct from 1918 to 1945, he did so in an open letter to Thomas Mann. The letter was apparently written in the summer of 1945 but not published until 1972.[18] Grimm regarded Thomas Mann as a civilization-writer (*Zivilationsliterat*) rather than a *völkisch* writer.[19] With the term *Zivilisationsliterat* Grimm accused Thomas Mann of the same thing of which Thomas Mann had accused his brother Heinrich Mann after the First World War. At that time Thomas Mann was in fact a Conservative Revolutionary while Heinrich Mann was liberal.[20] Because the goal of civilization-writers was the democratization and thus de-Germanization of Germany, Thomas Mann in effect accused his brother and others who wrote in his vein of being against nationalism and anti-German. Hans Grimm accuses Thomas Mann of insensitivity and an inflated sense of self-importance that he could only have acquired in America. With this in mind, and in the context of his usual litany of worries related to the protest years (1918–1932), Hans Grimm also listed the "clumsy self-importance of Jews" (*ungeschickte Vordringlichkeit der Juden*) (1972a: 19) and the "intrusion of Jews into key intellectual positions" (*Eindringen der Juden in unsere geistige Schlüsselstellungen*) (ibid.: 24).[21]

Grimm saw himself and saw other writers of his ilk as having to do a specific task during a dangerously impenetrable time for his *Volk*. He was a self-conscious political writer, not at all interested in the weaknesses, flaws and failures of individual psyches. Where individuals were concerned, he conceded that the great German classics from Goethe and Schiller to Thomas Mann remained unsurpassed. He did not see himself as having anything useful to contribute here. Grimm was driven to achieve something else. He called it "political art," an art of "experienced causes there, where formerly one talked of 'guilt' and where one lived as an I-person [*Ichmensch*] in what one thought to be a formed world, once and for all" (1954: 84). His favorite political poet was Rudyard Kipling (Grimm 1938).

Initially, Grimm's idea was to write a "novel of a country," and so he chose what at that time was called Cafraria in South Africa.[22] This is a part of the world with which he was personally familiar because he lived there as an employed and later independent businessman until 1908. It covered the eastern part of the Cape surrounding East London and reaching to the Transkei. Following the first conflict between English settlers and local Blacks, German legionnaires of the Crimean war were called in to help. When they failed, the English governor encouraged 450 landless German families from Pomerania and Brandenburg to settle there. Grimm's aim was not to write a history, but to write what he would write forever after, namely, a "fate-driven happening among human beings" (1954: 85).

It is possible that the work on Cafraria was never completed because its author lacked the second epitomizing experience, namely, the First World War and Germany's defeat. Defeat helped define how and why Grimm wanted to write political novels about countries rather than individuals.

One of Grimm's most self-aware ideological statements about what Germans in the 1920s and 1930s were up to was given in 1935 before a German-American audience in New York.[23] Grimm started his talk by raising a question that he thought Americans might ask, namely: what was the nature of the belief in humanity (*Menschheit*) that Germany, in an uncertain time, was trying to turn into a useful and duty- inspiring reality? (Grimm 1972b: 259). The belief was, said Grimm, "that the competent have more right than the incompetent, that the orderly have more right than the disorderly, that the healthy have more right than the sick, that the gifted have more right than the ungifted, that the innovator has more right than the imitator ... that these rights come from a man's gifts, achievements, and duties" (ibid.: 260).

And what is the other faith, the one opposed to the above, asks Grimm. "The other faith puts the masses before the *Volk*, class before nation, the dull before the gifted, the weak before the strong, the ignorant before the learned, the tired before the energetic ..." (ibid.: 260).

Then Grimm asks a third question that he imagined German-Americans might wish to have answered, namely, why Germans, who were once renowned for their universalism, had come to this new belief. His answer is revealing.

"My listeners, when we Germans in Germany lost the World War, when the guilt for the war was put solely on us without trial, when no state in the world had pity on us, when Wilson's fourteen points were ignored, when the hunger blockade was continued, when Versailles came, when the stupid injustice of Memel happened and the heavy injustice of Upper Silesia, when the Ruhr occupation occurred, then the other faith became attractive to the masses." The other faith was clearly Communism. It even won over some achievers (*Leistungsmenschen*) who were by nature deeply opposed to it (ibid.: 261). "Yes, where good German nationalists came together in those days one could hear them suggest that, being an oppressed people ourselves, we should get together with other oppressed people ... and destroy the thoroughly untruthful West." But Germany had stepped back from this passion for dissolution, revenge and destruction (ibid.: 262).

"My listeners, in Germany today under difficult circumstances we are leading the battle for the mind [*Geisteskampf*] in the direction of emphasizing the responsibilities of achievers but also their privileges, responsibilities of the healthy but also their privileges, and responsibilities of the gifted but also their preferential rights" (ibid.: 262). Grimm considered this elitism to be part of Nordic nature or of the rights of gentlemen (*Herrenrecht*). Beyond his untranslatable rhetoric, Grimm simply showed that Communism was warded off by National Socialism and the latter was but a form of hard-nosed social Darwinism. Grimm recognized the motive of revenge and destruction in Communism but not in National Socialism.

Hitler and Goebbels as writers

The genres of the 1920s that are guided by the above-mentioned experientially-based priorities emphasize subjectivity and experienced truth and reality (*Wahrheit* and *Wirklichkeit*) above objectivity and non-experienced, conceptual truth. Addressing academics, for example, Goebbels (1929: 78) called out, "Why do they not have the courage to practice free subjectivism." At any rate objectivity and conceptual truth were thought to be artificial and arbitrary—in other words, driven by special interests, especially those of Jews. By contrast, experiences are driven by destiny (*Schicksal*), especially that of the nation.[24] Thus Goebbels (1929: 35) wrote, for example, "political miracles occur only within things national. The international is only a teaching of reason directed against the blood,"[25] where "blood" stood for the combination of race, *Volk*, nation which reason undermined.

The greatest push to make the point that destiny drives experiences came of course from Adolf Hitler, whose two volumes of *Mein Kampf* (My Struggle) published in 1924 and 1925–1926 are an autobiography of a political pioneer and his party. It is significant that the book is not a theoretical work but a narrative about the young man Hitler who, according to his self-interpretation, experienced his society as having fallen on evil times. Disturbed by the decay and indifference that surrounded him, he began to search for their cause. Two major experiences soon took him to it: that of his youth in Vienna, where he viewed with despair the Czechoslovakianization[26] of society which marginalized things German; and that of his early manhood in the trenches of the First World War, with its bitter and unacceptable defeat.

Hitler's conclusions start with the demand for a united *Reich* of people who share the same blood and are prepared to fight against foreign rule. They end with his distinction between "pure force" and "real force." According to Hitler, pure force is merely destructive and therefore reactive. By contrast, real force, the only force that is capable of totally destroying the enemy, is motivated by a worldview that pushes its believers to achieve a positive goal (Zehnpfennig 2000: 93). The means to this end, suggests Hitler, are uncompromising determination and hardness, ruthless destruction of existing traditions, effective propaganda, political instrumentalisation of religion, and intolerance of anything not German (ibid.: 122). Hauer, Grimm and their colleagues helped cultivate these qualities in followers of the movement.

Zehnpfennig (2000: 44) points out that Hitler's book is intentionally written as a story that reveals chance happenings as actually guided by an unseen power toward a predetermined and necessary development. Readers are to discover for themselves that Hitler and his project are guided by destiny, but a destiny that affects not only one individual but the whole *Volk*. The story gives Hitler charisma, and the party its brutal determination.

Core National Socialist ideologues initially saw themselves as a small number of fanatical co-plotters, each with his own, personally organized circle of followers, and all fiercely loyal to their prophet-politician, the *Führer*. I think Hans Grimm may be believed when he reports that Hitler told him at their first meeting in Munich in 1926: "Until 1923 I made a big mistake. I thought that the important factor was quantity and especially the number of fellow combatants. What is necessary, however, is an unconditionally reliable circle of co-plotters among whom no one wants anything for himself" (Grimm 1954: 114).

In the 1920s most co-plotters saw themselves as preparers of the way, or as prophets calling in the wilderness. Thus during his born-again experience— born again as a National Socialist—Goebbels (who has his protagonist listening to Hitler) wrote: "That is not a speaker. That is a prophet!" (1929: 102). The implied biblical reference is not agreement with it, but nose-thumbing. It is to remind Christians that what was done within the context of one structure (namely, the church) can be done much more effectively within another structure; namely, the party. Christ is mere man (he is overcome) (ibid.: 50–65). Hitler is *the* man (*Persönlichkeit*) (whose hour has come).

As Payne (2002: 124) points out in his review of Emilio Gentile's *Historical Analysis and Taxonomy of Political Religions*, like Bolshevism, so

10.8 Erwin Ackerknecht, librarian, later Director of Schiller National Museum, Marbach

National Socialism shows the "recapitulation and secularist imitation of key traditional religious themes" at an early date; and, like Bolshevist liturgy, so National Socialism would develop its own liturgy.

To keep the reader focused on the secular impulse that directed his religious imitation, Goebbels wrote (1929: 114), "History is a flow of *manly* decisions. Not armies win, but *men* with armies. ... Art, discovery, ideas, battles, laws, states—at their beginning and end is always *Man*. Race is the fertile soil from which emerges all creative power. Humanity is but an assumption. *Volk* is reality" (ibid.: 114).[27] "Humanity is thought, *Volk* is grown" (ibid.: 115), and "all of life is war" (ibid.: 117). Without defeat, without Versailles, no one would have listened. The personal and collective experiences of defeat and denigration, specifically of German men, lent Hitler's, Goebbels' and Grimm's words substance.

Conclusion

There were also gentler voices that nevertheless made similar points and earlier, but after the defeat of World War I. On 12 December 1918 Erwin Ackerknecht, then a librarian who furthered those who were driven to be "servants of the word, the German word,"[28] wrote Hans Grimm a consoling letter. Both were in despair about the conditions of their country. As Ackerknecht expressed it, defeat was as if one's religion were shattered and trampled underfoot. "But some of us who provide national education [*Volksbildung*]," argued Ackerknecht, "are called to serve, although only in a preparatory way. When we approach the best of these men we cannot fail to recognize that they are comparable to the 'voice of a preacher in the wilderness.' One anticipates that someone bigger, something bigger, must come, namely a founder of a new religion."[29]

Ackerknecht, Grimm, and Hauer were believers in the "German word," not the Christian one. Their ideological writing was what Payne (2002: 124) said fascism is, namely, "the recapitulation and secularist imitation of key traditional religious themes."

Chapter 11

Scientific neo-paganism and the extreme Right then and today

Introduction

During the Weimar Republic, flourishing new religions and literary circles were harnessed to usher in the Cultural Revolution from the right that was soon dominated by the Nazis. Jakob Wilhelm Hauer's German Faith movement, an umbrella group for numerous new religions from versions of Hinduism to Nordic neo-paganism, all collaborated, as was shown, with Hitler and his party. This chapter looks at the continuity of core ideas from Mathilde Ludendorff's *Gotterkenntnis* to Hauer's German Faith Movement and, importantly, Sigrid Hunke's Unitarians (*Unitarier*).[1] It shows, further, the close connections between these forms of neo-paganism and the present day European New Right. The paradoxical co-occurrence in fascism of a religious populism and a metapolitical elitism, philosophical vitalism and dreams of national or European rebirth, has its roots in these French and German forms of neo-paganism.

The religious beliefs that galvanized the *Bünde* and Conservative Revolutionaries of the Weimar Republic also galvanize members of the European New Right today. These religions were part of the *völkisch* (folkish) movement (Mosse 1981a), which, along with numerous other associations including literary ones, constituted what Armin Mohler (1989a) called the Conservative Revolution. Although hesitatingly, Mohler also equated the guiding ideas of the Conservative Revolution with fascism (1989b: 103, 111).[2]

According to Roger Woods (1996: 5), the Conservative Revolution was an "intellectual movement which was driven by the interaction of culture and politics, ideas and ideology." While Woods probed the thought processes that shaped the extreme right by looking at a "broad mix of sources" including novels, diaries, philosophical works, cultural and political journalism, and political tracts (ibid.: 5), the present book has examined primarily religious issues that Woods ignored in the writings of Jakob Wilhelm Hauer, and here Mathilde Ludendorff and Sigrid Hunke.

The guiding ideas of the Conservative Revolution saturated the cultic milieu of Weimar. They were held by six hundred thousand German

11.1 Mathilde and Erich Ludendorff, 1935

Christians, by one hundred thousand adherents of Erich and Mathilde Ludendorff's movement (Mecklenburg 1996: 375), by Hauer's faith movement and the free religious, by numerous paramilitary groups such as Steel Helmet (*Stahlhelm*), by the four hundred thousand strong German Youth League (*Jungdeutscher Orden*) (Woods 1996: 3) and the millions of readers of literature that was at once religious, political, and militaristic. Neither academics nor the Christians who formed the Confessional Church were immune to these ideas (Fischer 1990; Lixfeld 1994; Dibelius 1927: 121–30). Worse still, most members of these groups were leaders of their own reading or student circles. The Hitler Youth, the NSDAP, and the SS were schooled in these ideas. The impact was overwhelming, and its presence is still felt today.

Mohler and links to the New Right

Because Armin Mohler is a natural link between the Conservative Revolution and the New Right, a few words about him are in order. Born 1920, Mohler sees himself as a fascist in the style of José Antonio Primo de Rivera, founder of the Spanish Phalanx in the 1930s, whose purpose it was to defend a Spanish way of life against capitalism, socialism, and liberalism. Like M. Ludendorff, Hauer, and Hunke, Mohler is highly educated. The last two, especially, are among the main metapolitical thinkers of the New Right, generally, and the Collegium Humanum and the Thule Seminar,[3]

11.2 Ludendorff house today

which are German New Right think tanks, specifically.[4] Since 1970 Mohler has been a member of the committee of patrons of the Nouvelle École and has given frequent talks at the national colloquia of G.R.E.C.E. (Group for Research on European Civilization, in France).[5] He writes for New Right journals such as *Criticón*, and has contact with political leaders such as Franz Schönhuber, one of the founders of the right wing *Republikaner* (Republicans, REP) party and Gerhard Frey, millionaire publisher and founder of the *Deutsche Volksunion* (German People's Union, DVU) (Mecklenburg 1996: 524–5; Kratz 1994: 196).[6]

There is a continuity of persons, ideas, and structures from the Conservative Revolution to National Socialism to the New Right. This continuity has to do with the fact that worldview ideologues, especially M. Ludendorff and Hunke, founded and refounded not only religious and worldview communities, but also publishing houses, academies, youth organizations, and memorial places. Their calendars are filled with conferences, seminars, and solstice festivities. Informally, members of the League for God-cognition (BfG) and Religious Community of German Unitarians (DUR) have contacts with political parties such as the Republicans, the National Democratic Party (NPD), even the Christian Democratic Union (CDU) and Social Democratic Party (SPD). They cultivate contacts with publishers of New Right and New Age books, and their ideas are alive in current New Right journals (Mecklenburg 1996: 374–5, 378–9).

The metapolitics of the Conservative Revolution and the New Right rests on a rejection of Christianity and the affirmation of paganism. In their eyes,

Christianity is totalitarian, Jewish, and dualistic. Its removal reveals neo-paganism, which is whole, organic, and "affirmative of all that is" (Mohler 1989a; de Benoist 1982: 56; Ludendorff 1921: 118; Hunke 1987; Lixfeld 1994: 69; Krebs 1981b: 15–22). Paganism is in fact the love of self and of one's own kind free of Christian influences.

The above thrust privileges *Schicksal* (Moira, fate) or cosmos (*Weltganze*) above individual, putting these in a part–whole relationship (de Benoist 1982: 57). Within the whole may be creative tension (*Spannungen*) but not,[7] as in the Judeo-Christian tradition, divisions owing to dualism (*Spaltungen*) (Mohler 1989a: 122). Rather than make radical moral judgments of good and bad,[8] fascists accept any and all happenings as meaningful. It is an aesthetic rather than a moral stance, so that the human being is not basically good (liberalism) nor bad (Christianity) but imperfect (*Unvollkommen*) and this by virtue of being but a part of a whole (ibid.: 124; de Benoist 1982: 57–8). The part–whole relationship does not debase, since the part shares in the dignity of the whole. Yahweh, by virtue of being "totally Other", debases totally the human being (de Benoist 1982: 59).

According to Mohler, the key to fascism is captured in Nietzsche's notion of "*amor fati*," meaning love of the world as it is, with its eternal dialectic between birth and destruction (*Vernichtung*)—the world, as it *now* is without hope of improvement in the beyond nor in the distant future (1989a: 125, his emphasis). Mohler, once private secretary to Ernst Jünger, captures perfectly Jünger's notion of heroic realism; heroic, Mohler writes (ibid.: 125), because this world is not to be seen as realistic (in the sense of true to reality) in order to allow us to postulate another and better one, but to affirm the world as it is (ibid.: 125).

Neo-pagans accuse Jewish-Christianity (*Judenchristentum*) of constituting a "dictatorship of morality." Premised on unworthiness and the Fall, its perspective is moral and time-linear (de Benoist 1982: 98). By contrast, for neo-pagans history is like life. It sits on the premise that, as human beings are innocent, so is historical development (ibid.: 108).

The thought processes of fascist ideologues from Weimar to the present vary in detail but follow the same basic pattern. Rejection of Christianity is the way to the recovery of neo-paganism. Neo-paganism affirms a Unitarian world-all. This Unitarian world-all manifests itself in a plurality of distinct organic peoples (*Völker*) and organic individuals.[9] What makes *Völker* and individuals distinct and different is, for M. Ludendorff, *Volksseele*, which refers simultaneously to the quality of genius (*Genialität*) and biological traits. Both are one's race-inheritance (*Rasseerbgut*), although genius is inherited and passed on through undying works of art and knowledge (Ludendorff 1921: 368). Hunke's ideas are an adaptation to present conditions. Rather than dwell on a single people or nation, she thinks in terms of Europe, and *Genialität* becomes a specific European thought-structure (Hunke 1987: 8). Their scheme sits on the same "heroic realist"

11.3 Mathilde Ludendorff, 1957

epistemology as that of Jünger, except that the *"amor fati"* of Nietzsche and
Jünger become the unity of natural science and religion for Ludendorff and
Hunke. The unity of natural science and religion is an expression of the fact
that "as the soul experienced" so "reason saw" (Ludendorff 1921: 9, 113).[10]
In the following sections we look at the person and thought of Ludendorff
and Hunke.

Mathilde Ludendorff (1877–1966)

Mathilde Ludendorff, born 4 October 1877, was the third daughter of a
Lutheran Minister, Dr Bernhard Spiess of Wiesbaden. In 1904 she married
the zoologist Gustav Adolf von Kemnitz (Haack 1981: 133). Two years
later she withdrew officially from the church, and in 1913 she received her
doctorate in neurology. With this science background, she criticized both
the occult and Christianity,[11] and prepared "a new religion" (Ludendorff
1921: 115).

Some years after she became widowed in 1916, Mathilde von Kemnitz
married a Major Kleine, whom she divorced in order to marry General Erich
Ludendorff (1865–1937) in 1926 (Haack 1981: 133). Erich Ludendorff was
also divorced.

Apparently, Mathilde von Kemnitz had met Ludendorff in 1923 while he
was still suffering from the defeat of the First World War. Unlike Ludendorff,

Mathilde brimmed with confidence, for according to the diary of Alfred Rosenberg, she offered herself to Hitler as *Führerin* (*Der Spiegel*, 17 February 1960: 30). While she was more right-wing than Hitler, she was a champion of gender equality (see also Payne 1995: 13; Kneller 1941: 232).

The book that made her name was *Triumph des Unsterblichkeitwillens* (Triumph of the Will to Immortality), published in 1921. This book, numerous other publications, the endorsement by Erich Ludendorff, and the organizations that Mathilde and Erich founded to disseminate their political and philosophic-religious ideas constituted Mathilde Ludendorff's science-based religion and/or worldview (Smart 1997).[12]

Because the organizational structure resembles that of the New Right today, it is worth describing. In 1925, Erich Ludendorff founded an umbrella organization called the Tannenberg League (*Tannenbergbund*) that had approximately 100,000 members (Mecklenburg 1996: 375). Its aim was to disseminate a specific metapolitics. Part of the umbrella organization was the German Volk Society (*Verein Deutschvolk*), founded in 1930. As indicated in Chapter 5, its purpose was to disseminate Mathilde Ludendorff's science-based religious views called *Gotterkenntnis*. These two organizations, which shared many ideas with National Socialism, were for that very reason prohibited in 1933 (Haack 1981: 139). The Ludendorff publishing house survived. What also survived is the pattern of combining "elitist" metapolitics with subliminal common-folk organicist spirituality.

In 1937, following a new rapprochement between Hitler and Ludendorff, the latter founded the Society for German God-knowledge (*Verein Deutsche Gotterkenntnis*). Its members were Mathilde's followers. Between 1945 and 1951 it was dormant, only to be reactivated under the new name of League for God-cognition (*Bund für Gotterkenntnis*). It had about 12,000 members when the Bavarian Administrative Court prohibited its existence in 1961 (Mecklenburg 1996: 374). As is done today, the court judged the organization to be hostile to the constitution (*verfassungsfeindlich*). The essential ideas of Mathilde's *Gotterkenntnis*, however, live on in the *Unitarier* of Sigrid Hunke.[13]

The *Bund für Gotterkenntnis* (Mathilde Ludendorff)

If a people [*Volk*] wants to be true to itself, it needs some unity [*Geschlossenheit*], otherwise the armed forces have no support.

This unity is achieved through the people's construction of their life which my wife's knowledge is bringing about. Her teachings unify race-inheritance [*Rasseerbgut*], belief, justice, culture and economy, and bring these into harmony [*Einklang*] with the findings of the natural sciences. It firmly roots the human being in his *Volk* and state and gives him freedom to experience his God (E. Ludendorff 1935).

This endorsement by Erich Ludendorff of his wife Mathilde's "findings" provided both the context and thrust of the new religion that she founded and named God-knowledge. It also guaranteed that her books would enjoy "phenomenal" sales, "rapidly approaching the million mark" (Kneller, 1941: 193 n. 40). The context was Germany's, and especially Ludendorff's, defeat in World War I and Germans' perceived denigration in Versailles. The thrust of Mathilde's religion, simultaneously metapolitical, elitist, and folk spiritual, was nothing other than the push of the extreme right to construct a new nationalism. This nationalism would be solidly rooted in the unity of all those things that make for conflict, disharmony, and factionalism. Conflicts between religion and science were resolved by basing both on the same style of thought (*gleichen Denkstil*) (Hunke 1987: 253).

Translated excerpts from Mathilde Ludendorff's book[14]

Mathilde von Kemnitz begins her religion with rhetorical questions and answers, both addressed to potential followers. "What do you want?," she asks. "Do you want sham consolation [*Scheintrost*] for your yearnings for good fortune [*Glückssehnsucht*], sham consolation for your aversion to suffering [*Leidscheu*], sham consolation for all the pain and misfortune that overcame you, or rather do you want the truth?" (M. Ludendorff 1935: 5; for similar emphasis, see Hunke 1997: 363).

"Only if you want truth, bared reality, whatever it might be, only then is there sense in listening to me. ... If you want sham consolation, it is better that you turn to a Christian or some other sort of non-Christian religion, or to any of the occult teachings ... for all of these promise good fortune before or after death, promise help for incurred injury [*Leid*], promise—and this is particularly important to many of you—that all bad deeds will be punished by God, all good ones rewarded" (M. Ludendorff 1935: 5).

Mathilde makes quite clear that her message is not for those who hanker after good fortune (*Glücksgier*) nor for those who avoid pain (*Leidscheu*) (ibid.: 6). For when she wrote her works, she claims, she only longed and asked for truth, and only researched to find reality. She left behind all her desire for good fortune and avoidance of pain. Consequently, writes Mathilde Ludendorff, her works contain only "uncovered reality" (*enthüllte Wirklichkeit*). If her works express sympathy at all, it is an unintended consequence of reality (*Tatsächlichkeit*). It is not the consequence of faith, fantasy, hope or desire (ibid.: 6). Rather, Mathilde's teachings place on the shoulders of each individual the uncomfortable responsibility for his own soul and for the fate (*Schicksal*) of his own people (*Volk*) (ibid.: 6; cf. Hauer 1938: 80). Only bared truth (*enthüllte Wahrheit*) will protect one's own people and other peoples from decline (Untergang) into degeneration (artung) (M. Ludendorff 1935: 7).

Christianity does not convince. "Natural science has replaced it. ... Furthermore, our race (ethnic-national) consciousness has become too strong to let us overlook the fact that all words of the Bible are purely Jewish or derived from Jewishness. Consequently, biblical teachings are a danger for our *Volk*" (ibid.: 8).

Her works, she claims, only give one a hold on life, suffering, and death because she recognized, in harmony with the facts, the sense of human life and the "necessity of death" (*Todesmuss*). Along with these go the sense of the imperfection (*Unvollkommenheit*) of the human soul, the sense of purity of race and maintenance of folk characteristics, the sense of freedom and its ethical (*sittliches*) limits, and, finally, the dangers that threaten the life of individuals and *Völker* (ibid.: 7–8).

She warned of the *Volk*-destructive tendencies of religion and the occult, writes Mathilde, but spared most philosophers. Excluded from the latter, however, are the Enlightenment philosophers, whose dangerous teachings about the unlimited freedom of the individual did not incorporate ethical constraints and duties to maintain the *Volk*. Consequently, *Völker* in full bloom were seriously harmed. Also harmed were peoples subjected to imperial greed and power under the guise of religion. Many of these peoples died out (ibid.: 14)—a fear also echoed by Krebs (1997).

Her works, writes Mathilde, are proof of the fact that, unlike individual human beings, *Völker* are not subject to the necessity of death (*Todesmuss*). Rather, the death of *Völker* is related to intellectual degeneration, weakening of the will to motherhood (*Mutterschaftswillen*) and consequent reduction in the number of births (M. Ludendorff 1935: 15). The will to truth (*Wille zur Wahrheit*) is a godly willing. Truth is discovered only by those who are worthy of it, because at least during the sacred hours of research they are above utilitarianism, avoidance of pain, and desire for good fortune (ibid.: 16).

Some of Ludendorff's "Basic Findings"

(a) The meaning of human life

The world-all (*Weltall*) is spiritualized (*durchseelt*) by the godly Being in all manifestations. This Being makes itself known as will, but in the human being is also self-consciously experienced.

The world-all is devoid of devils, angels and demons; it is also free of personal gods or a personal God who leads the world while outside of it (ibid.: 23). All concepts of God are nothing other than human reason gone wrong. The Being of all appearances of the world-all cannot be grasped by human reason, only its effects can be.[15]

According to Mathilde, reason is useless here. At best it does harm when it attempts to conceptualize the Being of all manifestations, as "God." The Being of manifestations is not conceivable, but it can be experienced. This experience in our soul is the only way to get to the Being of all manifestations, to the godly. One can only experience aspects of the godly in one's soul or perceive it allegorically in nature, words, deeds, and works (ibid.: 23–4).

We call the Being of all manifestations of the world-all "God" or "godliness," remembering however that this word has nothing to do with the notions of God (be it in the theistic, deistic or pantheistic sense) of other religions. Only a few peoples of the world surmised, as did the Samoans, that the becoming of the world and its life-forms was gradual, taking hundreds of thousands of years to develop (ibid.: 25). Mathilde's evolution is spiritualized. Thus, mechanical explanations of evolution based on notions of the survival of the fittest, battle for existence, or competition generally do not apply. Rather, Mathilde postulates for each rung of the developmental ladder the breakthrough of a new will, a godly will that strives toward the goal of ever greater awareness until full human consciousness is reached (ibid.: 25). One is reminded here of Nietzsche's "will to a stronger and higher existence," which played such an important role in National Socialism (Kneller 1941: 102).

(b) The meaning of Todesmuss, or the necessity of death

The necessity of death from old age was law, without exceptions, long before the arrival of human beings. To age and wither according to the laws of nature occurs only among multi-celled life forms. The necessity to die is not a later punishment, rather it is a *holy ability* (*heiliges Können*). The imperfection of human life has deep meaning.

The inevitability of death was the necessary precondition to make possible the human's godly right, as only life form of the godly aspect of the world-all, to experience, fulfill, and radiate godly volition unto present and future generations, and thus share in the godly (M. Ludendorff 1935: 28).

Every human who achieves harmony with godly volition is a unique personality who realizes a singularity of the godly experience, never before and never again to appear (ibid.: 28). But despite the multiplicity of self-conscious experiences of God, the maintenance of this unique personality into eternity, its immortality, would mean too much constricting of the godly. The human *must-die* protects the aware God-experience from such constriction. Allegorically speaking, the individual human being, who fulfilled the meaning of his/her life by the time of his/her death, is a "breath of God" (ibid.: 28).

Death from old age was the precondition of becoming human (ibid.: 29). Therefore, the necessity to die is the opposite of punishment. It is a holy ability that is in harmony with the facts uncovered by the natural sciences (ibid.: 29).

The necessity of death is the motive force behind evolution that culminated in the most aware life form, the human being (ibid.: 30). The human being, because of his/her ability to experience the fate (*Schicksal*) of necessary death,

11.4 Erich Ludendorff's pagan grave

who knows therefore his own fate long before it takes place, can through this death-knowledge receive a holy motivation to create himself. She can ennoble herself or perfect himself when s/he understands clearly that this death means vanishing for all eternity, so that the godly can only be self-consciously experienced before death.

The knowledge of the certainty of death warns the human being to use each day of his existence meaningfully. In death the self-consciousness of the human being disappears. Nothing other than a non-conscious godly volition that also lives in all material dwells in the cells of the body until these cells decay into the basic forms from which they were constructed. Before this death, however, the human being can as often and as long as he wants participate in the godly, or the immortal; he can experience "eternities" that are not subject to time. Furthermore, he can radiate his godliness-experience onto his undying *Volk*, just as he passes on his inheritance through his children to future generations. ... The human being dies for the sake of his sublime office, aware of *experiencing* immortality; immortal, however, *is* his *Volk* (ibid.: 33; see also Kneller 1941: 56, 57).

Völker are immortal.[16] They can, however, be exterminated by the enemy through war, or they can die from the known signs of a *Volk*'s disease, namely, the disappearance of the joy of motherhood. Other religions teach the opposite, namely that the individual is immortal among mortal *Völker*.

And now her fierce anti-Semitism is expressed fully, for she writes: "The imperialistic hegemonic goals of Jewish confessions (Mosaism, Mohammed-anism, and Christianity) believe only in the immortality of the 'chosen *Volk*,' all others were subject to extermination" (M. Ludendorff 1935: 33).

In sum, the core elements of Ludendorff's truth-only religion consist of an effort to strip life of all (false) religions and occult teachings. Judeo-Christianity, other religions, and the occult block the will and therefore destroy the *Volk*. Without the "*will* to truth and freedom," on one hand, and the "*must* to face death and inevitabilities," on the other, the purity and maintenance of the race and *Volk* is impossible. Necessary death and human imperfectability are the godly preconditions that *will* human beings to radiate godly volition unto present and future generations. Finally, Luden-dorff's religion distinguishes between *experiencing* (godliness and eternity) and *being* (mortal and imperfect).

Sigrid Hunke (1913–1999)

Sigrid Hunke was born on 26 April 1913. She studied philosophy, psychology, and science of religion with Martin Heidegger, Eduard Spranger, Karlfried Graf Dürckheim, Ludwig Ferdinand Clauss and Hermann Mandel. It will be remembered that the last two were closely associated with Hauer. In 1941, she received her PhD under the supervision of Clauss in the philosophical faculty at the University of Berlin (now Humboldt University) (Kratz 1994: 134). According to Kratz (ibid.), Clauss was then an SS race psychologist, and Hunke toed the party line in her dissertation. Hunke became a main ideologue of the Religious Community of German Unitarians (DUR), and the DUR still referred positively to the work of Ludwig Ferdinand Clauss into the 1980s (ibid.; cf. Hauer 1938: 70). The DUR was founded in 1950.[17] It has its headquarters in Hamburg, and has about 2,600 followers (Mecklenburg 1996: 378).[18]

In 1942 Hunke married the diplomat Peter H. Schulze, with whom she lived in Tangier until 1944 (Mecklenburg 1996: 474). She became a member of DUR in the 1950s. In the 1960s she wrote two significant books: (1) the bestseller *Allah's Sun Over the Occident* (*Allahs Sonne über dem Abendland*, 1960) and (2) *Europe's Other Religion* (*Europas andere Religion*, 1969). Her life in Tangier and her government-sponsored travels through several Arabic countries in 1967 crystallized her biases for, and notions of, a distinc-tive thought-structure or pattern of thought (*Denkstruktur*) of Europeans and Arabs, as against Orientals, including Greeks. The path is clear for a European religion that acknowledges its debt to medieval Arabic scholars but is irreconcilably opposed to the Judeo-Christian tradition also known as Orientalism (Hunke 1969; 1987).

Like most prominent fascist and New Right thinkers who anticipate becoming ancestors in the cult of ancestral veneration—the Ludendorffs, for example—Hunke helped found the Sigrid Hunke Society (*Sigrid-Hunke-*

Gesellschaft) in 1982. From 1971 to 1983 she was the vice president, and from 1985 to 1988 she was honorary president of DUR (Mecklenburg 1996: 378). During this time two further books that define the worldview of the *Unitarier* were published by her: (1) *Dialectical Unitarianism* (*Der dialektische Unitarismus*, 1982) cited in Mecklenburg (1996: 474) and (2) *Europe's Own Religion* (*Europas eigene Religion*, 1997).

Despite the fact that Hunke is connected with the elitist Thule Seminar[19] and with G.R.E.C.E., Hunke was honored with the Schiller prize for "German cultural works in the European Spirit." In 1988, she received the highest distinction for science and art from the Egyptian President Mubarak and became the only woman and only European to sit in the highest Council for matters concerning Islam.

In 1989, she left DUR to join a related body named League of German Unitarians (BDU). That same year, she also published the book entitled *From the decline of the West to the rise of Europe* (*Vom Untergang des Abendlandes zum Aufgang Europas*). As chief ideologue of DUR (and Thule), Hunke influenced deeply the ideological development of the New Right. Such New Right gurus as Alain de Benoist (*Heide sein*, Being Pagan, 1982) and Pierre Krebs (*Das Unvergängliche Erbe*, Undying Heritage, 1981a), both French by birth, are heavily indebted to the thought of Sigrid Hunke (interview with Pierre Krebs, summer 1997).

Deutsche Unitarier: their self-portrayal

On the Internet,[20] the German Unitarians describe themselves as a community of people on the move who do not have their beliefs anchored in any religious dogma. The echo of Hauer is obvious. Their central idea is that the source of personal religious truth is buried within the individual.[21] In the preamble of their basic ideas, the central notion is formulated as the "maintenance of the freedom to one's personal viewpoint." The Unitarian community stands on the common conviction that each human being has the capacity for religious independence.

To Unitarians, religion refers to experiencing, in a self-aware fashion, meaningful connections, and structuring one's own life so that it is fraught with meaning. Subject to ever-new discoveries, Unitarianism is the way to protect life from resignation. It begins with the religious conviction that there is security in the unity of all being, which is held together by the same numinous power that holds together personal unity.

For its development, religion requires loving encouragement and carefully directed challenges in a trustworthy environment. This is the reason why Unitarians need a religious community. Unitarian religion is therefore at once a religion of self-responsibility as well as a religion of mutual communication and understanding. It lives through personal responsibility, through responsibility for fellow human beings and for their environment.

Unitarianism is a demanding religion. It is not a comfortable religion (cf. M. Ludendorff 1935). No one is relieved of thinking for him- or herself. According to their self-description, Unitarianism demands and promotes thinking with, or with-thinking (*mitdenken*), and acting responsibly. Unitarians do not missionize; they convince.

As Unitarians have no dogma, they formulate common basic ideas and inform themselves of newly developed common insights on a continuous basis. They take into account actual developments, without creating conflicts between personal religious views and results of scientific research. According to Unitarians, no religion can claim that it alone has a hold on absolute and valid truth, for the source of religion lies within the (subconscious of the) human being. As with fascism generally, so religion too must grow naturally out of the human subconscious if it is to be the vital force of the national or European organism. It cannot admit any "absolute and universal moral norms: truth, justice, and law exist only in order to serve the needs of the collectivity" (Sternhell 1994: 10; Payne 1995).

Even in the knowledge of life's contradictions and harshness, Unitarians honor life. The diversity of human appearances, rather than uniformity, means wealth. Efforts to contain this multiplicity are opposed. The death of individual beings is a necessary precondition for the development of multiplicity (cf. M. Ludendorff 1935). The human being is one of the appearances of nature and thus is part of the evolution of life. He is an inseparable whole. Physically, spiritually, and intellectually humans develop in reciprocal play with their environment. Consequently, they have a right to their differences.

As the human being has the capacity to recognize and assess complex interrelationships, she is fully responsible for her behavior vis-à-vis her environment and herself. In all that she decides or that happens to her are found opportunities for development and possibilities of danger. Strengths and weaknesses, strokes of fate and guilty entanglements require her to grapple and come to terms with them.

Death ends life. Beyond death there is no certainty. This knowledge strengthens humans to live conscious and fulfilled lives. Each human being leaves his footprints behind and these outlast death.

The thought of Sigrid Hunke

Sigrid Hunke's thought, and the above self-description is an aspect of it, is but a variation and current version not only of Mathilde Ludendorff but importantly also of J. W. Hauer (1938: 64). What makes it current are some shifts in terminology; for example, away from Ludendorff's "a people's soul" (*Volksseele*) and Hauer's "West-Indo-Germans" (*Westindogermanen*), culture circle (*Kulturkreis*), or the intellectual history specific to the West-Indo-Germanic pattern of thought (*die artbestimmte Linie der westindogermanischen Geistesgeschichte*) (ibid.: 64) to European thought-structure (*europäische Denkstruktur*) or style of thought (*Denkstil*). Hunke's thought is similar in that Hunke, like Hauer who called it West-Indo-Germanic, traces a specifically European thought-structure (*spezifisch "europäischen" Denkstruktur*) (Hunke 1987: 8; 1969). Hunke finds this thought-lineage represented by Europe's heretics, who include: Pelagius, Johannes Scotus Eriugena, Gottschalk der Sachse, Hugo von St. Viktor, Francis of Assisi, and especially Meister Eckhart, Seuse, Tauler, and also Nikolaus Cusanus, Hans Denck, Sebastian Franck, Kaspar von Schwenckfeld, Valentin Weigel, Jakob Böhme, Paracelsus, George Fox, Johann Scheffler (Angelus Silesius), Franz von Baader and, finally, Schleiermacher, Novalis, Hölderlin, Goethe, Fichte, Hegel, Schelling, Rilke, even Teilhard de Chardin (Hunke 1969: 12). While her speculations resemble those of Houston Stewart Chamberlain, he is not mentioned.

Hauer and Hunke see the occurrence of a major separation in the early Middle Ages between, in the case of Hauer, West-Indo-Germanic thought-pattern (*westindogermanisches Denken*) and Christianity; in the case of Hunke, European thought-pattern (*europäisches Denken*) and Christianity (see also Krebs 1981b: 28). This parting of the way of two discrete thought-structures is linked, in the first instance, to the figure of Scotus Eriugena (Hauer 1938: 64–5; Hunke 1969: 134–7). In the early Middle Ages, writes Hauer (ibid.), we see a separation from Christianity of the west-Indo-Germanic history of thought (*Geistesgeschichte*) (Steuckers 1990: 68), as shown by the strongly characteristic line of thought that began with Scotus Eriugena in the ninth century. It was carried forward and developed independently by German mystics, humanism, and the Renaissance. Just such an independent line of thought, what Hunke calls an underground religion, centered primarily on "European" heretics, including, as we saw, Pelagius before and Eckhart after Eriugena, is the essence of Hunke's "other religion." While there were mutual influences between Christianity and Europe's other religion through the centuries, the absolute separation between them occurred with Nietzsche (Hauer 1938: 65; see also Kneller 1941: 102–3).

There are some other minor differences in the thinking of Hauer and Hunke. For example, Hauer thought in terms of culture circles (*Kulturkreise*) that were linked to specific epochs, each of which was penetrated by one major idea. Thus the Enlightenment period was consumed by the idea of autonomous reason, Idealism by the creative "I" (*das schaffende Ich*), Romanticism by the creative foundations of life (*schöpferische Lebensgründe*), the following epoch by the idea of natural law, and the current epoch (1930) by race (Hauer 1938: 65). Hunke's take, heeding current developments, is simpler. She argues that the same major idea, namely unity (*Einheit*), characterized "Europe's Own Religion" (1997) from its inception. It made a stark and unbridgeable contrast with the dualism of Christianity.

Conclusion

After denazification Hauer was contacted by the German Unitarians. One of their ministers, R. Stark, wrote Hauer that the German Unitarian Community was the only religious movement at the time that was rooted in the *völkisch* ground and expressed it in a manner relevant to the time.[22] Hauer received many letters from Unitarians affirming his influence on them. Otto Meyer, who built the German Unitarian Youth League (*Bund Deutscher Unitarischer Jugend*) in 1956 reminded Hauer that they first met in the *Köngener Bund* in 1921.[23] Hauer did not, of course, join the German Unitarians, because in 1956 he founded his own organization called the Free Academy (*Freie Akademie*), but they cooperated.[24] The Free Academy still functions today.

Conclusion

If there is one theme that emerges clearly from this study, it is that National Socialism was a national revolutionary movement determined to rid Germany of Jewish Christianity—in fact, of everything that reminded the Occident of the Oriental Jewish *Geist*. But of course Hauer's, Günther's and Grimm's primary motives were to usher in a holy new society that respected and groomed its race-specific biological and cultural heritage. To bring this about, to reverse the Spenglerian decline, they needed a race-specific religion. It was a form of paganism called German Faith. For Grimm, who was more comfortable with finding religion in poetics, his friend Moeller van den Bruck's notion of the Third Reich became the religious hope of salvation from the grinding needs of Germans during the Versailles era.

The turning point from the Old Right to what today is called, for lack of a better term, the New Right came in 1936. In April of that year Hauer was deposed as leader of the German Faith Movement. In his despair and still singing the tired radical song, namely, that the *Deutsche Christen* were raping the German *Volk* in the name of National Socialism, he appealed to Günther for help. Having never compromised his elitism, Günther gave Hauer the following advice: Leave radicalism to the young radicals, place your focus where it once was on the sophisticated segment of society, and find a new form for a truly free German Faith.[1] This is the insight that informs the strategy of the New Right today. The thinking elite, having rehabilitated the ideas and language of Hauer and his cohorts, work out their metapolitical program on a religious pagan foundation, while young radicals in national revolutionary parties, such as the NPD, do the work of radicalism.

It is fair to say, therefore, that in Germany as well as France neo-paganism was and is the heart of fascism and the New Right. It constitutes a radical criticism and rejection of Jewish-Christianity. It rejects Christianity for its imperialism (M. Ludendorff 1935), its radical judgments, its totalitarianism, its privileging of the sense of incurred injury (*Leid*) (ibid.; Hunke 1997: 33), its linear history, its denigration of woman and humanity, and its source in the culture of the *Hurriter* (Jews) (Hunke 1997: 31–3). One has to be blind not to see anti-Semitism here. Hunke's "sense of incurred injury" points directly at Neo-pagan impatience with the Holocaust. Memory culture, Jewish versus German, Holocaust versus civilian bombing is one of the footballs being kicked around the political arena defined by the pagan New Right and its loosely affiliated national-revolutionary parties.

European neo-paganism sees itself as the restorer of all that it claims Christianity removed from European life and thought, that is, human godliness, the seamless unity of religion and science, and the harmony of human beings with the environment. To neo-pagans, human beings are the measure of all things. There is no single God, any more than there is one truth, nor one humanity (de Benoist 1982: 107). The unnatural things (*Unnatur*) that burn in the soul of the *Hurriter* (Jews), the valley of suffering (*Jammertal*) from which they emerged and into which they turned the world, is rejected (Hunke 1997: 31, 32). And this rejection and the affirmation of unity Hunke finds in European heretics through the ages. This specific European structure of thought was Europe's other religion and is now its own.

Like Mohler and Vermeil, Kratz (1994) argues that not only the gods of neo-paganism, but also those of the (European) New Age are Nazi brown. The spiritual movement centred on godliness in harmony with nature and the cosmos, working in and through all things human, is today called New Age. In the twenties it was called the *völkisch* movement (*völkische Bewegung*) (ibid.: 8). For leftists and liberals, he argues, all this falls within the rubric of a constitutionally guaranteed freedom of religion, and this informs how we conduct our research. Fascists, by contrast, saw and see in this constitutional guarantee an opportunity to perpetuate their ideology for the most part at a metapolitical level (ibid.). Paganism is liked not only for its rituals and romanticism about nature but because it is a religion of *Verharmlosung*.[2] There are no sharp morals and no sharp contrasts, just one's own origins, heritage, nature, and landscape. And to the extent that renewal is necessary, it is achieved only by means of "one's own tradition."[3] The word "own" refers to what Hauer called *Volk* and what Hunke calls Europe.

The intellectual quarrel over whether or not New Age and neo-paganism are politically Left or Right, Green or Brown, also applies to National Socialism. The issue was first raised by Ernst Nolte (1966), who suggested that "racist anti-Semitism" which was "joined with a bias against the upper classes was rather a revolutionary provocation of this Right, and therefore essentially Left" (ibid.: 290).

While Nolte minimizes the importance of anti-Semitism to National Socialism and the New Right today, he partially corrects the general assumption that National Socialism was solely an extreme Right phenomenon. Even Haffner (2001b) did not buy that. He surmised that National Socialism was an extreme Left movement that, with the monarchy removed after World War I, took over Old Right ideas about aristocracy and hierarchy and, using Left methods, transformed them into revolutionary tools. For National

Socialists, aristocracy had nothing to do with the aristocracy of old. Their notion of aristocracy did not come from the Right but from the Left. With it they created a meritocracy that valued simultaneously hierarchy and comradeship as exemplified by the SS.

To Günther and Hauer, aristocracy meant *deutsch*-Germanic peoples who were becoming aware of being rooted in Indo-Germanic traditions and having the responsibility to groom their Nordic cultural and biological heritage. Using the Darwinian notion of natural selection, Günther advocated eugenics and social engineering (1930). Natural selection meant cultivating deliberately new cultural and social arrangements. Above all, Günther was clear from the beginning that the aim was the total separation of Jews from non-Jews and vice versa. With the Zionist dream of removing Jews to Palestine, anti-Semitism would disappear (ibid.: 345).

Of course it has not disappeared, and in Europe it cannot disappear so long as the New Right and its pagan base choose, in rehabilitated form, to play off against one another two irreconcilable worldviews (Krebs 1990), namely, Western representative democracy rooted in Christianity against European national democracy rooted in paganism. According to Hunke, the latter would not be a Hitler state. It would, however, be a Europe that acknowledged its roots in the notion of *Reich* (Hunke n.d.). The idea of the New Right and of leaders of national-revolutionary parties, such as the NPD leader Udo Voigt, is to oppose US imperialism and internationalism with a national Europe (that is, a Europe made of many specific nations, cultures, and religions without assimilation).

The European New Right is small, its pagan base generic. But in a world replete with conflict I cannot quite share Ernst Nolte's complacency about them when he writes that they "tend to do little more than try to correct certain exaggerations of Allied war propaganda" (1966: 303). What they are trying to correct has growth potential. My feeling is that what makes new religious phenomena harmless is their constitutionally guaranteed freedom, which takes the teeth out of any fanaticism. While the constitutions of western liberal democracies preserve the freedom of new religions, I am not sure whether new religions, including New Age and neo-paganism, preserve western liberal democracies. In Weimar they did not.

Notes

1 Introduction

1 *Völkisch* is the adjective derived from *Volk*. A *völkisch* worldview puts priority on group and personality above the individual and individualism. (Individuals subscribing to such a worldview could be described as *völkisch*.) Analogous to an individual, the group is a biological entity made up of a distinct racial, cultural, and intellectual substance. *Völkisch* writers translated this predilection into a very specific notion of nation. To them, a *völkisch* nation is to the democratic state as National Socialism is to liberalism. If democracy is made up of a state, an independent legislature, and the separation of state from church, then a *völkisch* nation is made up of a *Volksgemeinschaft* (a community of one people), a worldview-oriented police with law based on provisional measures, and the fusion of politics and religion. Such a political police defines its enemy from the *völkisch* perspective, meaning that it is focused on the racial integrity of the *Volks*body. Rather than being bound by the legal norms of the democratic state, the politicized arms of a *völkisch* nation are free to take arbitrary actions so long as these are responsible to the worldview that is expressed in the will of a brilliant personality.

2 A brilliant but controversial work on the nature of political religion is of course that of Eric Voegelin. It is discussed by Kraus (1997). In 1938, by now in America, Voegelin argued that the roots of a political religion were phenomena such as National Socialism.

3 *Geheimwissenschaft*: literally "secret science."

4 *Ergriffenheit* conveys the sense of being in the grasp of the godly or of the hidden original source of all being (Hauer 1922b: 50).

5 Originally published in 1938.

6 As determined by destiny (*Geschick*). The meaning of this concept is made especially clear by Heidegger who, according to Bambach (2003: 20), meant by it "the gathering together (*Ge-*) of the historical possibilities that the tradition has sent (*schicken*) to a community, possibilities that must constantly be worked out in and through a confrontations with their historical roots." For Hauer these historical roots included especially idealist philosophers and German heretics through the centuries. This notion is not all that different from Heidegger when he argues that the Volk (*Dasein*) can only become authentically what it is by struggling "to retrieve its roots (in history, language, and landscape)" (ibid.).

7 See also the letter of August Winnig to Hans Grimm, 18 September 1932, where Winnig announces that the Weimar system, the hegemony of the left, is broken: "... Nothing could be saved nor was the movement stoppable. A historical

necessity was executed" (A: Grimm, Briefe von August Winnig an H. Grimm, DLA, Marbach). The same hopelessness about events in 1932 and the expected ill fate of the national Right is also expressed in letters by Alfred Hugenberg (1865–1951) to H. Grimm 30 March 1932. Hugenberg was the media giant and leader of the DNVP. He favored an authoritarian regime. (A: Grimm, Alfred Hugenberg to Grimm 1930–1941, DLA, Marbach).

8 *Volksgemeinschaft* is what Schmitt, using more academically neutral language, described as a state based on *Artgleichheit* and *Führertum* (Schmitt 1933: 32).

9 I have also seen the date of Wüst's birth given as 1901.

10 For example, in his letter to Trautner, 23 April 1934, Hauer mentions that he had an important meeting about German Faith instruction with *Reichs-SS-Führer* Himmler (N1131 61, p. 366, BAK). I also thank Horst Junginger for pointing me to some 1939–1940 Himmler–Hauer correspondence then archived with the *Abteilung für Religionswissenschaft* at the University of Tübingen.

11 To Hauer Christianity was Jewish. As a form of Jewish imperialism, it was contrary and harmful to German thought and ways.

12 The research institute of the SS.

13 Klagges was inspired by Houston Stewart Chamberlain (1855–1927), who in turn was inspired by the religious studies scholar and orientalist Julius Wellhausen (Germann 1995: 29, 32, 37) To make his freethinking acceptable, Klagges also drew on the works of such philologists as Lachmann, Wilke, Weisse, and Holtzmann (ibid.: 36–7).

14 The word *artgemäss* is no longer found in ordinary German dictionaries because it was a Nazi expression. It means that it is characteristic and compatible with a specific race or ethnic group, here German.

15 *Bund* (pl. *Bünde*) is not easily translated into English. Crossmann, who wrote the Introduction to Laqueur's classic book and who himself experienced the German Youth Movement, wrote that the "*Bund* is neither a bond nor an association, but a nation wide (youth) organization consisting of local groups with a fairly strict discipline" and an emphasis on "collective life, on leadership and service" (see Crossmann in Laqueur 1962: xiv).

16 Letter from Lene Rukwied to Hauer, n.d. (thought to be 1925); N1131 10, pages 230–2, BAK.

17 Hans Endres, 1938, "*Der Erlösungsgedanke bei Nietzsche,*" *Deutscher Glaube,* 6: 303–7.

18 See Golomb 2004: 171. If Nietzsche appealed mainly to individuals, as Golomb claims, why was he a phenomenon in Zionism, National Socialism, and Italian fascism? Sadly, Aschheim's (1992) critique is not taken seriously enough.

19 During the war around 1942, some Nazi anthropologists made it their goal to define especially the psychological boundaries among races. Assuming Europe to be racially mixed, they made it their task to socially engineer selection in favor of Nordic elements. To that end, anything originating from the Near East or even Inner Asia, traditions that were once heralded as destroying Christianity, were now interpreted as being related to Christianity and intent on destroying Nordic Europe. Nazi anthropologists Günther, Clauss, and especially Bruno Beger of *Ahnenerbe-SS*, described "Near Asian Jewry" as the main enemy that was seriously corroding Europe. But they were not alone. Rather, they brought with them the combined weapons of Christianity, Islam, and now even Tibetan Lamaism. Carried by Jews, Lamaism influenced freemasons, Catholic rites, and Bolshevism. Beger saw its traits, those of immoderation and mercilessness, in Stalin (R 135/66 165976, BAB).

2 An overview

1 According to Hexham and Poewe (1986: xi; 1997) new religions are based on a framework that consists of primal experiences, new mythologies, and aspects of the great Yogic and Abrahamic traditions. Hauer's DGB falls within this framework although the Abrahamic tradition is violently opposed at the same time that he sees his religion as having emerged from it. Mathilde Ludendorff, founder of *Gotterkenntnis* and a major competitor in the religious-philosophical market place of Weimar, attacked the Yogic elements in Hauer's religion (Ludendorff 1933: 50–4). The concept "new religion" is sociological in nature and is here used independently of whether or not Hauer liked it. At times he denied having founded a religion, at other times he did not.

2 German scholars prefer to call their discipline "science of religion" and "history of religion" instead of "religious studies"; this because the latter gives no hint of the methods used by scholars in their research of religion.

3 The words quoted are from the translators' introduction to Hauer *et al.* (1937). Scott-Craig sent Hauer a letter dated 20 March 1937 informing him that the book "Germany's New Religion has just appeared on this side of the Atlantic, and I have already had letters of appreciation from those who had previously no idea of what the Glaubensbewegung really stood for." Apparently, Scott-Craig and his colleague had received permission from Hauer "to translate certain selections from your works and print them along with the replies of Professors Heim and Adam."

4 See also the correspondence between Hauer and Dr Erika Emmerich (30 November 1933 and 5 December 1933, N1131 56, BAK).

5 "November Revolution" (Hauer 1935: 10) is a derogatory term used by the nationalistic and national socialistic Right to refer to those who agreed to the armistice of 11 November 1918 and therefore were accused of having ushered in the much-hated Republic. In the early 1920s already Hitler called the political leaders of the Weimar Republic "November criminals" (Benz *et al.* 1997: 617).

6 *Köngener* comes from the name of the castle *Köngen* by the Neckar River where the *Bund* was founded. Even as professor, Hauer was a cult figure. His followers called him Chancellor (*Kanzler*) and addressed him with the informal *Du*. Also in the 1920s, words like *Heil* and *Führer* were used in the Hauer correspondence.

7 Heinrich (2002: 158–9), following Dierks, sees Hauer's 1935 biographical sketches as having an ideological coloring, which, if removed, shows Hauer as Christian rather than *völkisch* in the 1920s. In other words, Heinrich tries to highlight the Christian element in the *Köngener Bund* mix at the expense of its *völkisch* leanings. Furthermore, like Junginger, Heinrich ignores Hauer's correspondence and involvement with other Youth Movement leaders and thereby misses his German Faith and political development. At any rate, Hauer quarreled with the leader of the *Köngener Bund*, Rudi Daur, and found his continued links with Christianity disappointing.

8 The organization was first known as the ADGB. A year later, in 1934, it became simply the DGB.

9 His journal is called *Deutscher Glaube*.

10 See *Darmstädter Echo*, Tuesday, 15 August 2000, 14.

11 Hans Grimm was a German nationalist and a onetime businessman in South Africa and Namibia, whose South African novels (1913) and his political novel *A People Without Space* (*Volk ohne Raum*) (1926), although written before and during Weimar, became bestsellers during the Nazi era. The book title became a Nazi slogan, and paperback versions were sent to frontline soldiers. Throughout the Nazi era Grimm organized Conferences for Poets and Writers. These conferences took on special meaning after the war because they gave the Old Right a voice and a means of transforming itself into the New Right (see Poewe 1999).

12 A: Grimm, letters from Grimm to Dierks, 1951–1959, DLA, Marbach.
13 Hans Baumann (1914–1988) was a German author of children's and youth literature, a dramatist, and a songwriter, whose songs became popular with the Hitler
   Youth, to which he belonged. After the war he became embroiled in a controversy
   when one of his dramas, deliberately submitted under a pseudonym, won a prize
   that he had to forfeit upon revelation of his Nazi past. By mentioning him, Dierks
   intends to underline the point that past Nazi affiliation must be kept separate
   from authors' works. Some think Baumann distanced himself from National
   Socialism upon return from Russian imprisonment; others see Nazism encoded in
   some of his children's books.
14 There are two PhD theses on Hauer; one in Hebrew by Shaul Baumann, the other
   in Japanese by Hiroshi Kubota (personal communication, Shaul Baumann, 16
   November 1999). These scholars look at Hauer in relationship to the ADGB,
   which he co-founded with Graf Ernst zu Reventlow in the thirties.
15 Hauer to Mande, 25 February 1931, N1131 13, Doc 205, BAK.
16 Some intellectual Nazis associated liberal and liberal theology (also called the
   "free direction of theology," "radicalism," or "comparative history of religion")
   with radical breakthrough (von Leers 1938). This "liberal" experience was
   German but mislabeled by its enemies. Other Nazis, however, associated liberalism with mercenary individualism, the ideas of the French Revolution, and
   above all with Jews who "dominated German economic and intellectual life
   between 1918 and 1933" to the detriment of *völkisch* ways (Frenssen 1941: 233).
   As such, liberalism became part of four major foreign ideas from which
   "Germany" supposedly suffered: Christianity, French liberalism, Jewish liberalism (Weimar), and Communism. The *völkisch* writer Frenssen, and not just he,
   called these Semitic, Roman, French, American, and Russian ideas foreign and
   therefore a danger to the German *Volksseele* (ibid.: 232–4).
17 It is not too far-fetched to hypothesize that the radical liberal forces of a mori-
   bund democracy, which is what Weimar was, were as ready and willing to
   produce an authoritarian dictatorship, one that would restore pride and undo
   humiliation, as was the radical Right (see Gregor 2000: 5). One is reminded of
   Russia's Vladimir Zhirinovsky, among others (ibid.: 114).
18 Hauer's correspondence shows some contact with Gregor Strasser (1892–1934),
   who, at the time that Goebbels worked for him, was for a *"deutschen Sozialismus"*
   (Reuth 2000: 86, 90). By contrast, Gregor's brother Otto Strasser (1897–1974)
   was once a member of the SPD. Already in 1925, however, he became a member of
   the NSDAP and led the *Kampf-Verlag*, a small publishing firm founded by his
   brother. After a furor with Hitler, Otto left the NSDAP. Thereupon Gregor
   distanced himself from Otto, swore loyalty to Hitler, and became the national
   organizing leader of the NSDAP (*Reichsorganisationsleiter*). He fell out with Hitler
   in 1932 over Schleicher's invitation to make him Vice-Chancellor in Schleicher's
   cabinet, and was murdered during the *Röhm Putsch* in 1934.
19 In a letter to Paul Zapp, 26 June 1933 (N1131 16, Doc 223, BAK), when Hauer
   thought of writing a pamphlet (which captured Hitler's sentiment) entitled *A Christian or a German State*, Hauer instructed Zapp to contact various people in Berlin.
   They included Gregor Strasser (1892–1934) and, importantly, the co-founder of
   the ADGB, Ernst Graf zu Reventlow (1869–1943). A fanatical National Socialist,
   Reventlow was the founding editor of the *Reichswart*, a severe critic of the Weimar
   Republic, and a defender of Equal Rights for German non-Christians (Scholder
   1988: 451). Like Goebbels, as said, Reventlow too was sympathetic toward
   Strasser's view of German socialism but then shifted to Hitler's position and
   became a member of the *Reichstag* for the National Socialist party.

20 See the very different view of Scholder (1988: 453, 488, 526), who acknowledges the DGB's growth, its attraction of important Nazi officials and especially Nazi youths, and its serious rivalry with the *Deutsche Christen.* "The training leader of the National Socialist German Student Union, Dr von Leers, was a member of the *Führerrat* of Hauer's DGB," among others (Scholder 1988: 526).

21 Hauer to Zapp, 26 June 1933, N1131 16, Doc 223, BAK. See also Kater 2001: 17 and Reuth 2000.

22 Haffner (2001a: 195–214) argues that the relationship between liberalism and National Socialism is a "radical nihilism that equally denies all values be they capitalistic, a matter of civil rights, or proletarian ..."

23 Hauer to Best, 9 March 1934, N1131 66, Doc 52, BAK.

24 Common German notion also thought by one of the most prominent leaders of the conservative party Julius Stahl (1802–1861). Stahl had Jewish parents but embraced Christianity. He distinguished between political parties that embraced revolution and those that embraced legitimacy. He preferred the latter. The former included Liberals who he thought, because of their inner instability, prepared the way for socialism and their own destruction. He preferred the state to be founded on God not the will of human beings.

25 The German Christians were the radical branch of Christianity. Many rejected the Old Testament, Paul's teachings, and so on, because they were Jewish. Their aim was to unite Christianity with National Socialism, turning it into a "positive Christianity" as per Article 24 of the NSDAP Party Program. While the German Christians became a popular phenomenon in the 1930s, the idea is older. Ernst Moritz Arndt (1769–1860) talked about *deutsches Christentum* und *eine deutsche Kirche* (German Church) in 1815. The prophet of German Faith is Paul Anton de Lagarde (real name Paul Anton Bötticher) and later Arthur Bonus (1864–1941) (Meyer 1915: 182–4). In his poetry, Lagarde presented his German Faith as a "*Wodankult*" (ibid.: 183).

26 Hauer, *Aus der Front der Gegner und Kompromissler*, 1 October 1934, Berlin. N1131 63, Doc 105, BAK.

27 Hauer *Aus der Front der Gegner und Kompromissler*, 1 October 1934, Berlin. Doc 106, BAK. See also Gloege (1934a: 393–415; 1934b: 464–505) and Hutten (1934: 510–33), who discuss the liberal theological origins of the *deutsch-germanisch* religions and worldviews and Rosenberg's liberalism in *völkisch* garb (1930: 105). Walter Künneth, who edited the volume with chapters by Gloege and Hutten, was a controversial Protestant theologian (in our view a liberal one) who initially approved of National Socialism then turned to criticizing it.

28 Called *SS-Führerpersonalakten.*

29 Hauer, *Aus der Front der Gegner und Kompromissler*, 1 October 1934, Berlin. 27 March 1936, N1131 62, Doc 128, BAK.

30 Hauer, *Aus der Front der Gegner und Kompromissler*, 1 October 1934, Berlin. 27 March 1936, N1131 62, Doc 128, BAK.

31 Albert Speer (1969: 39) too mentioned the cooperative role of the civil servants who simply carried on under Hitler and in a sense helped him succeed.

32 Nanko (1993) looked at 545 DGB members (between 1933 and 1935) for whom he could find relevant data.

33 After World War II, Ackerknecht became director of the Schiller National Museum in Marbach, of which the DLA is a part. (A: Grimm, Ackerknecht to Grimm, 1919, 1925, 1933-35, DLA)

34 Frobenius (1921: 4) writes that, being a natural scientist, he used the term "*drittes Reich*" in 1898 to add a third category, culture, to the notions of organic and

inorganic nature. Nature was therefore organic, cultural, and inorganic. Thus culture is not created by human beings but "lives on them" or "lives through them" (ibid.: 4). "The organic life of the third Reich (culture)," which is "carried by" human beings, this nature-based cultural life, is accessible by our "living intuition" (ibid.: 6–7). One sees even here some foundational elements of National Socialism with, however, this difference. Frobenius considered the Orient and the Occident (the space-paideuma and the cave-paideuma) as *Ur*-phenomena that "fertilized" one another, that were complementary rather than antagonistic (ibid.: 99), hence no hostility toward Jews.

35 See the von Leers files, N2168, 2, 3, 25 in BAB.

36 Reventlow, the editor of *Reichswart* and co-founder of the ADGB, mentioned that about 2½ million people declared themselves to be followers in 1935. In that year too, the movement referred to itself as a "movement of millions" (*Millionen-bewegung*) (Bartsch 1938: 68). A large membership increase occurred after the Sport Palace meeting in Berlin, 26 April 1935. Because the crowd filled the Sport Palace even after its 20,000 seats were occupied, it had to be closed by the police. Apparently vigorous propaganda preceded the meeting, with as many as 90 talks per month being given all over Germany (ibid.: 68).

37 Von Leers, N2168 9, *Gustav Frenssen wird 75 Jahre alt*, BAB, also von Leers about Hölderlin and others (ibid.).

38 Letter dated 13 January 1937 from *SS Obersturmführer* to *Brigadeführer*, in von Leers files, N2168 2, BAB.

39 20 November 1933, N1131 56, Doc 106, BAK.

40 N1131 55, Doc 30, BAK.

41 19 December 1933, N1131 55, Doc 29, BAK.

42 19 December 1933, N1131 55, Doc 29, BAK.

43 One can only speculate whether the pietistic environment had any influence on Hauer other than to reject it. It may be, however, that his interest in religious experiences, mysticism, visions, religious eclecticism, Swedenborgian theosophy, an anti-church sentiment, and a preference for small intimate confidential groups may have received a first impulse here. On Hahn see Brecht (1995: 283–6). Nanko (1998: 73) claims Hauer was influenced by Hahn but gives no primary source evidence.

44 Translated as *What is Christianity?* (Harnack 1901). He also read Schleiermacher and Albrecht Ritschl.

45 Von Leers, 1938, *Gustav Frenssen wird 75 Jahre alt*, in von Leers files, N2168 9, BAB.

46 Macalpine to Hauer, 21 October 1923, 23 March 1924; illegible signature to Hauer, 10 August 1921, N1131 8, BAK. Correspondence in this file dealt primarily with the cruelty of Versailles, worthless money, the German youth movement as a turning away from militarism, and common memories.

47 For an interpretation of Plato's Theory of Forms or Ideas and the Nazis, see Popper (1963: 20–31) and Günther (1928).

48 A thesis written separately from and after the PhD, as a qualification for lecturing in a German university.

49 A Nazi term used for anything that in terms of its form, appearance, or content could be German in accordance with the usage of those days, even if its origins were foreign.

50 More than Frobenius, Hauer is interested in the notion of *Völkerwanderungen* that he relates to prehistorical *Indogermanen* (Indo-Germanics) (1923: 165–7). Hauer attempts to answer the question whether there is a historical-genetic connection between the oldest Stone Age cultures of Europe and the lowest ranks

of cultures of other parts of the world (ibid.: 164). He works with the analogy of a living tree so that the "deep levels of religious life," its roots, are uniform across all humanity. Only the highest ranks of development branch out, far above their roots, with specific characteristics represented by different races and cultures (ibid.: 162).

51 The *Bhagavad Gita* is Hindu scripture. Literally translated "The Song of the Lord," it is probably the most popular book of Hindu scripture in the West. For many modern Hindus it represents the essence of their religion, with its message that there are many ways to salvation. The Buddhist scholar Edward Conze and others, but not Hauer, have argued that the devotional tone of the *Gita* reflects the influence of Christianity and that it was probably written to counter Christian teaching.

52 See letter 5 April 1930, N1131 31, Doc 41, BAK.

53 For a similar "camouflaged" approach see Herwig's study (1999) of the geopolitician, Karl Haushofer. The latter similarly worked for the Nazis and, specifically, with Hess behind the scenes (Hipler 1996).

54 In a letter to Buber, for example, Hauer wrote "… for us, the Jewish question is a problem, for surely one cannot disagree with the fact that for example especially Jews have had a bad influence on our theater and literature. Or do you think I am wrong?" (Hauer to Buber, 18 October 1932, N1131 13, Doc 15, BAK). He makes stronger comments to Werner Best, "That cleansing the German *Volk* of Jewish elements, especially in the leading classes, was necessary forced itself upon me from year to year through my observations of academic life and of different German universities, especially, also through my observations within literature, art, and so on. I therefore made a firm effort at this university and tried already in 1929 to prevent a professor who was a baptized Christian, but was of Jewish descent, from coming here" (Hauer to Best, 9 March 34, N1131 66, Doc 55, BAK).

55 He also helped students interested in topics related to his. For example, writing a student, Emil Blum, 20 December 1930, he suggested that Blum read his work *Die Religionen*, but also Frazer, Wilhelm Wundt, Theodor Preuss, Pater Wilhelm Schmidt, Söderblom and Levy-Bruhl. (Letter, 20 December 1930, N1131, 124, Doc 350, BAK).

56 In German, *Kommende Gemeinde*.

57 Hauer to Gebser, 31 March 1932, N1131 14, BAK.

58 See letters in N1131, Band 10, BAK.

59 Letter, 1 November 1928, N1131, Band 38, BAK.

3 Hauer and the *Bünde*: becoming a National Socialist

1 See chapter 2, note 4.

2 See chapter 2, note 5.

3 See chapter 2, note 6.

4 See chapter 2, note 7.

5 See chapter 2, note 8.

6 During a seminar at the C. G. Jung Institute, Hauer spoke about Kundalini Yoga (1932c). Regarding the word *satyagraha*, he said that it is a symbol that has been adapted to political life and sets free certain powers that are working in the people; in this situation they are thus mobilized by a genius. "There is no situation for which man has not a remedy; out of some depth in humanity which we do not see, springs that helpful power" (Hauer 1932c: 65).

7 If Mohler does not want to discuss the fact that the CR was responsible for the success of National Socialism, Neurohr (1956), who first wrote his manuscript in London in 1933, does. According to him, Mohler's definition of conservatism is

untenable anyway because he excludes virtually all historical forms of conservatism except the one that has as its inner core the revolutionary idea of Nietzsche about the "eternal return" (Neurohr 1956: 11). Trying to give a voice to silenced ex-Nazi writers and scholars after 1945, Armin Mohler (1999: 63–7) singled them out as the minds behind a "Conservative Revolution" rather than National Socialism. Evidence does not support Mohler's claim (Herbert 1996; Herbert 2001; Neurohr 1956). Regarding the phrase "conservative revolution", Hauer claimed to have first coined it while applying it to himself.

 8 Geuter (1994: 17) quotes a witness of the 1920s as estimating that 30 percent of the young men had inclinations toward their own gender. A wave of sexual inversion (*Inversionswelle*) characterized the times (ibid.: 286). It is not that homosexuals came out, although that too happened; rather love toward boys and men was wrangled about and discussed (ibid.: 287). Machtan (2001: 109) quite rightly concludes, "In short, ideologically charged homosexual eroticism and sexuality were cornerstones of the fascist male-bonding culture prior to 1933."

 9 Kloppe to Hauer, 24 October 1933, N1131 57, Doc 63; 13 November 1933, N1131 57, Doc 61; all BAK.

10 Discussions about matriarchy were popular among *völkisch* thinkers and go back to Ludwig Klages (1872–1956) and Alfred Schuler's (1865–1923) popularization of Bachofen's (1815–1887) *Das Mutterrecht* (1861). These *people* were just as inclined toward Nordic and racist ideas as were National Socialists. For example, see Carola Struve (1933). She sees Bachofen and Morgan as the two pillars of a new world picture. Struve (ibid.: 150–2) criticizes "Nietzsche, the philosopher of power" for his proclamation of a "hysterical kind of *Herrenmoral*," and argues that with World War I the world became intoxicated with this "man-based amoral *Herrengeist*." Nevertheless, she sees Versailles as an attempt to deliberately destroy the German *Volk* (*völkervernichtende Agonie*), which National Socialism must stop. Likewise, P. Sophie Rogge-Börner in her book *Zurück zum Mutterrecht?* (1932) argues against Bergmann's depiction of men as amoral sex-driven nomads. Nevertheless, she sees the cause of Germany's and the West's despair as born of the "gruesome, bloodthirsty, money-grabbing spirit of the Old Testament," a spirit that wants to "devour all peoples." This spirit that she calls Liberalism is the "legitimate androcentric birth of the OT" (ibid.: 46). Her antidote to "Jewish imperialism" is heroic, Nordic, nationalistic and *völkisch* pride (ibid.: 74).

11 Hauer differed only from such desperate, fanatical PhDs as Goebbels, among others, in that Hauer had a secure position at a university. The others did not. For them it was the party or the dole.

12 Fritz Borinski and Werner Milch divide the *Jugendbewegung* (German Youth Movement) into three phases. The early *Wandervogel* years of Karl Fischer from 1896 to 1912 was the first phase. Fischer's philosophy was to "maintain the right attitude" (*Haltung*) which was to value the "new mode of life" and cast aside the old "bourgeois mode of life," meaning "the mode of life of the post-Bismarck era in Germany" (1967: 10). The second phase started with the Meissner Rally of 1913 and its formula "The Freideutsche Jugend is determined to fashion its life on its own initiative, on its own responsibility and in inner sincerity" (ibid.: 13). The poetry and philosophy of Stefan George, Rilke, Lagarde, Nietzsche, Paul Natorp, Leonhard Nelson, and Hölderlin were popular (ibid.: 14). After 1919, however, religious attitudes received emphases and youths read the *Poetic Edda*, Laozi (Lao-Tse), Master Eckhart, and Rudolf Steiner (ibid.: 20). False prophets surfaced, from Friedrich Muck-Lamberty, who was clearly influenced by Klages and like him taught "fire is spirit" (*Glut ist Geist*) and "reality was only appearance" (*Wirklichkeit ist nur Schein*), to Adolf Hitler (ibid.: 45–6, 21–2). This soon led to

the third phase, the ever-more-nationalistic *Bündische Jugend* (ibid.: 27). This phase parallels Laqueur's post-*Wandervogel* phase, although Borinski and Milch, having both been part of the Youth Movement and wanting to use it in post-World War II Germany, highlight to excess its positive features. The correspondence between Hauer, other leaders, and followers does not bear this out.

13 Bartsch (1938: 48) writes that *Köngener* joined the Volunteer Corps in 1927. In fact Hauer's documents show it to have been in 1926.

14 The following is a long excerpt from Schoeps' letter to Hauer (26 August 1927, N1131 30, BAK):

> ... der Geist dieser Bewegung, dieser mit dem Namen "freideutsch" gekennzeichnete Haltung im übergeschichtlichen, methaphysischen Sinne (ist) von einem ganz bestimmten Menschentypus gefordert ... Was wir unter dieser Haltung verstehen zu müssen glauben ... (ist folgendes): Wir glauben dass es noch eine ganz bestimmte freideutsche Sendung gibt, der heute weder im Bund der Wandervögel und Pfadfinder noch im proletarischen Lager entsprochen wird. Es geht uns um die "Revolution des Gewissens" auf allen Gebieten gegen den Geist des Bürgertums als den der Sattheit, Geistesstarre, und Gewissensenge, dem es heute noch genau so wie 1913 das freideutsche Lebensbekenntnis entgegenzusetzen gilt ... Dem Menschenbild der bündischen Jugend ... setzen wir für unsere Jungmannschaft das Bild des brüderlich-liebenden Menschen gegenüber, dem aber auch der Begriff zuchtvoller Männlichkeit nicht fremd ist. Er allein wird die wahre Volksgemeinschaft, gegründet auf sozialer Gerechtigkeit und gegenseitiger Hilfsbereitschaft, erbauen können.

15 Schoeps to Hauer, 26 August 1927, N1131 30, BAK. It is not known whether Hauer knew at the time that Schoeps was Jewish. A person's Jewish identity was often not known, as the quarrel between anthropologists Thurnwald and Krickeberg shows. See Krickeberg (1937; 1938) and Fischer (1990).

16 *Um das Bild des Bundes*, N1131 22, BAK.

17 Lutzhöft (1971: 19) defines *völkisch* as referring to groups who are defined as being essentially formed by blood, where blood can mean race, *Volk*, or tribe.

18 While imperialism usually refers to dominating the economic and political affairs of weaker countries that were once part of an empire, to *völkisch* and Nazi ideologues it meant that a defeated nation was controlled by a foreign religion, namely Jewish Christianity. It simply reflected the fact that nationalists and *völkisch*, who equated religion with politics, did not like the politics of internationalists, that is, of the enemy.

19 26 August 1927, N1131 30, BAK.

20 In the twenties, Gogarten still shared basic ideas of Barth's biblical theology. In 1933, Gogarten switched to the position of the *Deutsche Christen*, whose theology was based on the reification of *Volk* and *Volkstum* as concrete creations of God.

21 26 August 1927, N1131 30, BAK.

22 *Altwandervogel* was a periodical of the German Youth Movement. It was in circulation from 1906 to *c.* 1920 (Laqueur 1962: 246).

23 It seems to have been since birth.

24 Letter 1 May 1930, N1131 32, BAK.

25 Letter Hauer to Möller, 21 October 1929, N1131 32, Doc 407, BAK.

26 N1131 14, n.d., Doc 2, BAK.

27 Hauer, N1131 14, Doc 2, BAK.

28 Hauer to Schramm, 24 September 1929, N1131 31, BAK. Also Hauer to Umfried, 20 July 1929, N1131 32, BAK.

29 Comburg is simply the place where the annual Workweek took place.

30 Hauer to Umfried, 21 June 1930, N1131 13, BAK.
31 Dr med Karl Strünckmann to Hauer, 10 November 1931, N1131 31, BAK.
32 23 November 1926, N1131 10, Doc 207, BAK.
33 Lene to Hauer, n.d., Doc 230, and 22 October 1926, N1131 10, BAK.
34 N1131 30, BAK.
35 Hauer to Boden, 20 November 1931; Hauer to Dannemann, 18 September 1931, N1131 14, BAK.
36 N1131 13, BAK.
37 27 January 1930, N1131 13, BAK.
38 Leaders and followers of *Bünde* visited Grimm in Lippoldsberg, where he had his estate. Also followers of the Ehrhardt brigade and of the Ludendorffs, with more of a fighting spirit, visited him. According to Grimm, all of these leaders and followers came from an established bourgeoisie (1954: 13).
39 Further editions appeared 1926 and 1931.
40 *Die Kommenden* could also be taken to refer to *commendam*, a benefice held in trust because there is no proper incumbent.
41 Hauer to Borinski, 6 June 1930, N1131 22, BAK.
42 Hauer and Borinski 12 July 1930, N1131 22, BAK.
43 13 May 1930, N1131 22, BAK.
44 19 May 1930, N1131 22, BAK.
45 Hauer to Ahlborn, 20 July 1930, N1131 22, BAK.
46 8 November 1930, N1131 22, BAK.
47 14 November 1930, N1131 22, BAK.
48 19 January 1931, N1131 13 BAK.
49 25 February 1931, N1131 13 BAK.
50 23 November 1926, N1131 195, Doc 102, BAK.
51 9 February 1928, N1131 195, Doc 90, BAK.
52 21 February 1931, N1131 195, Doc 46, BAK.
53 16 February 1931, N1131 195, Doc 47, BAK.
54 25 January 1930, N1131 10, BAK.
55 25 April 1931, N1131 13, BAK.
56 Mergenthaler was a well-known National Socialist who became the Minister President of Württemberg and Kultusminister (Minister of Culture, Education and Church Affairs) when the Nazis took over in 1933.
57 Hauer to Dannemann, 18 September 1931, N1131 14, BAK; Junginger 1999: 125.
58 Hauer to Dannemann, 18 September 1931, N1131 14, BAK.
59 Hauer to Frau Oberin, 22 January 1931, N1131 13, BAK.
60 Hauer to Craemer, 11 January 1930, N1131 13, BAK.
61 N1131 74, BAK.
62 Otto Strasser founded the Schwarze Front in 1930–1931. It consisted of a collection of disappointed Nazis and Communists, former people from the *Landvolkbewegung*, and sectarian Right radicals, among others. Membership never exceeded more than 5000. It was banned in February 1933.
63 Hauer to Backofen, 19 July 1935, N1131 86, BAK.
64 Hauer to Backofen, 19 July 1935, N1131 86, BAK.
65 The Youth section of Hauer's *Bund*.
66 31 March 1932, N1131 14, BAK.
67 Hauer to Heldt, 6 April 1938, N1131 85, BAK.
68 Bebermeyer, 7 September 1933, N1131 209, BAK.
69 Hauer to Ehlen, 21 July 1932, N1131 13, Doc 89, BAK.
70 13 October 1932, N1131 13, Doc 149, BAK.
71 Hauer to Buber, 18 October 1932, N1131 13, Doc 15, BAK.

4 The push toward Nazism: youths and leaders

1 Letter of Grimm to Hugo Gutsche, 11 October 1933. A: Grimm/Africa, Grimm to Gutsche 1933–1955, DLA.
2 A: Grimm, Hirsch to Grimm, 1941–1953, DLA.
3 See the open letter by seven professors, dated 3 April 1932. A: Grimm, Hirsch to Grimm, DLA.
4 *Die Arbeiter*, 1932, Hamburg: Hanseatische Verlagsanstalt.
5 Hirsch to Grimm, 2 November 1932. A: Grimm, letters Hirsch to Grimm 1927–1936, DLA.
6 A: Grimm, letters Hirsch to Grimm 1941–1954, DLA.
7 8 January 1931, N1131 13, Doc 225, BAK.
8 Ibid.
9 10 January 1931, N1131 13, Doc 223, BAK.
10 10 January 1931, N1131 13, Doc 224, BAK.
11 21 January 1931, N1131 13, Doc 220, BAK.
12 Ibid.
13 25 February 1931, N1131 13, Doc 204, BAK.
14 *Zielwillen* means literally the will to (reach) a goal.
15 25 February 1931, N1131 13, Doc 204, BAK.
16 One of his PhD professors in 1948 was Hans-Joachim Schoeps, who was one of the *Bünde* philosophers and corresponded with Hauer. The son of Hans-Joachim Schoeps is Professor Dr Julius H. Schoeps, who is director of the Moses Mendelssohn Zentrum, which was founded in 1992.
17 25 February 1931, N1131 13, Doc 204, BAK, explanation added.
18 25 February 1931, N1131 13, Doc 204, BAK.
19 By "Democrat" Hauer was, no doubt, thinking of Gertrud Bäumer, whom he initially identified as a "Liberal" until she insisted that she was a "Democrat." There were no democrats—for example, real supporters of the Weimar Republic —in Hauer's *Bund*.
20 25 February 1931, N1131 13, Doc 205, BAK.
21 Ibid.
22 The Young Plan of 1929 was to establish terms for clearing the reparations burden. It stirred a new wave of nationalist agitation (Kershaw 1998: 257).
23 E. Hirsch (1888–1972), *Erinnerungen and das Jahr 1929*, A: Grimm, Hirsch to Grimm 1941–1953, DLA. Kershaw (1998: 339) mentions the meeting between Brüning, Treviranus, Frick, Gregor Strasser, and Hitler.
24 *Volkskonservative Partei* was a short-lived attempt to form a political party of conservative revolutionaries. The party did poorly in the 1930 elections and eventually disappeared. According to Mohler (1999: 59, 421) the organizations of conservative revolutionaries tended not to become parties but consisted of elite gatherings that shied away from the public. They included small literary circles and followers of journals, but also extra-parliamentary *Kampfbünde* (Fighting Leagues), secret orders, and the like. This party is the same as Eyck's *Konservative Volkspartei* (1956: 344).
25 Hauer to Mande, 25 February 1931, N1131 13, Doc 205, BAK.
26 Hauer to Mande, 25 February 1931, N1131 13, Doc 205, BAK.
27 25 February 1931, N1131 13, Doc 205, BAK.
28 Hugenberg to Grimm, 30 March 1932, A: Grimm, Alfred Hugenberg to Grimm 1930–1941, DLA.
29 25 February 1931, N1131 13, BAK.
30 25 February 1931, N1131 13, Doc 506, BAK.
31 29 March 1931, N1131 13, Doc 200, BAK.

32 22 October 1931, N1131 13, Doc 196, BAK.
33 22 October 1931, N1131 13, Doc 196, BAK.
34 The left wing of the NSDAP was centered on Gregor and (especially) Otto Strasser, who in some sense wanted a National Socialism with the emphasis on Socialism.
35 24 October 1931, N1131 13, Doc 194, BAK.
36 24 October 1931, N1131 13, Doc 194, BAK.
37 The DVP, *Deutsche Volkspartei* (German People's Party) founded 1918 by Gustav Stresemann, who was honored by all Europeans for his foreign policy achievements, consisted of the right wing of the National Liberal Party and some left-wingers of the People's Party. When it went over to the NSDAP, liberals in Germany shrank further.
38 Reflecting on these events in a document that Hugenberg sent his friend Grimm 6 October 1947, Hugenberg argued that Hitler's meeting with Hindenburg on 10 October 1931 torpedoed Harzburg. From that meeting Hitler took away two things that had an important psychological effect on him: the full recognition that the Reichspresident was the commander-in-chief of the army, the only real power in Germany at the time, and the knowledge that he did not need the help of others any longer.
39 Forell to Hauer, 14 October 1930, N1131 45, BAK.
40 Brüning's remark. See A: Grimm, Hugenberg to Grimm, 6 October 1947, DLA.
41 20 May 1932, N1131 14, Doc 313, BAK.
42 25 May 1932, N1131 14, Doc 313, BAK: my emphasis.
43 Wilhelm Stapel to Grimm, 2 July 1931, A: Grimm, Hans Grimm, letters to him from Wilhelm Stapel, 1931–1947, DLA.

5 Hauer's view of religion

1 See Hauer's correspondence with Martin Buber.
2 Idealism assumes that mind and spiritual values are fundamental in the world as a whole. It is opposed to naturalism, materialism and realism. Fichte opposed determinism, which he called dogmatism and instead argued for a critical idealism. German idealists include beside Fichte, Schelling, Hegel, and the neo-Hegelians who spread idealism to England through Coleridge and Carlyle and to the USA primarily through Unitarian writers.
3 Also spelled Eckehardt.
4 The lineage of German thinkers was one leg on which German Faith stood. As we see later, the other leg was the *Bhagavad Gita*.
5 See chapter 1, note 3.
6 See chapter 1, note 4.
7 Vedanta is one of the six classical schools of Hindu philosophy and the one that is best known in the West. There are three main schools of Vedanta: (1) Advaita, which promotes monism; (2) Viaiadvaita, or qualified nondualism; and (3) Dvaita, which is a form of dualism. All three are similar to Platonism in aiming to go beyond the limits of empirical observation to explore the nature of Brahman. Since the nineteenth century scholars have noted similarities between the Vedanta and Western forms of idealism. Hauer's favoring of monism, nondualism, going beyond empirical observation, and Platonism has their source here.
8 Bhakti means "devotion" and denotes movements within Indian religions, especially Hinduism, that emphasizes the love of God or the gods.
9 5 April 1930, N1131 31, BAK.
10 5 April 1930, N1131 31, BAK.
11 See chapter 2, note 51.

12 5 April 1930, N1131 31, BAK.
13 5 April 1930, N1131 31, BAK, emphasis added.
14 Ibid. See also Hauer's letter to Otto, 20 June 1930, N1131 45, BAK.
15 Hauer to Buber, 26 April 1929, N1131 45, Doc 223, BAK.
16 Hiller to Hauer, 10 February 1934, N1131 66, Doc 366, BAK.
17 Hiller to Hauer, 10 February 1934, N1131 66, Doc 366, BAK.
18 *Seelentum* is an ambiguous term. It is often a substitute for "culture" or "psychology."
19 Hauer to Hiller, 19 February 1934, N1131 66, Doc 365, BAK.
20 This section translates as much and as closely as possible what Hauer and others wrote in his journal, *Deutscher Glaube*. Translation is never totally verbatim. Rather the aim is to have it make sense in English while yet maintaining the peculiar writing style, mood, and deliberate ambivalence of, especially, Hauer.
21 Also another word for God or World-all.
22 ADGB stands for *Arbeitsgemeinschaft der Deutschen Glaubensbewegung*.
23 Postmodernism sits on certain principles which are already found in the work of Ludwig Klages. See Poewe (1996). Related here is Aschheim's point that: "Nazism was, after all, a regenerationist, postdemocratic, post-Christian social order where the weak, decrepit and useless were to be legislated out of existence" (1992: 239).
24 According to Dierks (1986: 27), as a youth Hauer read a free adaptation of the Edda (*Nachdichtung der Edda in Prosa*).
25 23 June 1934, N1131 61, Doc 248, BAK.
26 23 May 1934, N1131 61, Doc 315, BAK.
27 21 June 1934, N1131 61, Doc 316, BAK.
28 28 June 1934, N1131 61, Doc 314, BAK.
29 Mathilde gives her father the title of Professor Dr (1931: 149). He was not a professor but a teacher whose scholarship is in doubt.

6 The Germanic-*deutsch* leg of Hauer's German Faith

1 The title of his three-volume work published between 1929 and 1932 is *Der Geist als Widersacher der Seele* (Rationality as Adversary of Symbolism, or Reason as the Adversary of the Soul).
2 Implied is that, if Christianity disappears, so will logocentrism, since both are Jewish.
3 To German encyclopedists, Pelasgians are relations of the legendary pre-Indo-Germanic original inhabitants (*Urbevölkerung*) of Greece.
4 To translate *Dichter* with "poet" and *Dichtung* with "poetic composition" would not give the full sense of what is subsumed under these terms in German. Hence I translate *Dichtung* as "language art" and *Dichter* as "language artists."
5 One could translate *Deutsche Gottschau* as beholding godliness in the German way. Hauer used the term "God" when convenient politically, but voiced often enough not liking it or believing in a personal one. He is actually referring to something he sees as Indo-Germanic faith, but he thought it politically unwise, given various criticisms, to have Indo- on the front cover of a book that was to capture the essence of National Socialism.
6 *Arteigen, Artung,* and *Rasse* are difficult terms to define, because even race is given different meanings by different Nazis and Hauer followers. One of Hauer's favorite co-workers, Ludwig Ferdinand Clauss, an anthropologist whose methods were based on mimicry and experience, defined *Artung* or *Rasse* as follows: "The terms *Artung* or *Rasse* do not refer to a collection of distinctive features or traits; rather they refer to a style of experiencing [*Stil des Erlebens*] that reaches through the whole of a living person. The two words *Artung* and

Rasse mean the same here" (Clauss 1932: 17). "When two souls are governed by the same style of experiencing and respond to their environment with the same gesture or attitude, then we say they are of the same *Artung* [kind, style] or same *Rasse* [race]" (ibid.: 16). "The only thing that one soul has wholly in common with another soul is the style of the experience, the manner in which something is experienced, the gesture of the soul [*seelische Gebärde*]; and only this is purely understandable between soul and soul" (ibid.: 16).

7 On 11 July 1951 Hans Buchheim, then with the *Deutsches Institut für Geschichte der Nationalsozialistischen Zeit*, carried by the *Bund und die Länder der Bundesrepublik Deutschland*, wrote Hauer that he had been commissioned to write about the religious-politics of National Socialism from the non-Confessional or non-Church side (11 July 1951, N1131 148, BAK). Whereupon Hauer, who in the past had denigrated objective research, answered that he "was pleased that the religious-politics of National Socialism would be thoroughly and objectively researched" (n.d. to Hans Buchheim, München, N1131 148, BAK). "I hold the purely negative judgment, one not supported by experience, that has gained momentum since 1945 not only as scientifically insupportable, but as dangerous from the perspective of the *Volksgemeinschaft*" (ibid.). What Hauer meant was, as usual, that he objected to the Church's version of that time and that it should be told, not objectively (although he used that word) but from his position. To that end he was prepared to point to or present known material (ibid.).

8 Lemcke still thought in terms of *Bünde*, namely, each *Bund* gave expression to a specific attitude and had a specific way or style of experiencing the world. Hauer now argued, in effect, that the *Urwille* was expressing itself in larger communities. The psychology on which all this thinking is based is not only that of Klages and Jung, but also of Ludwig Ferdinand Clauss (1926).

9 5 May 1934, N1131 61, Doc 22, BAK.

10 Ibid.: Doc 22–23.

11 Ibid.: Doc 23.

12 28 May 1934, N1131 61, Doc 20, BAK.

13 30 May 1934, N1131 61, Doc 19, BAK.

14 11 June 1934, N1131 61, Doc 16, BAK.

15 Ibid., Doc 17.

16 14 June 1934, N1131 61, Doc 15, BAK.

17 June 1934, N1131 61, Doc 24, BAK.

18 Ibid.: Doc 25–26.

19 Ibid.: Doc 27.

20 Ibid.: Doc28.

21 Ibid.: Doc 29–30.

22 Ibid.: Doc 30.

23 2 July 1934, N1131 61, Doc 13, BAK.

24 For the sole Heydrich version, see Buchheim (1953: 185, 196).

25 *Seelengrund im Menschen* means literally the foundation of the soul in the human being. Hauer uses the word as concept, however, and adjusts its meanings according to context.

7 Organizational help from *Wehrwolf* and the SS

1 A play on the word *Werwolf*, the mythological werewolf, but *Wehr-* refers to defense or resistance. It was a *Bund* of young fighters, especially popular in villages and the rural areas generally. At the time of writing, the *Wehrwolf* was in liquidation, no doubt because it had been taken over by the Hitler Youth.

2 After Scharzfeld the German Faith Movement became the German Faith Community. The change of name was to underline that the movement consisting of many *Bünde* had now become a unitary community.

3 In a letter to a comrade Weber, Hauer wrote on 5 May 1942 that within the two years after 1933 he spoke before about 10 million Germans (Hauer to Kamerad Weber, 5 May 1942, N1131 4, BAK).

4 Frick participated in the Hitler *Putsch* in 1923, led the party in Parliament in 1928, and became Minister of the Interior in 1933. It is in this capacity that Hauer knew and dealt with him. Frick's execution in Nürnberg 1946 had to do with his role of transferring police sovereignty from the *Land* (province) to the *Reich*, which helped the SS become all-powerful. Wilhelm Frick is not to be confused with Heinrich Frick, a professor at Marburg

5 Jäger was brought before a Polish court on 13 December 1948 and executed on 17 June 1948 for "the organization and execution of war crimes and crimes against humanity" (Scholder 1988: 351).

6 *Obergruppenführer* is a rank in the SS (among other Nazi formations) equal to the status of General.

7 After his law degree in 1928, Werner Best served as judge. He joined the Nazi party in 1930 and the SS in 1931. When Hauer knew him in 1933 and 1934 he was *Landespolizeipräsident* in (the *Land* of) Hessen. In 1935 he worked with the Gestapo in Berlin. From 1939 to 1940 he led Bureau II of the National Security Headquarters, which had to do with the administration, organization and law pertaining to deprivation of citizenship, confiscation of property harmful to the state, the construction of gas wagons, and so on. He served in France 1940 and Denmark 1942. In 1944 be was promoted to SS-*Obergruppenführer* (General). In 1949 he was sentenced to death in Copenhagen, only to be pardoned and released in 1951. In 1972 there was a new case against him because of the organization of the *Einsatzgruppen* in Poland in 1939, but no proceedings followed, owing to his poor health. He died 1989.

8 9 December 1933, N1131 66, Doc 77, BAK.

9 Hauer to Boge, 29 December 1933 / 3 January 1934, Doc 76.

10 Ibid.

11 Gottfried Feder (1883–1941) was a civil engineer who was an economic expert for the NSDAP and a Member of Parliament for them. He belonged to G. Strasser's social-revolutionary wing of the Party (1932). Along with Strasser he lost favor, and he was given a professorship at the Technical University in Berlin.

12 Franz Seldte (1882–1947) joined the NSDAP and became *Obergruppenführer* (General) of the SA 1933. In 1918 he had founded the *Stahlhelm*, which he led until its dissolution in 1935. He was also the *Reichsarbeitsminister* and the *Preussische Wirtschaftsminister*. Hauer no doubt knew him to be favorably inclined toward the ADGB from his SA and *Freiwilligen Arbeitsdienst* association. Seldte worked closely with Grimm's friend Alfred Hugenberg. Seldte died in an American military hospital.

13 15 January 34, N1131 66, Doc 74, BAK.

14 Rosenberg, who likewise hated Christianity, did not leave the Church officially until 15 November 1933, after the Sports Palace spectacle, which marked the beginning of the break-up of the *Deutsche Christen*.

15 This was also the view of the Thuringian *Deutsche Christen* led by Leutheuser. To him Adolf Hitler was "the spokesman for a savior" who had become "flesh and blood in the German *Volk*" (Scholder 1988: 560).

16 Bormann was at the time the *Reichsleiter* of the NSDAP and, as of July 1933, Hess's chief of staff. Hauer met with him in Berlin and considered him favorably inclined toward the German Faith Movement.

17 Kloppe to Hauer, 24 October 1933, N1131 57, Doc 63, BAK.
18 2 November 1933, N1131 57, Doc 62, BAK.
19 13 November 1933, N1131 57, Doc 61, BAK.
20 After the *Reich*, the *Gau* was the largest organized body led by a *Gauleiter*. A *Gau* consisted in turn of circles, local groups (*Ortsgruppen*), cells, and blocks.
21 13 November 1933, N1131 57, Doc 61, BAK.
22 14 November 1933, N1131 57, Doc 60, BAK.
23 14 November 1933, N1131 57, Doc 60, BAK.
24 Hauer to Kloppe, 16 November 1933, N1131 57, Doc 59, BAK.
25 17 November 1933, N1131 57, Doc 58, BAK.
26 Ibid.
27 20 November 1933, N1131 57, Doc 56, BAK.
28 17 November 1933, N1131 56, Doc 301, BAK.
29 17 November 1933, N1131 56, Doc 301, BAK.
30 17 November 1933, N1131 56, Doc 302, BAK.
31 20 November 1933, N1131 57, Doc 56, BAK.
32 20 November 1933, N1131 57, Doc 54, BAK.
33 20 November 1933, N1131 57, Doc 54, BAK.
34 25 November 1933, N1131 57, Doc 52, BAK.
35 25 November 1933, N1131 57, Doc 52, BAK.
36 1 December 1933, N1131 57, Doc 45, BAK.
37 1 December 1933, N1131 57, Doc 45, BAK.
38 Ibid.
39 Ibid.
40 Ibid.
41 n.d., N1131 57, Doc 43, BAK.
42 Ibid.
43 7 December 1933, N1131 57, Doc 41, BAK.
44 Ibid.
45 5 December 1933, N1131 56, Doc 120, BAK.
46 5 December 1933, N1131 56,j Doc 120, BAK.
47 Stammler's real name was Ernst Emanuel Krauss. He adopted the pseudonym Stammler 1913 when he had established himself as an author. A group of followers published *Das neue Volk. Sendblätter von Georg Stammler* (The New *Volk*: Georg Stammler's Leaflets). Around this time, after Stammler had become a member of the National Socialistic Freedom Movement in 1924, Erich Röth's *Urquell*-Press took over Stammler's works. Röth belonged to the extreme right of the Youth Movement, with which Stammler too identified. In 1925 he became the leader of the *Deutschen Richtwochen* (German Guidance Weeks) that offered a cultural and national pedagogical program for the Youth Movement. Stammler was, therefore, a core figure of the extreme Right youths and the *völkisch* movement. (Puschner *et al.* 1999: 927–8).
48 31 October 1933, N1131 57, Doc 322, BAK.
49 19 October 1933, N1131 57, Doc 323, BAK.
50 Ibid.
51 *Sturmführer* is about the equivalent rank of a second lieutenant.
52 A *Standarte* was a unit of the SS (also the SA) consisting of several *Sturmbanne* (smaller units) holding altogether between 3000 and 4000 men.
53 7 May 1934, N1131 61, Doc 234, BAK.
54 Ibid.
55 11 May 1934, N1131 61, Doc 235, BAK.
56 31 May 1934, N1131 61, Doc 267, BAK.

57 4 June 1934, N1131 61, Doc 264, BAK.
58 Ibid., Doc 265.
59 Ibid., Doc 265.
60 9 June 1934, N1131 61, Doc 263, BAK.
61 9 June 1934, N1131 61, Doc 263, BAK.
62 9 June 1934, N1131 61, Doc 263, BAK.
63 27 October 1933, N1131 57, Doc 250, BAK.
64 27 October 1933, N1131 57, Doc 250, BAK.
65 9 November 1933, N1131 57, Doc 249, BAK.
66 Ibid.
67 7 December 1933, N1131 56, Doc 414, BAK.
68 Ibid.
69 Ammerlahn to Hauer, 27 September 1933, N1131 56, Doc 8, BAK.
70 Ball to Hauer, 4 October 1933, N1131 56, Doc 13, BAK.
71 Ball to Hauer, 4 October 1933, N1131 56, Doc 13, BAK.
72 6 November 1933, N1131 57, Doc 230, BAK.
73 Bänsch to Hauer, 19 November 1933, N1131 56, Doc 15, BAK.
74 Fuhrmann to Hauer, 16 November 1933, N1131 56, Doc 282, BAK.
75 Eudaemonia or eudemonia refers to an Aristotelian notion of achieving happiness derived from a life of activity governed by reason. Eucken, like the other writers, poets, and life philosophers who attracted Hauer or were attracted by Hauer, were all against materialism, modernism and reason. They were in varying degrees for irrationalism and for things experiential. Two famous students of Eucken were Fritz Medicus, the editor of Fichte's works, and Max Scheler, the life philosopher who defended Eucken's anti-formalistic heroic ethic of love and criticized psychologism in philosophy.
76 It is hard to know who is meant here: Werner von Siemens (1816–1892), inventor in the area of electronic technology, or Werner Siemens (1873–1964), a sea captain.
77 4 June 1934, N1131 61, Doc 368, BAK.
78 n.d., N1131 61, Doc 367, BAK.
79 The Nazis founded the *Deutsche Arbeitsfront* in November 1933 to replace the unions. The founding became effective 1 January 1934. In October of 1934 it became an organization of the NSDAP and received its own constitution. All Germans in professions or jobs were to be members, so that its membership number was twenty-five million. The *Kraft durch Freude* (Power through Joy) ship was one of its organizations; it offered holidays for workers.
80 4 June 1934, N1131 61, Doc 368, BAK.
81 4 June 1934, N1131 61, Doc 368, BAK.
82 Dehne to Hauer, 11 December 1933, N1131 56, Doc 157, BAK.

8 Hauer and the war of attrition against Christianity

1 Friedrich von Bodelschwingh was a Protestant theologian who led the Betheler Institutes for the handicapped that were founded by his father. After his resignation as *Reichsbischof*, Bodelschwingh worked against the euthanasia program with some success. In opposition to these events Martin Niemöller (1892–1984) and his Berlin colleagues Jacobi and von Rabenau called into being the *Pfarrernotbund* (Pastors' Emergency League), which became the *Bekennende Kirche* (Confessional Church). By 15 January 1934 they had 7036 Protestant ministers in their fold, half of the Protestant clergy (Zipfel 1965: 40).
2 See letter, Hauer to Backofen, 19 July 1935, N1131 86, BAK.

3 Eisenach was not Luther's birthplace as Cancik claims (1982: 176); it was, however, the place where Luther attended boarding school, and the Wartburg was the castle where Luther translated the New Testament into German. The place was chosen for its symbolic significance and for the respectability that it guaranteed.

4 The new Evangelical Church Constitution of 11 July came into effect on 14 July 1933.

5 A play on Luther's famous phrase, "Here I stand, I cannot do otherwise." Only Hauer says, "We cannot do otherwise."

6 26 June 1933, Doc 223, N1131 16, BAK.

7 26 June 1933, Doc 223, N1131 16, BAK.

8 Gregor Strasser was shot by the SS in 1934.

9 26 June 1933, Doc 223, N1131 16, BAK.

10 Hauer's German Faith was in fact a concoction of the *Edda*, *Bhagavad Gita*, *Upanishads*, Platonism, and German (heretical) authors from Goethe to Nietzsche, Kolbenheyer, Rosenberg, and many others (Scholder 1988: 452). It is the Indian material—things from the Yogic tradition—that Mathilde Ludendorff saw as occult. By contrast, Hauer justified it as being part of the Indo-Germanic tradition, although he selectively de-emphasized the Indian contribution when expediency demanded it.

11 26 June 1933, Doc 223, N1131 16, BAK.

12 29 June 1933, Doc 155, N1131 16, BAK.

13 Grabert to Hauer, 9 November 1933, N1131 56, BAK.

14 Herber Grabert's son, Wigbert Grabert, still runs the Grabert Verlag in Tübingen. The publishing firm was founded by the father who died 1978 and has been run by the son since 1972. Wigbert Grabert is connected with the Nouvelle Droite and has published translations of Alain de Benoist. He still publishes the *Euro-Kurier*. His books could sell 80,000 copies per title in the 1990s, although now he is complaining that the readership is shrinking. His readers included many descendants of the DGB. See 2004 editions of his *Euro-Kurier*.

15 23 October 1933, N1131 56, Doc 315, BAK.

16 Ibid.: emphasis his.

17 This is Grabert's second book. His first was *Religiöse Verständigung: Wege zur Begegnung der Religionen bei Nicolaus Cusanus, Schleiermacher, Rudolf Otto und J.W. Hauer* (1932). It is a defense of Hauer's line while he was still working within the *Third Commission of the World Conference*, when he argued that not syncretism but a strong rooted faith, rooted within something Hauer called *letzte Wirklichkeit*, final reality, is the path to a religious brotherhood. At the time Hauer attempted to reconcile universalism with particularism without being totally relativistic. His notion of a godliness or spirituality that he called Final Reality as the common ground in which diverse religions were rooted did that (ibid.: 81). Then too Hauer argued that there was such a thing as an Islamic soul, a Christian-oriental soul, even a Christian-German soul (ibid.: 84). But there were two kinds of absoluteness. The first is relative because it refers to the absoluteness of experience-, thought- and conceptual forms. The second is not relative because it refers to the absoluteness of a human being's relationship with eternal reality (ibid.: 86, 94). By the time the book was published, Hauer already thought that Christianity and German faith were irreconcilable.

18 23 October 1933, N1131 56, Doc 315, BAK.

19 30 October 1933, N1131 56, Doc 314, BAK.

20 Ibid.

21 13 November 1933, N1131 56, Doc 311, BAK.

22 14 November 1933, N1131 56, Doc 310, BAK.
23 20 November 1933, N1131 56, Doc 307, BAK.
24 21 November 1933, N1131 56, Doc 306, BAK.
25 16 January 1934, N1131 58, Doc 216, BAK.
26 Ibid. Up to now Krause had "argued not for an abolition of the confession but,"
     like Hauer earlier, "for broadening it, so that all the members of the *Volk* could
     be united in one *Volkskirche*" (Scholder 1988: 557).
27 16 January 1934, N1131 58, Doc 216, BAK.
28 15 February 1934, N1131 58, Doc 215, BAK.
29 For more details about Zapp, see Schaul Baumann (2005: 178–84).
30 5 October 1933, N1131 57, BAK.
31 Ibid.
32 20 October 1933, N1131 56, BAK.
33 Ibid.
34 Ibid.
35 9 November 1933, N1131 56, BAK.
36 Ibid.
37 13 November 1933, N1131 56, BAK.
38 21 October 1933, N1131 56, BAK.
39 25 October 1933, N1131 57, BAK.
40 7 November 1933, N1131 56, BAK. Hauer did not like Manfred Boge because
     the latter had sharply criticized Bergmann and Hauer. Boge claimed that their
     attitude was "if you don't believe as we do, then you are not a National Socialist."
     On 21 March 1934 Hauer cut off all correspondence with Boge (Hauer to Boge,
     21 March 34, N1131 58, BAK, Doc 35).
41 14 November 1933, N1131 56, BAK.
42 21 November 1933, N1131 56, BAK.
43 10 November 1933, N1131 57, BAK.
44 Ibid.
45 Ibid.
46 Theodor Fritsch (1855–1938) was an extreme anti-Semite. According to von
     Leers, Fritsch took up the fight against Jews starting 1880 with his publishing
     house called *Hammer*. He published the *Antisemitenkatechismus* 1887 and later
     Handbuch der Juden. Fritsch argued that Jewry constituted a Race-*Bund* focused
     on hating all non-Jews. During the Weimar regime he was taken to court (von
     Leers, N2168 9, BAB).
47 12 November 1933, N1131 57, BAK.
48 14 November 1933, N1131 57, BAK.
49 15 November 1933, N1131 56, BAK.
50 Ibid.
51 The real title was *Blätter zur Pflege persönlichen Lebens*, from 1914 to 1941.
     From 1933 he dedicated himself entirely to Germany's "national rebirth."
52 Wolfgang Kapp, director-general of the East Prussian agricultural credit banks,
     led a *putsch* after anti-republican *Freikorps* units occupied Berlin on 13 March
     1920. The chancellor at the time, Gustav Bauer, fled to Stuttgart and from there
     defeated the *putsch* within five days. From then on, however, the democratic
     parties never again had a majority and had to coalesce with "openly or latently
     antidemocratic parties" (Schulze 1998: 205–7).
53 15 November 1933, N1131 56, BAK.
54 Refers to the socialist republic of Bavaria of 1919. The author implies that he
     deliberately did not leave the church then because, if he had, it might have given
     the impression that he was communist or socialist.

55 18 November 1933, N1131 56, Doc 107, BAK.
56 This may refer to the split that occurred in the *Glaubensbewegung Deutsche Christen* in November 1933 after a provocative speech given by the chief district officer of Berlin (*Berliner Gauobmann*) Dr Reinhold Krause. The *Deutsche Christen* split into the *deutschgläubigen* (those with a German faith) who were obviously heretical and the others who still held to the Old and New Testament. The latter remained within the Church Movement of German Christians, the former became the Reich's Movement of German Christians and as of 1938 the Luther Germans (Benz *et al.* 1997: 420).
57 20 November 1933, N1131 56 Doc 106, BAK.
58 The group was called *Bund der Gemeinden eines freien deutschen Glaubens.*
59 23 November 1933, N1131 55, BAK.
60 Ibid.
61 Ibid.
62 29 November 1933, N1131 55, BAK.
63 Ibid.
64 Ibid.
65 Ibid.
66 30 December 1933, N1131 55, BAK.
67 No doubt doing her *Habilitation.*
68 The person wrote to ask about the seeming conflict between, on the one hand, the *Reichswart* calling itself the organ of *Die Brüder völkischer Europäer* (Brothers of *völkisch* Europeans) and, on the other, that of the ADGB. She wanted to know the nature of their interrelationship. Hauer answered that the two organizations, BVE and ADGB, had nothing to do with one another. The BVE was purely a Reventlow effort to gather race-conscious peoples of Europe into groups and, on the basis of the knowledge of racial power, come to some sort of understanding (5 December 1933, N1131 56, BAK).
69 30 November 1933, N1131 56, BAK.
70 Her emphasis, ibid.
71 5 December 1933, N1131 56, BAK.
72 Hauer to Heinz Leonhardt, 14 November 1933, N1131 57, Doc 130, BAK.

9 Werner Best: Hauer's contact in the SS

1 Bruno Beger to Schäfer, 23 September 1942, R135/48, *Blätter* 164046–164049, BAB.
2 Hauer to Trautner, 23 April 1934, N1131 61, Doc 366, BAK.
3 According to Gründel's scheme Joseph Goebbels would be part of the "young front generation"—those born between 1890 and 1900. Owing to the deformation of his foot incurred during childhood, Goebbels could not serve. Although his heightened sense of drama made him a rather different individual from Best, they shared many of the characteristics discussed in the text.
4 The free religious movement consisted of the *Bund freireligiösen Gemeinden Deutschlands* (League of Free Religious Communities in Germany), which was renamed *Bund der Gemeinden deutschen Glaubens* (League of Communities of German Faith) when it joined the ADGB in 1933. The leaders were Carl Peter, Professor Drews, BfG Minister Raschke, and Preacher Elling. Once they joined the ADGB, Hauer became the *Bund* leader, Carl Peter the treasurer; the others oversaw different regions. There was also a *Verband der freireligiösen Gemeinden* led by a Dr Pick. Pick's group did not join the ADGBB, although some of his communities may have. The free religious were under constant

surveillance by the secret police after the Hitler takeover because they were suspected of having harbored freemasons, communists, and the rare Jew.

5 Werner Best became an official member of the *Führerrat* on 28 January 1934 (Nanko 1993: 170).

6 Hauer to Reventlow, 20 and 23 December 1933, in Nanko (1993: 324–5).

7 19 February 1934, N1131 66, Doc 58, BAK.

8 19 February 1934, N1131 66, Doc 66, BAK.

9 27 February 1934, N1131 66, Doc 56, BAK.

10 27 February 1934, N1131 66, Doc 57, BAK.

11 Hauer to Best, 9 March 1934, N1131 66, Doc 52, BAK.

12 Actually, Paul Krannhals was not "Dr"; his brother was.

13 First published 1928; a new *Volks*-edition appeared in 1934 and again in 1936.

14 Hauer to Best, 9 March 1934, N1131 66, Doc 52, BAK.

15 9 March 1934, N1131 66, Doc 52, BAK.

16 9 March 1934, N1131 66, Doc 52, BAK.

17 9 March 1934, N1131 66, Doc 52, BAK.

18 9 March 1934, N1131 66, Doc 52, BAK.

19 9 March 1934, N1131 66, Doc 53, BAK.

20 GGG stands for *Germanische Glaubens-Gemeinschaft*, Germanic Faith Community.

21 9 March 1934, N1131 66, Doc 53, BAK.

22 9 March 1934, N1131 66, Doc 53, BAK.

23 9 March 1934, N1131 66, Doc 53, BAK.

24 9 March 1934, N1131 66, Doc 53, BAK.

25 What this means exactly only Hauer knew. He could not be explicitly political. What is clear, however, is that he told Best that only under his leadership would all this happen.

26 Hauer to Best, 9 March 1934, N1131 66, Doc 52, BAK.

27 Hauer is referring to the story of the suspended curate, Johannes Ronge, and the Deutschkatholizismus (1844–1852). Ronge wrote an open letter to Bishop Arnoldi of Trier, 1 October 1844 (not 1843 as Hauer says), in which he attacked the teachings of the Catholic Church, specifically, the display of the holy robe of Trier. In this struggle Ronge conjured up German national feelings against the tyrannical power of Rome (Leesch 1938: 10–11). Ronge was a radical liberal raised in the liberal atmosphere of those days.

28 Hauer to Best, 9 March 1934, N1131 66, Doc 52, BAK.

29 Ibid.

30 9 March 1934, N1131 66, BAK, Doc 54, my emphasis.

31 9 March 1934, N1131 66, Doc 54, BAK.

32 9 March 1934, N1131 66, Doc 54, BAK.

33 Ibid.

34 Ibid.

35 9 May 1938, Niels Diederichs wrote von Leers about their publishing firm's new book, *Engländer, Juden, Araber in Palestine*, which threw a most powerful light on Near East problems. Von Leers replied almost immediately, 11 May 1938, that he wanted Wirsing's book because he was himself preoccupied with just these issues (N2168 3, Johannes von Leers, BAB; see also Wirsing 1942: 118).

36 9 March 34, N1131 66, Doc 55, BAK.

37 Ibid., Doc 15.

38 9 March 34, N1131 66, Doc 15, BAK.

39 See also Buber to Hauer, 4 October 1932, Doc 44, N1131 13, BAK.

40 Ibid., Doc 50.

41 7 August 1935, N1131 88, BAK, 133.
42 13 August 1935, N1131 88, BAK, 133.
43 24 September 1935, N1131 88, 235, BAK.
44 Hauer to Dr Gräter of the National Political Institute of Education, 24 December 1935, N1131 88, Doc 246, BAK.
45 Hauer to Günther, 4 October 1935; Günther to Hauer, 6 October 1935; Hauer to Günther, 7 October 1935, N1131 88, Doc 299–301, BAK.
46 1 April 1936, N1131 88, BAK. The actual resignation was made in a letter of 29 March 1936 to the *Landesgemeindeleiter* of the German Faith Movement. Following much vagueness, Hauer ends with the words that he would return the administration of the German Faith Movement "into your hands" (Dierks 1986: 264–5).
47 2 April 1936, N1131 88, BAK.
48 Hauer to Gutbrod, 15 April 1936, N1131 88, BAK.

10 The faith of the Nationalists: narrative and the Third Reich

1 Letter by Erwin Ackerknecht to Hans Grimm, 27 December 1918. A: Grimm, letters from Ackerknecht to Grimm 1916–1921, DLA, Marbach.
2 "Max Weber über Deutschlands Not." *Stuttgarter Neues Tagblatt*, Saturday, 19 February 1921: 7.
3 It should be noted that Peter Kratz of the *Berliner Institut für Faschismus-Forschung und Antifaschistische Aktion* objects to Machtan's book *Hitlers Geheimnis* (2003, Fischer). I have only read Machtan's book, *The Hidden Hitler* (2001). Kratz, who excels in uncovering links between extreme right wing personalities past and present and politicians currently in power, argues that Machtan's new thesis claims that the origins of Nazi Germany are Hitler's inhibited sexuality as a disguised homosexual. This would of course be absurd. I can only assume that Kratz has made a mistake in his interpretation of Machtan's work.
4 Schmitt (1938: 614) wrote citing Dr Georg Daskalakis, a Greek scholar, "… the total [totalitarian] state is not a state in itself, but only a moment in the life of a state …" (My insertion). Every state has the potential to be totalitarian, but a state only follows through with totalitarianism in very specific dangerous situations (ibid.: 614).
5 Grimm used the terms "new faith" (referring to the nationalism of National Socialism) and "other faith" (referring to Communism and/or Socialism) in his American speech in New York before a German-American audience on 6 October 1935. It is explained later in the chapter.
6 The German title is *Michael: Ein deutsches Schicksal in Tagebuchblättern*. Goebbels published plays and diary-form books some years before he became propaganda minister under Hitler. Most were a type of political confessional autobiography, a mixed genre that combined his own life experiences, primarily political ones, with those of his friends. The aim was to describe paths toward becoming a committed National Socialist. Stations on the way always included a *Bünde* phase, overcoming Christianity, and discovering a vengeful anti-Semitism.
7 Grimm (1931: 10–14). The 1980 reprint is as the original.
8 Grimm's female characters are not developed. Usually, they play a secondary role to men.
9 For example, he refers to the 11 September 1897 issue of *Saturday Review*. The article seems to give a Darwinian capitalist explanation of why England's immediate enemy was Germany. Grimm is intrigued by this and other *SR* arguments because, of course, they feed his developing ideas about Nordic elitism, the white man, and survival of the fittest nation (Grimm 1954: 58–9).

10 He claims the *SR* article ended with "*Germaniam esse delendam*" (Grimm 1954: 59). This 1954 book he started to write in 1945, after the defeat and in response to Thomas Mann, who condemned German atrocities. Grimm used Mann's letter as an excuse to be heard himself in England (Grimm to Stapel, 12 September 1945, A: Grimm, DLA, Marbach).

11 Grimm to Hugenberg, 15 March 1932 and 31 March 1932, A: Grimm, from Grimm to Alfred Hugenberg 1930–1951, DLA, Marbach. Grimm had occasional doubts about the National Socialists but none about the Nationalists. Nor did he doubt that, in the end, the Nazis would serve the Nationalists.

12 Grimm to Ilse Hess, 6 May 1938, A: Grimm, DLA, Marbach. The explanation in brackets is inserted by me.

13 Letter of librarian Erwin Ackerknecht to novelist Hans Grimm, 27 December 1918, where he talks about faith in the "German Reich in us" being inexhaustible. A: Grimm, DLA, Marbach.

14 From a speech Grimm gave in October 1931 entitled "Political Interpreters" (*Politische Dolmetscher*) (Grimm 1931: 10–14). Grimm responded here to a specific event where a Jewish woman, a Social Democrat and parliamentarian, informed the government about Ernst Krieck. Krieck was professor at the Pedagogical Academy in Frankfurt, from which he was subsequently removed to another post. The informer told the government about a nationalistic vigil that he held with his students during which he hailed the Third Reich. It will come up later.

15 1923 is the publication date of Moeller van den Bruck's book, *The Third Reich*.

16 Grimm's book, *Die Olewagen Saga*, was first published in 1918 by the Albert Langen Verlag in Munich. In a 1942 Preface to the 1972 reprint of this book from his own publishing firm, called Klosterhaus Verlag, he discussed the importance of "silence" (ibid.: III). "I wondered," he wrote, how much, by virtue of its form, was not said in the saga only to be expressed anyway by virtue of having been kept silent or unspoken. All of Grimm's writing fascinates by virtue of what his "silences," his self-imposed discretion, in fact say without being said.

17 Acta Bekenntniskirche, 1934/36, Ref. IV, Kirchenkampf und Luth. Vereinigung, Berlin Mission Society, Berlin, Germany.

18 On 30 October 1945 Grimm wrote Alfred Hugenberg that his Thomas Mann answer was finished but that he was not sure whether it would pass American censorship. (See A: Grimm, letter from Grimm to Hugenberg, 30 October 1945, DLA, Marbach).

19 The play is on the civilization versus culture differences.

20 Grimm is thinking of Thomas Mann's 1918 book, *Betrachtungen eines Unpolitischen.*

21 In fairness to Grimm, the worry about Jewish intrusiveness was but one worry among many in what Grimm called the protest years between 1918 and 1932. The more important worries included the Scheidemann revolution, the broken promise of Wilson's fourteen points, Versailles, and the profiteering attitude of parliamentarianism (Grimm 1972a: 19). These were popular perceptions during Weimar and Nazi Germany. Jewish success was presented as statistics about Jews in the general population as against their presence in the professions, media, and Weimar government.

22 *Kaffernland* was written between 1911 and 1915 and never completed. Fragments were first published in 1935 (Grimm 1978: 266) and then in 1961 by Grimm's Klosterhaus Verlag, Lippoldsberg. It was reprinted in 1978. *Kaffernland* is his most anthropological narrative, perhaps because it is not as ideologically determined as are his post-1918 publications. Like most of his works it sits

on variously archived documents. His first paragraph is reminiscent of Alan Paton's *Cry, the Beloved Country*, but beyond that lacks entirely Paton's Christian viewpoint. Grimm begins his book with a description that celebrates Africa's beauty with all senses. He starts: "There is a smell in the air as of open fires. It sounds as if cattle ..." (1978: 7).

23 Grimm received an invitation to give his talk before German-Americans on the 6 October 1935, the occasion of German Day (Grimm to Gutsche, 4 September 1935, A: Grimm, Grimm to Hugo Gutsche, 1933–1955, DLA).

24 For example, 11 June 1931, Emanuel Hirsch, a nationalistic Protestant theologian wrote Hans Grimm "a Mr Mendelssohn—he is baptized—is outraged in the name of Christ about our political phrases and he made the glorious suggestion that we replace the word '*Nation*' with '*Heimat*'." Hirsch worried that Jewish voices in the church might become strong enough to disavow "German conscience and will." (A: Grimm, Emanuel Hirsch to Hans Grimm, DLA).

25 Goebbels (1929: 35) makes reference to what Russians call international, namely, a mix of "Jewish kabalistic, cowardly blood-terror," and such that he sees as forced onto the world by but one man, Lenin. "Without Lenin, no Bolshevism."

26 Hitler argued that Slavs and their culture were being favored.

27 Here is the big man theory that was also popular among anthropologists of the time.

28 The German Word not the Word of God.

29 Dr Erwin Ackerknecht to Hans Grimm, 27 December 1918. A: Grimm, letters from Ackerknecht, Erwin to Grimm, DLA, Marbach. After the war Ackerknecht became the director of the Schiller Museum and this archive.

11 Scientific neo-paganism and the extreme Right then and today

1 The *German Unitarian Religious Community* was founded in 1950. Because they attracted *völkisch* and German Christians, these Unitarians are seen as a successor to Hauer's German Faith Movement, whose religious philosophy they adopted. In the fifties, Nazi and SS scholars who had lost the right to teach in German institutions were hired by this organization as speakers. Aside from Hauer's religious philosophy, Sigrid Hunke's notion of Europe's own religion and Hubertus Mynarek's ecological religion are foundational (Mecklenburg 1996: 378–9). Hunke traces the origin of the Unitarian movement back to the 1500s when, she claims, the "pure Monotheism" of Islam encouraged Antitrinitarianism (Hunke 1969: 477). German Unitarians insist that religion is the expression of a specific mentality (*Denkart*), a euphemism for race. Consequently, they encourage Europeans to express their religious needs independently of, and against, an imposed Christianity. Unlike British and American Unitarians, German Unitarians are decidedly non- and anti-Christian. There were natural affinities for National Socialism that are now denied. (See also W. Paysen to Hauer, 26 August 1952, N1131 147, BAK, where Paysen informs Hauer that American and the English Unitarians are also no longer loyal to the Christian tradition: "If Americans today still hold it necessary to use the Christian teachings of compassion in their practical politics, then they do it only in the sense of Albert Schweitzer or perhaps Professor Kurt Leese of Hamburg").

2 Edmond Vermeil (1944), *Hitler et le christianisme*, does *not* distinguish between conservative revolution and national socialism. Already in 1946, the French called these phenomena neo-paganism (Mohler 1989a: 222).

3 The Thule Seminar is small but can still be found on the Internet. One of its leaders, Pierre Krebs, a lawyer and political scientist, also put out the magazine

called *METAPO* (now discontinued), the *Thule-Briefe* (2002–2004), and the Pagan pocket planner *Mars Ultor* (2001–2005). He has a publishing firm called edition de facto in Kassel. In 2003 it published, in the form of a fairytale, a book entitled *Zabiba und der König*. Its author wanted to be anonymous but is "said to be" Saddam Hussein. Editio de facto also publishes the conspiracy books by the French journalist and political scientist Thierrey Meyssan about 9/11, the Pentagon, and the Bush family.

4 There are also connections to Franz Schönhuber, Horst Mahler, news journals such as *Junge Freiheit*, *National-Zeitung*, and *Nation and Europa*. The latter was one of the first New Right magazines and was known to Grimm and Hauer. Grimm wrote an essay for it in 1951 (Grimm to Stapel, 18 August 1951, A: Grimm, Grimm letters to Stapel, DLA).

5 Payne (1995: 510) is only half right when he argues that the *nouvelle droite* "rejects the mysticism and idealism of Evola, affirming the importance of science in modern life and relying heavily on the new sociobiology" (ibid.: 510). The science emphasis, already seen in Ludendorff and Hunke, and the emphasis on sociobiology (Krebs 1981a) is correct. But despite this, Evola is a leading light of both G.R.E.C.E. and the Thule Seminar (personal interview with Pierre Krebs, summer 1997; also Krebs 1997: 13, 26, 32, 40, 43, 46, 49, 66, 69; Trimondi 2002: 227–44).

6 Currently (2005) the NPD, an extreme right party like the DVU, has twelve members in the Sachsen parliament. They caused uproar because one of their members, Jürgen Gansel talked about the "bombing holocaust of Dresden" and complained about the "selective memory-culture" in Germany.

7 Woods (1996: 6, 88–100, 115–32) argues that the ideas of Conservative Revolutionaries were "expressions of tensions," like finding meaning in the sacrifice of World War I. It is by studying the changing responses of diverse writers (Jünger, Zehrer, Spengler) to these tensions that Woods is able to chronicle the transition from democracy to activism, struggle for its own sake, leadership principle and National Socialist dictatorship.

8 In fact, their thinking is dualistic, only it is directed against those outside of the whole.

9 Organic individualism refers to the responsibility of everyone doing his or her own thing, in harmony with godliness, and within the context of being rooted in a distinct ethnic group or nation.

10 "*Wie es die Seele erlebte*" and "*Wie die Vernunft es sah*" are the headings of the two parts of her book (1921).

11 Her criticisms were published by J. F. Lehmann Verlag, part of the publishing infrastructure of the Conservative Revolution. Lehmann also produced a series on South Africa to which Afrikaner nationalists such as Rompel, Kestell, Viljoen, President Paul Krüger contributed (Poewe 1998).

12 Smart (1997) says the dimensions of religions and secular world views are the same.

13 Hunke's books are best-sellers.

14 The book is called *Aus der Gotterkenntnis meiner Werke* (From the God-knowledge of my works).

15 Schopenhauer's *Welt als Wille und Vorstellung* (1819).

16 One of several corollaries of the individualism of unequals is the National Socialist teaching that "*Volk* is eternal" (Kneller 1941: 56) or "man comes and goes but his people are eternal" (ibid.: 57).

17 DUR traces its origins back to the liberalism of the free religious and free Protestants of previous centuries and, like most new religions, inclines toward pantheism.

18 One of the main ideologues of DUR, in addition to Hunke, is Hubertus Mynarek

(Ökologische Religion) (Mecklenburg 1996: 379). For Mynarek, born 1929, religiosity is a biological fact (*Tatsache*) (Kratz 1994: 120–1).
19 The Thule Seminar of approximately fifty members was founded in 1980 (Mecklenburg 1996: 311–14). Its name recalls the tradition of the Thule-Gesellschaft and its connection to National Socialism (Rose, 1994). Thule Seminar is connected with the Grabert Verlag, Tübingen, which published the Rose book as well as the books of Krebs and de Benoist. Payne (1995: 151) only mentions the Thule Society that grew out of the Germanen Orden and was founded by Sebottendorf in 1917–1918. He does not mention the elite, intellectual, and influential Thule Seminar of today.
20 Deutsche Unitarier Religionsgemeinschaft can be easily found on the Internet.
21 This is what Hauer (1937: VII) means by *Glaube*, the original experience of ultimate reality and the realm of inner power that is buried deep within the foundation of the soul of races and *Völker*.
22 R. Stark to Hauer, 14 March 1951, N1131 148, BAK.
23 Otto Meyer to Hauer, 27 March 1961, N1131 215, BAK.
24 Otto Meyer to Hauer, 27 March 1961, N1131 215, BAK.

12 Conclusion

1 Günther to Hauer, 2 April 1936, 9 April 1936, N1131 88, BAK.
2 It minimizes, plays down, makes harmless.
3 For an uncritical, romantic, but well-researched portrayal of new Germanic paganism, see Schnurbein 1993.

Bibliography

Almond, Ian 2003 "Nietzsche's Peace with Islam: My Enemy's Enemy is my Friend." *German Life and Letters* 56(1): 43–55.

Anonymous 1934 "Von der Not durch christliche Erziehung." *Deutscher Glaube*, 1934 no. 10 (October): 449–55.

Aschheim, Steven E. 1992 *The Nietzsche Legacy in Germany: 1890–1990*. Berkeley: University of California Press.

Axmann, Arthur 1995 *Das kann doch nicht das Ende sein: Hitlers letzter Reichsjugendführer erinnert sich*. Koblenz: S. Bublies Verlag.

Bachofen, Johann Jakob 1861 *Das Mutterrecht: Eine Untersuchung über die Gynaikokratie der alten Welt nach ihrer religiösen und rechtlichen Natur*. Basel: Benno Schwabe.

Bambach, Charles R. 2003 *Heidegger's Roots: Nietzsche, National Socialism, and the Greeks*. Ithaca and London: Cornell University Press.

Banach, Jens 1998 *Heydrichs Elite: Das Führerkorps der Sicherheitspolizei und des SD 1936–1945*. Paderborn: Ferdinand Schöningh.

Barnett, Victoria 1992 *For the Soul of the People: Protestant Protest Against Hitler*. New York: Oxford University Press.

Bärsch, Claus-Ekkehard 1995 *Der junge Goebbels: Erlösung und Vernichtung*. Düsseldorf: Klaus Boer Verlag.

—— 2002 *Die politische Religion des Nationalsozialismus*. München: Wilhelm Fink Verlag.

Barth, Karl 1938 Introduction, in Arthur Frey, *Cross and Swastika: The Ordeal of the German Church* (tr. J. Strathearn McNab). London: SCM Press, pp. 9–32.

Bartsch, Heinz 1938 *Die Wirklichkeitsmacht der Allgemeinen Deutschen Glaubensbewegung der Gegenwart*. Breslau: Otto Ludwig.

Baumann, Schaul 2005 *Die Deutsche Glaubensbewegung und ihr Gründer Jakob Wilhelm Hauer (1881–1962)*. Marburg: Diagonal-Verlag.

de Benoist, Alain 1982 *Heide Sein: Zu Einem Neuen Anfang. Die europäische Glaubensalternative*. Tübingen: Grabert-Verlag.

Benrath, Gustav Adolf 2000 "Die Erweckung innerhalb der deutschen Landeskirchen," in Ulrich Gäbler (ed.) *Der Pietismus im neunzehnten und zwanzigsten Jahrhundert*. Göttingen: Vandenhoeck & Ruprecht, pp. 150–271.

Benz, Wolfgang, Hermann Graml and Hermann Weiß 1997 *Enzyklopädie des Nationalsozialismus*. München: Deutscher Taschenbuch Verlag.

Bergen, Doris L 1996 *Twisted Cross: The German Christian Movement in the Third Reich*. Chapel Hill: The University of North Carolina Press.

Bergmann, Ernst 1934 "Arbeit und Religion." *Deutscher Glaube* 1934 no. 1 (January): 10–15.

Berlin, Isaiah 1999 *The Roots of Romanticism*. Princeton: Princeton University Press.

Bethge, Eberhard 1970 *Dietrich Bonhoeffer: Theologian, Christian, Contemporary* (tr. Eric Mosbacher, Peter and Betty Ross, Frank Clarke, William Glen-Doepel; ed. Edwin Robertson). London: Collins.

Biehl, Michael 1990 *Der Fall Sadhu Sundar Singh*. Frankfurt/Main: Verlag Peter Lang.

Black, Edwin 2004 *War Against The Weak: Eugenics and America's Campaign to Create a Master Race*. New York: Thunder's Mouth Press.

Blunck, Hans Friedrich 1936 *König Geiserich: Eine Erzählung von Geiserich und dem Zug der Wandalen*. Hamburg: Hanseatische Verlagsanstalt.

Boge, Manfred 1935 *Volk ringt um Gott*. Breslau: Verlag Priebatsch's Buchhandlung.

Borinski, Fritz and Werner Milch 1967 *Die Geschichte der deutschen Jugend 1896–1933*. Frankfurt/Main: Dipa-Verlag.

Brady, Robert A. 1969 *The Spirit and Structure of German Fascism*. New York: Howard Fertig (originally published London: Victor Gollancz, 1937).

Bramsted, Ernest K. 1965 *Goebbels and National Socialist Propaganda 1925–1945*. Michigan State: The Cresset Press.

Bramwell, Anna 1985 *Blood and Soil: Walther Darré and Hitler's Green Party*. Abbotsbrook: The Kensal Press.

Braun, Walter 1932 *Heidenmission und Nationalsozialismus*. Berlin: Heimatdienst Verlag.

Brecht, Martin 1995 "Der württembergische Pietismus," in Martin Brecht and Klaus Deppermann (eds.) *Der Pietismus im achtzehnten Jahrhundert*. Göttingen: Vandenhoeck & Ruprecht, pp. 225–95.

Buchheim, Hans 1953 *Glaubenskrise im Dritten Reich*. Stuttgart: Deutsche Verlags-Anstalt.

Burleigh, Michael 2000 "National Socialism as a Political Religion." *Totalitarian Movements and Political Religions* 1(2): 1–26.

—— 2001 *The Third Reich: A New History*. London: Pan Books.

Campbell, Colin 1972 "The Cult, the Cultic Milieu, and Secularization," in Michael Hill (ed.) *A Sociological Yearbook of Religion in Britain 5*. London: SCM Press, pp. 119–36.

Cancik, Hubert 1982 "'Neuheiden' und totaler Staat," in Hubert Cancik (ed.), *Religions- und Geistesgeschichte der Weimarer Republik*. Düsseldorf: Patmos Verlag, pp. 176–94.

Chamberlain, Houston Stewart 1899 *Die Grundlagen des XIX. Jahrhunderts*. München: Bruckmann (16th edn., 1932).

—— 1916 *Arische Weltanschauung*. München: Bruckmann.

Clauss, Ludwig Ferdinand 1926 *Rasse und Seele: Eine Einführung in die Gegenwart*. München: J. F. Lehmann Verlag.

—— 1932 *Die nordische Seele*. München: J. F. Lehmann Verlag.

Conway, J. S. 1968 *The Nazi Persecution of the Churches 1933–1945*. Toronto: The Ryerson Press.

Cranston, Maurice 1967 "Liberalism," in Paul Edwards (ed. in chief), *The Encyclo-*

pedia of Philosophy, Vol. 3. New York: Macmillan and The Free Press; London: Collier-Macmillan, pp. 458–61.

Darmstädter Echo 2000 "Streit um Nazi-Vergangenheit einer Schriftstellerin." *Darmstädter Echo*, Tuesday, 15 August: 14.

Der Spiegel, 1960 "Antisemitismus: Mathilde Ludendorff." *Der Spiegel* 14(8), 17 February: 22–32.

Dibelius, Otto 1927 *Das Jahrhundert der Kirche*. Berlin: Furche-Verlag.

Dierker, Wolfgang 2003 *Himmlers Glaubenskrieger: Der Sicherheitsdienst der SS und seine Religionspolitik 1933–1941*. Paderborn: Ferdinand Schöningh.

Dierks, Margarete 1939 "Die preußischen Altkonservativen und die Judenfrage 1810/1847." PhD dissertation, Philosophy Faculty, Universität Rostock.

—— 1986 *Jakob Wilhelm Hauer 1881–1962: Leben, Werk, Wirkung*. Heidelberg: Verlag Lambert Schneider.

Dohnke, Kay 1999 "Artur Dinter," in Uwe Puschner, Walter Schmitz, and Justus H. Ulbricht (eds.), *Handbuch zur "Völkischen Bewegung" 1871–1918*. München: K. G. Saur, pp. 902–3.

Dönhoff, Marion Gräfin 1994 *Um der Ehre Willen: Erinnerungen an die Freunde vom 20. Juli*. Berlin: Siedler Verlag.

Endres, Hans 1938 "Der Erlösungsgedanke bei Nietzsche." *Deutscher Glaube* 1938 no. 6 (June): 303–7.

Evans, Richard J. 2004 *The Coming of the Third Reich*. New York: Penguin.

Evans-Pritchard, Edward E. 1965 *Theories of Primitive Religion*. Oxford: Clarendon Press.

Eyck, Erich 1956 *Geschichte der Weimarer Republik*. 2 vols. Erlenbach-Zürich und Stuttgart: Eugen Rentsch Verlag.

—— 1967 *A History of the Weimar Republic*, 2 vols. (tr. Harlan P. Hanson and Robert G. L. Waite). Cambridge, Mass.: Harvard University Press.

Fischer, Hans 1990 *Völkerkunde im Nationalsozialismus: Aspeckte der Anpassung, Affinität und Behauptung einer wissenschaftlichen Disziplin*. Berlin: Dietrich Reimer Verlag.

Frenssen, Gustav 1941 *Lebensbericht*. Berlin: G. Grote.

—— 1942 *Der Weg unseres Volkes*. Berlin: G. Grote'sche Verlagsbuchhandlung.

Fritsch, Theodor 1923 *Handbuch der Judenfrage*. Leipzig: Hammer-Verlag.

Fritzsche, Peter 1999 *Germans into Nazis*. Cambridge, Mass: Harvard University Press.

Frobenius, Leo 1921 *Paideuma: Umrisse Einer Kultur-Und Seelenkunde*. München: C.H. Beck'sche Verlagsbuchhandlung.

Germann, Holger 1995 *Die politische Religion des Nationalsozialisten Dietrich Klagges*. Frankfurt/Main: Peter Lang.

Geuter, Ulfried 1994 *Homosexualität in der deutschen Jugendbewegung*. Frankfurt/Main: Suhrkamp.

Gloege, Gerhard 1934a "Die Deutschkirche," in Walter Künneth and Helmuth Schreiner (eds.), *Die Nation vor Gott*. Berlin: Wichern Verlag, pp. 393–415.

—— 1934b "Die Weltanschauung Hermann Wirths," in Walter Künneth and Helmuth Schreiner (eds.), *Die Nation vor Gott*, Berlin: Wichern Verlag, pp. 464–505.

Goebbels, Joseph 1926 *Die zweite Revolution: Briefe an Zeitgenossen*. Zwickau: Streiter-Verlag.

—— 1927 *Wege ins Dritte Reich*. München: Verlag Franz Eher.

—— 1929 *Michael: Ein deutsches Schicksal in Tagebuchblättern.* München: Zentral-verlag der NSDAP, Franz Eher Nachf. (Unpublished MS, 1923, Michael Voor-mann, NL118 127, BAK)

Goldhagen, Daniel 1996 *Hitlers willige Vollstrecker.* Berlin: Siedler.

—— 2002 *A Moral Reckoning: The Role of the Catholic Church in the Holocaust and its Unfulfilled Duty of Repair.* New York: Knopf.

Golomb, Jacob 2004 *Nietzsche and Zion.* New York: Cornell University Press, pp. 159–88).

Goodrick-Clarke 1992 *The Occult Roots of Nazism.* New York: New York University Press.

—— 1998 *Hitler's Priestess: Savitri Devi, the Hindu-Aryan Myth, and Neo-Nazism.* New York: New York University Press.

Grabert, Herbert 1932 *Religiöse Verständigung: Wege zur Begegnung der Religionen bei Nicolaus Cusanus, Schleiermacher, Rudolf Otto und J. W. Hauer.* Leipzig: C. L. Hirschfeld.

—— 1936 *Der protestantische Auftrag des deutschen Volkes: Grundzüge der deutschen Glaubensgeschichte von Luther bis Hauer.* Stuttgart: Karl Gutbrod.

Gregor, A. James 2000 *The Faces of Janus: Marxism and Fascism in the Twentieth Century.* New Haven: Yale University Press.

Grimm, Hans 1918a *Die Olewagen Saga.* München: Albert Langen (reprinted 1972 Lippoldsberg: Klosterhaus Verlag).

—— 1918b *Der Ölsucher von Duala.* Berlin: Verlag Ullstein.

—— 1926 *Volk ohne Raum.* Munich: Albert Langen.

—— 1931 "Politische Dolmetscher," reprinted 1980 in id., *Der Schriftsteller und Seine Zeit: Aufsätze, Zeitungsantworten, Politische Briefe.* Lippoldsberg: Kloster-haus Verlag, pp. 10–14.

—— 1938 "Vom politischen Dichter, geistige Begegnung mit Rudyard Kipling," reprinted 1977 in id., *Forderung An Die Literatur.* Lippoldsberg: Klosterhaus Verlag, pp. 61–92.

—— 1954 *Warum – Woher – Aber Wohin?* Lippoldsberg: Kosterhaus Verlag.

—— 1972a *Die Thomas Mann Schrift.* Lippoldsberg: Klosterhaus Verlag.

—— 1972b "Amerikanische Rede (6.10.1935)," in id., *Von der verkannten Wirk-lichkeit.* Lippoldsberg: Klosterhaus Verlag, pp. 242–66.

—— 1978 *Kaffernland.* Lippoldsberg: Klosterhaus Verlag.

Gründel, Ernst Günther 1932 *Die Sendung der jungen Generation: Versuch einer umfassenden revolutionären Sinndeutung der Krise.* München: C. H. Beck.

Günther, Hans F. K. 1926 *Adel und Rasse.* München: J. F. Lehmanns Verlag.

—— 1928 *Platon als Hüter des Lebens.* München: J. F. Lehmanns Verlag.

—— 1930 *Rassenkunde des jüdischen Volkes.* München: J. F. Lehmanns Verlag.

—— 1934 *Die Nordische Rasse bei den Indogermanen Asiens.* München: J. F. Lehmanns Verlag.

—— 1935a *Ritter Tod und Teufel: der heldische Gedanke.* München: J. F. Lehmanns Verlag.

—— 1935b "Zum Tode des Verlegers J. F. Lehmann." *Rasse* 2: 155–156.

—— 1936 *Führeradel durch Sippenpflege.* München: J. F. Lehmanns Verlag.

—— 1941 *Gattenwahl zu ehelichem Glück und erblicher Ertüchtigung.* München: J. F. Lehmanns Verlag.

—— 1969 *Mein Eindruck von Adolf Hitler.* Pähl: Franz von Bebenburg.

Gutmann, Bruno 1928 *Freies Menschentum aus ewigen Bindungen*. Kassel: Bären-reiter Verlag.

Haack, Friedrich-Wilhelm 1981 *Wotans Wiederkehr: Blut-, Boden- und Rasse-Religion*. München: Claudius Verlag.

Haffner, Sebastian 2001a *Germany: Jekyll & Hyde. 1939 – Deutschland von innen betrachtet* (retrans. Kurt Baudisch from English edn., London: Secker & Warburg, 1940). München: Knaur.

—— 2001b *Anmerkungen zu Hitler*. Frankfurt/Main: Fischer Taschenbuch Verlag.

—— 2002 *Geschichte eines Deutschen: Die Erinnerungen 1914–1933*. München: Deutscher Taschenbuch Verlag.

Hakl, Hans Thomas 2001 *Der verborgene Geist von Eranos: Unbekannte Begeg-nungen von Wissenschaft und Esoterik*. Bretten: Scientia Nova – Verlag Neue Wissenschaft.

Hamann, Brigitte 1996 *Hitlers Wien: Lehrjahre eines Diktators*. München: Piper.

Harnack, Adolf 1901 *What is Christianity?* (tr. Thomas Bailey Saunders). London: Williams and Norgate.

Hauer, Jakob Wilhelm 1921a "Das Wesen des Prophetischen," *Stuttgarter Neues Tagblatt*, Saturday 5 February: 7.

—— 1921b "Das prophetische Erlebnis." *Stuttgarter Neues Tagblatt*, Saturday 19 February: 7.

—— 1922a *Die Anfänge der Yogapraxis. Eine Untersuching über die Wurzeln der indischen Mystik nach Ṛgveda und Atharvaveda*. Stuttgart: W. Kohlhammer Verlag.

—— 1922b *Werden und Wesen der Anthroposophie*. Stuttgart: W. Kohlhammer Verlag.

—— 1923 *Die Religionen*. Berlin: W. Kohlhammer Verlag.

—— 1932a *Indiens Kampf um das Reich*. Stuttgart: Kohlhammer.

—— 1932b *Der Yoga als Heilsweg*. Stuttgart: Verlag von W. Kohlhammer.

—— 1932c *The Kundalini Yoga. Notes on the Seminar given by Prof. Dr. J. W. Hauer*. San Francisco: C. G. Jung Institute.

—— 1933a *Verfassungsänderung oder Revolution der Kirche*. Leipzig: E. L. Hirschfeld.

—— 1933b *Wo bleibt die deutsche Intelligenz? Gedanken eines Hochschullehrers zur Verständigung und zur Entscheidung*. Leipzig: E. L. Hirschfeld.

—— 1934a *Eine indo-arische Metaphysik des Kampfes und der Tat: Die Bhagavadgita in neuer Sicht*. Stuttgart: Kohlhammer.

—— 1934b "Zum Geleit." *Deutscher Glaube* 1934 no. 1 (January): 1–3.

—— 1934c "Deutscher Glaube?" *Deutscher Glaube* 1934 no. 1 (January): 3–8.

—— 1934d "Wesen und Ziel der Deutschen Glaubensbewegung." *Deutscher Glaube*, 1934 no. 2 (February): 49–57.

—— 1934e *Deutsche Gottschau: Grundzüge eines Deutschen Glaubens*. Stuttgart: Karl Gutbrod.

—— 1935 "Skizzen aus meinem Leben," *Deutscher Glaube*. Hartung 1935: 5–11.

—— 1937 *Das Religiöse Artbild der Indogermanen und die Grundtypen der Indo-Arischen Religion*. Stuttgart: Verlag W. Kohlhammer.

—— 1938 "Religion und Rasse," in id. (ed.), *Glaube und Blut: Beiträge zum Problem Religion und Rasse*. Karlsruhe and Leipzig: Verlag Boltze, 1938, pp. 64–152.

—— 1958 *Der Yoga: Ein indischer Weg zum Selbst*. Stuttgart: Verlag W. Kohlhammer.

Hauer, Wilhelm, Karl Heim and Karl Adam 1937 *Germany's New Religion: The German Faith Movement* (tr. T. S. K. Scott-Craig and R. E. Davies). New York: The Abingdon Press.

Heer, Friedrich 1982 "Weimar – Ein religiöser und weltanschaulicher Leerraum," in Hubert Cancik (ed.), *Religions- und Geistesgeschichte der Weimarer Republik*. Düsseldorf: Patmos Verlag, pp. 31–48.

—— 1998 *Der Glaube des Adolf Hitlers: Anatomie einer politischen Religiösität*. Wien: Amalthea Verlags GmbH.

Heinrich, Fritz 2002 *Die Deutsche Religionswissenschaft und der Nationalsozialismus*. Petersberg: Michael Imhof Verlag.

Herbert, Ulrich 1996 *Best: Biographische Studien über Radikalismus, Weltanschauung und Vernunft 1903–1989*. Bonn: Verlag J. H. W. Dietz.

—— 2001 "Ideological Legitimisation and Political Practice of the Leadership of the National Socialist Secret Police," in Hans Mommsen (ed.), *The Third Reich Between Vision and Reality*. Oxford: Berg, pp. 95–108.

Herwig, Holger 1999 "*Geopolitik*: Haushofer, Hitler and Lebensraum," in C. S. Gray and G. Sloan (eds.), *Geopolitics, Geography and Strategy*. London: Frank Cass, pp. 218–41.

Hexham, Irving and Karla Poewe 1986 *Understanding Cults and New Religions*. Grand Rapids, Mich: William B. Eerdsmans.

—— 1997 *New Religions as Global Cultures*. Boulder, Colo: Westview Press.

Hipler, Bruno 1996 *Hitlers Lehrmeister: Karl Haushofer als Vater der NS-Ideologie*. St. Ottilien: EOS-Verlag.

Hitler, Adolf 1940 *Mein Kampf*. München: Zentralverlag der NSDAP, Franz Eher Nachf.

Hofer, Hans 1934 *Die Weltanschauung der Neuzeit*. Elberfeld: Verlag "Die Aue."

Höhne, Heinz 2002 *Der Orden unter dem Totenkopf: Die Geschichte Der SS*. München: Orbis Verlag.

Hunke, Sigrid 1960 *Allahs Sonne über dem Abendland*. Stuttgart: Deutsche Verlags-Anstalt.

—— 1969 *Europas andere Religion*. Düsseldorf: Econ Verlag.

—— 1982 "Der dialektische Unitarismus," in Manon Maren-Grisebach and Ursula Menzer (eds.), *Philosophinnen: Von Wegen ins 3. Jahrtausend*. Mainz: Tamagnini-Verlag, pp. 10–22.

—— 1987 *Glauben und Wissen: Die Einheit europäischer Religion und Naturwissenschaft*. Hildesheim: Georg Olms Verlag.

—— 1989 *Vom Untergang des Abendlandes zum Aufgang Europas. Bewußtseinswandel und Zukunftsperspektiven*. Stuttgart: Horizonte Verlag.

—— 1997 *Europas Eigene Religion: Die Überwindung der religiösen Krise*. Tübingen: Grabert.

—— n.d. *Das Reich und das werdende Europa*. Kreuzau-Stockheim: Alma Verlag.

Huntington, Samuel 1996 *The Clash of Civilization and the Remaking of World Order*. New York: Simon & Schuster.

Hutchinson, George P. 1977 "The Nazi Ideology of Alfred Rosenberg: a study of his thought 1917–1946." PhD thesis, University of Oxford.

Hutten, Kurt 1934 "Die Deutsche Glaubensbewegung," in Walter Künneth and Helmuth Schreiner (eds.), *Die Nation vor Gott*. Berlin: Wichern Verlag, pp. 510–33.

Johnson, Eric A. 2000 *Nazi Terror: the Gestapo, Jews, and Ordinary Germans*. New York: Basic Books.

Jooss, Rainer 1998 "Erich Keller (1894–1977)," in Rainer Lächele and Jörg Thierfelder (eds.), *Wir konnten uns nicht entziehen*. Stuttgart: Quell Verlag, pp. 287–98.

Jünger, Ernst 1931 *Die Arbeiter*. Hamburg: Hanseatische Verlagsanstalt.

Junginger, Horst 1999 *Von der philologischen zur völkischen Religionswissenschaft*. Stuttgart: Franz Steiner Verlag.

—— 2001 "Der Gescheiterte Religionsgründer," *Schwäbisches Tageblatt*, Friday, 5 January: 30.

Kater, Michael 2001 *Das "Ahnenerbe" der SS 1935–1945. Ein Beitrag zur Kulturpolitik des Dritten Reiches*. München: R. Oldenbourg Verlag.

Kershaw, Ian 1998 *Hitler 1889–1936: Hubris*. New York: W. W. Norton & Co.

—— 2000 *Hitler 1936–45: Nemesis*. London: Allen Lane, The Penguin Press.

Keynes, John Maynard 1920 *The Economic Consequences of the Peace*. New York: Harcourt, Brace and Howe.

Klages, Ludwig 1929a *Der Geist als Widersacher der Seele*. Vol. 1: *Leben und Denkvermögen*. Leipzig: Johann Ambrosius Barth.

—— 1929b *Der Geist als Widersacher der Seele*. Vol. 2: *Die Lehre vom Willen*. Leipzig: Johann Ambrosius Barth.

—— 1932 *Der Geist als Widersacher der Seele*. Vol. 3, Part II: *Das Weltbild des Pelasgertums*. Leipzig: Johann Ambrosius Barth.

Klagges, Dietrich 1926 *Das Urevangelium Jesu, der deutsche Glaube*. Wilster: Meister Ekkehart Verlag.

—— 1934 *Heldischer Glaube*. Leipzig: Armanen Verlag.

Knak, Sigfried 1931 *Zwischen Nil und Tafelbai*. Berlin: Heimatdienst Verlag.

—— n.d. *Geschichte der Berliner Mission 1924–1949*. Unpublished manuscript of Professor Knak. Archive of the *Berliner Missionswerk*.

Kneller, George Frederick 1941 *The Educational Philosophy of National Socialism*. New Haven: Yale University Press.

Krannhals, Paul 1936 *Das Organische Weltbild: Grundlagen einer neuentstehenden deutschen Kultur*. Vols. 1 and 2. München: F. Bruckmann.

Kratz, Peter 1994 *Die Götter des New Age*. Berlin: Elefanten Press.

Kraus, Hans-Christof 1997 "Eric Voegelin redivivus? Politische Wissenschaft als Politische Theologie," in Michael Ley and Julius H. Schoeps (eds.) *Der Nationalsozialismus als politische Religion*. Bodenheim b. Mainz: Philo Verlagsgesellschaft, pp. 74–88.

Krebs, Pierre (ed.) 1981a *Das Unvergängliche Erbe: Alternativen zum Prinzip der Gleichheit*. Tübingen: Grabert-Verlag.

—— 1981b "Weltanschauung: Gedanken zu einer kulturellen Wiedergeburt," in Krebs (1981a), pp. 13–31.

—— 1990 "Eine Epoche in der Krise." *Elemente der Metapolitik zur europäischen Neugeburt* 4, 1990: 8–19.

—— 1997 *Im Kampf um das Wissen: Ethnosuizid in der Multirassischen Gesellschaft, der Judäochristlichen Zivilisation des Westens oder Ethnokulturelle Neugeburt Europas in der Organischen Demokratie Indoeuropäischer Prägung?* Horn: Burkhart Weecke.

Krickeberg, W. 1937 "Lehrbuch der Völkerkunde. Ed. Konrad Theodor Preuss (Stuttgart: Enke)." *Zeitschrift für Ethnologie* 1937 no. 6: 464–6.

—— 1938 "Abwehr." *Zeitschrift für Ethnologie* 1938 no. 1/2: 119–23.

Kulick, Don and Margaret Willson (eds.) 1995 *Taboo*. London: Routledge.

Kwiet, Konrad 2004 "Paul Zapp – Vordenker und Vollstrecker der Judenvernichtung," in Klaus-Michael Mallmann and Gerhard Paul (eds.), *Karrieren der Gewalt: Nationalsozialistische Täterbiographien*, Darmstadt: Wissenschaftliche Buchgesellschaft, pp. 252–62.

Laqueur, Walter Z. 1962 *Young Germany: A History of the German Youth Movement*. London: Routledge & Kegan Paul.

—— 1972 *A History of Zionism*. New York: MJF Books.

Lauryssens, Stan 1999 *The Man who Invented the Third Reich*. Stroud, UK: Sutton Publishing.

Leers, Johannes von 1938 *Gustav Frenssen wird 75 Jahre alt*. N2168 9, BAB.

—— n.d. *Mustafa Kemal Pascha*. N2168 9, BAB.

Leesch, Wolfgang 1938 *Die Geschichte des Deutschkatholizismus in Schlesien (1844–1852)*. Breslau: Priebatschs Buchhandlung.

Leggewie, Claus 1998 *Von Schneider zu Schwerte*. München: Carl Hanser Verlag.

Liebs, Ludwig 1976 *Glauben an Gott und die Götter*. Heidenheim/Brenz: Südmarkverlag Fritsch KG.

Lixfeld, Hannjost 1994 *Folklore & Fascism* (tr. James R. Dow). Bloomington: Indiana University Press.

Lohalm, Uwe 1970 *Völkischer Radikalismus: Die Geschichte des Deutschvölkischen Schutz- und Trutz-Bundes: 1919–1923*. Hamburg: Leibniz-Verlag.

Ludendorff, General Erich von 1935 Preface, in M. Ludendorff (1935), p. 3.

Ludendorff, Mathilde 1921 *Triumph des Unsterblichkeitwillens*. Stuttgart: Verlag Hohe Warte.

—— 1931 *Erlösung von Jesu Christo*. München: Ludendorffs Volkswarte-Verlag.

—— 1933 *"Induciertes" Irresein durch Occultlehren*. München: Ludendorffs Volkswarte-Verlag.

—— 1935 *Aus der Gotterkenntnis meiner Werke*. München: Ludendorffs Verlag.

—— 1937 *Ein Blick in die Dunkelkammer der Geisterseher: Moderne Medium-Forschung*. München: Ludendorffs Verlag (first published 1913, München: J. F. Lehmann).

Lutzhöft, Hans-Jürgen 1971 *Der Nordische Gedanke in Deutschland 1920–1940*. Stuttgart: Ernst Klett Verlag.

Machtan, Lothar 2001 *The Hidden Hitler* (tr. John Brownjohn). New York: Basic Books.

Malefijt, Annemarie de Waal 1974 *Images of Man*. New York: Alfred A. Knopf.

Mandel, Hermann 1931 *Wirklichkeitsreligion*. Kiel: Walter G. Mühlau Verlag.

—— 1934 "Thesen Deutscher Reformation." *Deutscher Glaube* 1934 no. 1 (January): 25–31.

Mann, Thomas 1918 *Betrachtungen eines Unpolitischen*. Berlin: Fischer.

Martin, Bernd 1991 "Universität im Umbruch: Das Rektorat Heidegger 1933/34," in E. John, B. Martin, M. Mück, and H. Ott (eds.), *Die Freiburger Universität in der Zeit des Nationalsozialismus*. Freiburg: Verlag Ploetz, pp. 9–24.

Mecklenburg, Jens 1996 *Handbuch Deutscher Rechts Extremismus*. Berlin: Elefanten Press.

Meyer, Johannes D. 1915 *Deutscher Glaube und christliches Bekenntnis*. Berlin-Lichterfelde: Edwin Runge Verlag.

Moeller van der Bruck, Arthur 1923 *Das Dritte Reich*. Berlin: Ring-Verlag.

Mohler, Armin 1989a *Die Konservative Revolution in Deutschland 1918–1932: Ein Handbuch*. Darmstadt: Wissenschaftliche Buchgesellschaft.

—— 1989b *Die Konservative Revolution in Deutschland 1918–1932: Ergänzungsband*. Darmstadt: Wissenschaftliche Buchgesellschaft.

—— 1999 *Die Konservative Revolution in Deutschland 1918–1932*. 5th edn. Graz: Leopold Stocker Verlag.

Moore, Gregory 2003 "From Buddhism to Bolshevism: Some Orientalist Themes in German Thought." *German Life and Letters* 56(1): 20–42.

Mosse, George L. 1981a *The Crisis of German Ideology: Intellectual Origins of the Third Reich*. New York: Schocken.

—— 1981b *Nazi Culture*. New York: Schocken.

Mühlberger, Detlef 2003 *The Social Bases of Nazism 1919–1933*. Cambridge: Cambridge University Press.

Müller, Jan-Werner 2003 *A Dangerous Mind: Carl Schmitt in Post-War European Thought*. New Haven and London: Yale University Press.

Nanko, Ulrich 1989 "Deutsche Gottschau, 1934: Eine Religionsstiftung durch einen deutschen Religionswissenschaftler," in Peter Antes and Donate Pahnke (eds.), *Die Religion von Oberschichten*. Marburg: Diagonal-Verlag, pp. 165–316.

—— 1993 *Die Deutsche Glaubensbewegung: Eine historische und soziologische Untersuchung*. Marburg: Diagonal-Verlag.

—— 1998 "Jakob Wilhelm Hauer (1881–1962)," in Rainer Lächele and Jörg Thierfelder (eds.), *Wir konnten uns nicht entziehen*. Stuttgart: Quell Verlag, pp. 61–76.

Nassen, Ulrich 1987 *Jugend, Buch und Konjunktur 1933–1945*. München: Wilhelm Fink Verlag.

Neurohr, Jean F. 1956 (written 1933) *Der Mythos vom Dritten Reich: Zur Geistesgeschichte des Nationalsozialismus*. Kettwig: Akademische Verlagsgesellschaft.

Nigg, Walter 1937 *Geschichte des religiösen Liberalismus*. Zürich and Leipzig: Max Niehans Verlag.

Nolte, Ernst 1966 "Germany," in Hans Rogger and Eugen Weber (eds.), *The European Right: A Historical Profile*. Berkeley: University of California Press, pp. 261–307.

Overy, Richard 2001 *Interrogations: The Nazi Elite in Allied Hands, 1945*. New York: Viking Press.

Padfield, Peter 2001a *Himmler Reichsführer-SS*. London: Papermac.

—— 2001b *Hess: the Führer's Disciple*. London: Cassell.

Paetel, Karl Otto 1999 *Nationalbolschewismus und nationalrevolutionäre Bewegungen in Deutschland*. Schnellbach: Verlag Siegfried Bublies.

Payne, Stanley G. 1995 *A History of Fascism 1914–1945*. Madison: University of Wisconsin Press.

—— 2002 "Emilio Gentile's Historical Analysis and Taxonomy of Political Reform." *Totalitarian Movements and Political Religion* 3(1): 122–30.

Peters, Ludwig 1998 *Volkslexikon Drittes Reich*. Tübingen: Grabert Verlag.

Poewe, Karla 1993 "Theologies of Black South Africans and the Rhetoric of Peace versus Violence." *Canadian Journal of African Studies* (Ottawa) 27(1), 1993: 43–65.

—— 1996 "Writing Culture and Writing Fieldwork: The Proliferation of Experimental and Experiential Ethnographies." *Ethnos* 61(3/4), December 1996: 177–206.

—— 1998 "Affinities and Links between German and Afrikaaner Nationalism: Politicians, Berlin Missionaries, and Committed Writers." Unpublished manuscript.

—— 1999 "Scientific Neo-Paganism and the Extreme Right then and today: from Ludendorff's *Gotterkenntnis* to Sigrid Hunke's *Europas Eigene Religion.*" *Journal of Contemporary Religion* 14(3): 387–400.

Poliakov, Leon 1974 *The Aryan Myth* (tr. Edmund Howard). New York: Basic Books.

Popper, Karl R. 1963 *The Open Society and its Enemies.* New York: Harper Torchbooks.

Puschner, Uwe, Wlater Schmitz and Justus H. Ulbricht 1999 *Handbuch zur "Völkischen Bewegung" 1871–1918.* München: K. G. Saur.

Rennstich, Karl 1992 *Der Deutsche Glaube: Jakob Wilhelm Hauer (1881–1962): Ein Ideologe des Nationalsozialismus.* Stuttgart: Evangelische Zentralstelle für Weltanschauungsfragen.

Reuth, Ralf George 2000 *Goebbels: Eine Biographie.* München: Piper.

Reventlow, Graf Ernst zu 1920 *Reichswart* (published 1920–1941). Berlin: Reichswart-Verlag.

—— 1934 "Luther und Deutscher Glaube." *Deutscher Glaube* 1934 no. 1 (January): 15–23.

Rimmele, Eva 1999 "Leers, Johann von: NS-Publizist," in Hermann Weiß (ed.), *Biographisches Lexicon zum Dritten Reich.* Frankfurt/Main: S. Fischer Verlag, pp. 293–4.

Rogge-Börner, P. Sophie 1932 *Zurück zum Mutterrecht? Studie zu Professor Ernst Bergmann "Erkenntnisgeist und Muttergeist".* Leipzig: Adolf Klein Verlag.

Rose, Detlev 1994 *Die Thule-Gesellschaft.* Tübingen: Grabert Verlag.

Rosenberg, Alfred 1930 *Der Mythus des 20. Jahrhunderts.* München: Verlag Hohenreichen.

Rychlak, Ronald 2003 "Daniel Goldhagen's Assault on Christianity." *Totalitarian Movements and Political Religions* 4(2): 184–94.

Salomon, Ernst von 1999 *Der Fragebogen.* Hamburg: Rowohlt Verlag (first edn., 1954).

Schmidt, Wilhelm 1931 *Der Ursprung der Gottesidee.* Münster (Westfalen): Aschendorffsche Verlags-Buchhandlung.

Schmitt, Carl 1933 *Staat, Bewegung, Volk.* Hamburg: Hanseatische Verlagsanstalt.

—— 1934 *Politische Theologie.* München: Verlag von Duncker & Humboldt.

—— 1936 "Die deutsche Rechtswissenschaft im Kampf gegen den jüdischen Geist." *Deutsche-Juristen-Zeitung* 41(20), 15 October 1936: 1194–9.

—— 1938 "Völkerrechtliche Neutralität und völkische Totalität." *Monatshefte für auswertige Politik* 5: 613–18.

Schnurbein, Stefanie von 1993 *Göttertrost in Wendezeiten.* München: Claudius Verlag.

Scholder, Klaus 1988 *The Church and the Third Reich*, Vol. 1. Philadelphia: Fortress Press.

—— 2000 *Die Kirchen und das Dritte Reich: Vorgeschichte und Zeit der Illusion 1918–1934.* München: Propyläen Taschenbuch of the Econ Ullstein List Verlag.

Schopenhauer, Arthur 1819 *Die Welt als Wille und Vorstellung.* Leipzig: Brockhaus.

Schröder, Hans Eggert 1966 *Ludwig Klages: Die Geschichte seines Lebens. Erster Teil: Die Jugend.* Bonn: H. Bouvier u. Co. Verlag.

Schulze, Hagen 1998 *Germany: A New History* (tr. Deborah Lucas Schneider). Cambridge, Mass.: Harvard University Press.

Schuppan, Erich 2000 "Bekennen – Sich Anpassen – Widerstehen," in Erich Schuppan and Christian R. Homrichhausen (eds.), *Bekenntnis in Not*. Berlin: Wichern Verlag, pp. 213–94.

Smart, Ninian 1997 *World's Religions: Old Traditions and Modern Transformations*. Cambridge: Cambridge University Press.

Speer, Albert 1969 *Erinnerungen*. Berlin: Propyläen Verlag.

Spengler, Oswald 1920 *Der Untergang des Abendlandes*. München: C. H. Beck'she Verlagsbuchhandlung.

Stachura, Peter D. 1981 *The German Youth Movement 1900–1945*. London: Macmillan.

Stapel, Wilhelm 1931 "'Literarische Diktatur' des Deutschnationalen Handlungs-gehilfen-Verbandes?" *Die deutsche Handels-Wacht*, 25 June. (A: Grimm, DLA, Marbach).

Steigmann-Gall 2003 "Rethinking Nazism and Religion: How Anti-Christian were the 'Pagans'?" *Central European History* 36(1): 75–105.

Stern, Fritz 1961 *The Politics of Cultural Despair: a study in the Rise of the Germanic Ideology*. Berkeley: University of California Press.

Sternhell, Zeev 1994 *Birth of Fascist Ideology: From Cultural Rebellion to Political Revolution* (tr. David Maisel). Princeton University Press.

Steuckers, Robert 1990 "Postmoderne, Technizität und Heidnisches Erbe." *Elemente der Metapolitik zur europäischen Neugeburt* 4: 61–68.

Stevenson, William 1973 *The Bormann Brotherhood*. New York: Harcourt Brace Jovanovich.

Strauß, Lulu von and Torney-Diederichs 1936 *Eugen Diederichs: Leben und Werk*. Jena: Eugen Diederichs Verlag.

Streicher, Julius (ed. and publ.) 1923 *Der Stürmer* (published 1923–1945). Nürnberg: Wilhelm Härdel Verlag until 1935; then Nürnberg: Verlag Der Stürmer until 1945.

Struve, Carola 1933 *Frauenfreiheit und Volksfreiheit auf kameradschaftsrechtlicher Grundlage*. Heidelberg: Bündischer Verlag.

Trimondi, Victor and Victoria (pseudonyms for Herbert and Mariana Rèottgen) 2002 *Hitler, Buddha, Krishna: Eine Unheilige Allianz vom Dritten Reich bis Heute*. Wien: Ueberreuter.

Ustorf, Werner 2000 *Sailing on the Next Tide: Missions, Missiology and the Third Reich*. Frankfurt/Main: Peter Lang.

Vermeil, Edmond 1944 *Hitler et le christianisme*. London: Penguin.

Wagner, Gottfried 1999 *Twilight of the Wagners: The Unveiling of a Family's Legacy* (tr. Della Couling). New York: Picador.

Weiß, Hermann 1999 "Dinter, Artur: Gauleiter, Schriftsteller," in Hermann Weiß (ed.), *Biographisches Lexicon zum Dritten Reich*. Frankfurt/Main: S. Fischer Verlag, pp. 90–1.

Werner, Hermann 1986 *Tübingen, 1945: eine Chronik*. Stuttgart: K. Theiss.

Wielandt, Rudolf 1908 *Der politische Liberalismus und die Religion*. Göttingen: Vandenhoeck und Ruprecht.

Wirsing, Giselher 1942 *Engländer, Juden, Araber in Palästina*. Jena: Eugen Diedrichs Verlag (first edn., 1938).

Wischnath, Johannes Michael 1998 "Wilhelm Pressel (1895–1986)," in Rainer Lächele and Jörg Thierfelder (eds.), *Wir konnten uns nicht entziehen*. Stuttgart: Quell Verlag, pp. 299–310.

Woods, Roger 1996 *The Conservative Revolution in the Weimar Republic*. New York: St. Martin's Press.

Wüst, Walther and Kurt Schrötter 1942 *Tod und Unsterblichkeit: im Weltbild indogermanischer Denker*. Berlin-Dahlem: Ahnenerbe-Stiftung Verlag.

Zapp, Paul 1934 "Die Aufgaben der deutschen Glaubensbewegung." *Deutscher Glaube* 1934 no. 11 (November): 501–5.

Zehnpfennig, Barbara 2000 *Hitlers Mein Kampf: Eine Interpretation*. München: Wilhelm Fink Verlag.

Ziegler, Herbert F. 1989 *Nazi Germany's New Aristocracy: The SS Leadership, 1925–1939*. Princeton University Press.

—— 2001, 2002 personal communications. 16 January 2001, 17 January 2001, 7 January 2002.

Zipfel, Friedrich 1965 *Kirchenkampf in Deutschland 1933–1945*. Berlin: Walter de Gruyter & Co.

Index

The Paganism Reader

Edited by Chas S. Clifton and Graham Harvey

Paganism is one of the world's fastest-growing religions, practised in a huge variety of ways. *The Paganism Reader* provides a definitive collection of key sources in Paganism, ranging from its ancient origins to its twentieth-century reconstruction and revival. Chronologically organized sections include extracts from ancient Greek, Norse and Celtic literature, inspirational texts from the early twentieth-century, writings by leaders of the Pagan revival, and newer perspectives showing the diversity of Paganism today. Witchcraft, nature religion, shamanism and goddess worship are considered, as is the influence of environmental and feminist movements. Fully introduced, with editors' prefaces to all extracts and suggestions for further reading, this comprehensive book is an invaluable guide to Paganism and critical issues in its study.

Hb: 0-415-30352-4
Pb: 0-415-30353-2
Available at all good bookshops
For ordering and further information please visit:
www.routledge.com

Related titles from Routledge

The Routledge Companion to the Study of Religion

Edited by Professor John R. Hinnells

The effective study of religion involves many disciplines and methods, from psychology to sociology, and from textual analysis to case studies in the field. It also requires an awareness of key thematic issues such as gender, science, fundamentalism, ritual, mysticism, and new religious movements.

Containing everything needed for a full understanding of theory and methods in religious studies, *The Routledge Companion to the Study of Religion*:

- surveys the history of religious studies and the key disciplinary approaches
- shows how to apply theories and methods to practical study
- highlights contemporary issues such as globalization, diaspora and politics
- explains why the study of religion is relevant in today's world

Beginning by explaining the most important methodological approaches to religion, including psychology, philosophy, anthropology and comparative study, the text then moves on to explore a wide variety of critical issues. Written entirely by renowned international specialists, and using clear and accessible language throughout, it is the perfect guide to the problems and questions found in exams and on courses.

Hb: 0-415-33310-5
Pb: 0-415-33311-3
Available at all good bookshops
For ordering and further information please visit:
www.routledge.com

New Religious Movements in the 21st Century: Legal, Political and Social Challenges in Global Perspective

Edited by Phillip Charles Lucas and Thomas Robbins

New religious movements are proliferating in nearly every region of the world. From new sects within larger global movements such as Islam, Christianity, or Buddhism, to the growth and spread of minority religions (e.g. ISKON, Unification Church, and Scientology) and the development of completely new religions, the future of these new religious movements will increasingly come to be played out on a political battlefield. Governments in many countries in both the industrialized and the developing worlds have enacted new policies and legislation that dramatically affect not only marginal and minority religious groups but also the broader power relationships between states and the religious freedom of their citizens.

New Religious Movements in the 21st Century is the first volume to examine the urgent and important issues facing new religions in their political, legal, and religious contexts in global perspective. With essays from prominent new religious movement scholars and usefully organized into four regional areas covering Western Europe, Asia, Africa, and Australia, Russia and Eastern Europe, and North and South America, as well as a concluding section on the major themes of globalization and terrorist violence, this book provides invaluable insight into the challenges facing religion in the twenty-first century. An introduction by Tom Robbins provides an overview of the major issues and themes discussed in the book.

Hb: 0-415-96576-4
Pb: 0-415-96577-2
Available at all good bookshops
For ordering and further information please visit:
www.routledge.com

Related titles from Routledge

Children of the New Age:
A History of Spiritual Practices

Steven Sutcliffe

The first true social history of the phenomenon known as New Age culture, *Children of the New Age* presents an overview of the diverse varieties of New Age belief and practice from the 1930s to the present day. Drawing on original ethnographic research and rarely seen archival material, it calls into question the assumption that the New Age is a discrete and unified 'movement', and reveals the unities and fractures evident in contemporary New Age practice.

Hb: 0-415-24298-3
Pb: 0-415-24299-1
Available at all good bookshops
For ordering and further information please visit:
www.routledge.com